World Wrestling Entertainment BOOKS

MAIN EVENT

WWE in the Raging 80s

Brian Shields

POCKET BOOKS
New York London Toronto Sydney

POCKET BOOKS, a division of Simon & Schuster, Inc.
1230 Avenue of the Americas, New York, NY 10020

This book is a publication of Pocket Books, a division of Simon & Schuster, Inc., under exclusive license from World Wrestling Entertainment, Inc.

Library of Congress Cataloging-in-Publication Data

Shields, Brian.
Main event : WWE in the raging 80s / Brian Shields.
p. cm.
1. World Wrestling Entertainment, Inc.—History. 2. World Wrestling Federation—History. 3. Wrestling—History. I. Title.

GV1195.S45 2006
796.881209—dc22 2006049818

ISBN 978-1-4165-3257-6

This Pocket Books trade paperback edition November 2006

10 9 8 7 6 5 4 3 2

POCKET and colophon are registered trademarks of Simon & Schuster, Inc.

Designed by Richard Oriolo

Visit us on the World Wide Web
http://www.simonsays.com
http://www.wwe.com

Manufactured in the United States of America

For information regarding special discounts for bulk purchases, please contact Simon & Schuster Special Sales at 1-800-456-6798 or business@simonandschuster.com.

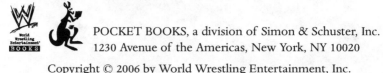

CHRONOLOGY

1980

JANUARY

2: Hulk Hogan defeats Ben Ortiz and Angelo Gomez in a Handicap match.

FEBRUARY

17: World Wrestling Federation Champion Bob Backlund defeats Ken Patera via countout. Pat Patterson was special guest referee.

MARCH

23: The Wild Samoans defeat Ivan Putski and Tito Santana for World Wrestling Federation World Tag Team Championship.

APRIL

1: Ken Patera defeats Pat Patterson for World Wrestling Federation Intercontinental Championship to become the second Intercontinental Champion in World Wrestling Federation history.

MAY

27: World Wrestling Federation World Champion Bob Backlund defends the title against "The American Dream" Dusty Rhodes in Osaka, Japan.

JUNE

2: World Wrestling Federation Champion Bob Backlund, Andre the Giant & Tito Santana face Antonio Inoki, Riki Choshu & Kengo Kimura in Hamamatsu, Japan.

16: Hulk Hogan defeats Gorilla Monsoon in front of a sell-out Madison Square Garden crowd.

JULY

18: Hulk Hogan wins a sixteen-man battle royal at the Civic Arena in Pittsburgh, Pennsylvania.

AUGUST

3: World Wrestling Federation Champion Bob Backlund defeats Florida Champion Don Muraco.

9: *Showdown at Shea:* Over 36,000 fans pack Shea Stadium to see Andre the Giant vs. Hulk Hogan, Pedro Morales & Bob Backlund vs. the Wild Samoans, and Bruno Sammartino vs. Larry Zbyszko in a steel cage!

SEPTEMBER

22: In the historic World Wrestling Federation/National Wrestling Association supercard, a capacity Madison Square Garden crowd witnesses World Wrestling Federation Champion Bob Backlund defeat NWA Champion Harley Race via disqualification.

30: World Wrestling Federation World Heavyweight Champion Bob Backlund defends the championship against the unpredictable Stan "The Lariat" Hansen in Tokyo, Japan.

OCTOBER

20: Dusty Rhodes & Pat Patterson defeat World Wrestling Federation World Tag Team Champions the Wild Samoans in a Best-Two-Out-of-Three Falls match via referee's decision.

NOVEMBER

8: Rick Martel & Tony Garea defeat World Wrestling Federation Tag Team Champions the Wild Samoans when Martel gets the pin with a sunset flip.

DECEMBER

8: Pedro Morales defeats Ken Patera to capture the Intercontinental Championship. Morales became the first Superstar in World Wrestling Federation history to hold World Wrestling Federation World, Intercontinental, and Tag Team titles, which today is known as "The Triple Crown."

1981

JANUARY

14: Hulk Hogan defeats Angelo Gomez and Steve King in a Handicap match.

FEBRUARY

15: World Wrestling Federation World Champion Bob Backlund, Intercontinental Champion Pedro Morales & S. D. Jones vs. the Moondogs & Capt. Lou Albano.

MARCH

8: Bruno Sammartino defeats Sgt. Slaughter.

APRIL

23: The first ever meeting between Tiger Mask and Dynamite Kid in Sumo Hall in Tokyo, Japan.

MAY

2: Killer Khan leaps onto Andre the Giant from the top rope and breaks his ankle. This ignites a bitter feud that ends in a Stretcher match.

4: Sgt. Slaughter meets Pat Patterson in a no-holds-barred Alley Fight match after Slaughter attacks Patterson during the $10,000 Cobra Clutch Challenge two months earlier.

JUNE

1: World Wrestling Federation World Champion Bob Backlund, Dusty Rhodes & Antonio Inoki defeat Stan Hansen, Hulk Hogan & Bobby Duncum in a Best-Two-Out-of-Three Falls match in Okayama, Japan.

JULY

11: World Wrestling Federation Champion Bob Backlund defeats George "The Animal" Steele in the Boston Garden.

AUGUST

24: Andre the Giant defeats Killer Khan in a Texas Death match. Pat Patterson and Gorilla Monsoon are special guest referees.

SEPTEMBER

21: Mr. Fuji and Mr. Saito co-win a twenty-man battle royal in Madison Square Garden. Other participants included Pedro Morales, Curt Hennig, Killer Khan, Tony Garea, Rick Martel, S. D. Jones, and Mil Mascaras.

OCTOBER

9: Andre the Giant defeats Killer Khan in a Stretcher match; World Wrestling Federation World Champion Bob Backlund fights Intercontinental Champion Don Muraco to a sixty-minute draw.

NOVEMBER

23: Pedro Morales defeats Don Muraco in a Texas Death match for the Intercontinental title after he hits Muraco with his own foreign object.

DECEMBER

5: World Wrestling Federation World Champion Bob Backlund defeats Don Muraco in a Steel Cage match when he escapes through the door as Muraco's head is entangled in the ropes.

1982

JANUARY

1: Japan's Tiger Mask defeats Dynamite Kid for the vacant World Wrestling Federation Junior Heavyweight Championship. This is the first of two title reigns for the future Japanese legend.

6: World Wrestling Federation World Champion Bob Backlund & Intercontinental Champion Pedro Morales defeat Jesse "The Body" Ventura & Adrian Adonis via countout.

FEBRUARY

15: World Wrestling Federation Intercontinental Champion Pedro Morales defeats Greg Valentine in a Brass Knuckles Alley Fight with Ivan Putski as special guest referee.

MARCH

7: The Cadillac tournament from Toronto's Maple Leaf Gardens sees Jimmy Valiant defeat Jesse Ventura in the finals.

APRIL

26: Jimmy "Superfly" Snuka defeats World Wrestling Federation Champion Bob Backlund via disqualification when Backlund refuses to break a chokehold. After the match, Snuka leaps from the top rope, and Backlund has to be carried out on a stretcher.

MAY

28: Hulk Hogan appears in *Rocky III* alongside Sylvester Stallone as Thunderlips.

JUNE

26: "Mr. USA" Tony Atlas wins a twenty-man Over the Top Rope battle royal in Philadelphia's Spectrum. Other participants are Pedro Morales, Greg Valentine, Blackjack Mulligan, the Strongbows, Ivan Putski, Stan Hansen, Adrian Adonis, and more.

28: Jimmy "Superfly" Snuka dives off the top of the steel cage during his title match against World Champion Bob Backlund, who moves out of the way and crawls out the cage door and on to victory.

JULY

4: World Wrestling Federation World Champion Bob Backlund fights NWA Champion Ric Flair to a double countout in Atlanta's Omni.

13: Mr. Fuji & Mr. Saito defeated World Wrestling Federation World Tag Team Champions The Strongbows in a Best-Two-Out-of-Three Falls.

AUGUST

11: World Wrestling Federation Champion Bob Backlund defeats International Champion Billy Robinson.

30: World Wrestling Federation Junior Heavyweight Champion Tiger Mask pins Dynamite Kid. This is the Madison Square Garden debut for both Superstars.

SEPTEMBER

18: World Wrestling Federation World Champion Bob Backlund pins Jimmy "Superfly" Snuka in Philadelphia's Spectrum. After the bout, Backlund and Snuka shake hands. "Superfly" shakes Arnold Skaaland's hand as well as the referee's before Backlund gives him his towel, which reads "World Wrestling Federation Champion." S. D. Jones is the special guest referee.

OCTOBER

4: The Strongbows defeat Mr. Fuji & Mr. Saito for World Wrestling Federation World Tag Team Championship in a Best-Two-Out-of-Three Falls.

NOVEMBER

22: World Wrestling Federation Champion Bob Backlund defeats returning former champion Superstar Billy Graham at Madison Square Garden.

DECEMBER

28: Jimmy "Superfly" Snuka meets with Ray "Crippler" Stevens in New York City's Madison Square Garden. This match solidifies the "Superfly" as a bona fide fan favorite.

1983

JANUARY

22: The Magnificent Muraco pins Intercontinental Champion Pedro Morales when Morales's injured knee gives out on him as he attempts a bodyslam.

FEBRUARY

18: Andre the Giant & Jimmy "Superfly" Snuka defeat the Wild Samoans in Madison Square Garden when Snuka leaps off Andre's shoulders and onto Sika for the pinfall.

MARCH

5: Andre the Giant wins a battle royal in San Diego, California.

12: Andre the Giant wins a twenty-man $10,000 battle royal. Some participants are Big John Studd, the Wild Samoans, Rocky Johnson, Chief Jay Strongbow, and Pedro Morales.

APRIL

25: Andre the Giant beats "Big" John Studd via countout. Studd escapes a scoop slam attempt from Andre and leaves the ring.

MAY

15: The teacher and the student team up as Fabulous Moolah & Leilani Kai face Princess Victoria & Susan Starr.

JUNE

3: World Wrestling Federation Champion Bob Backlund defeats former champion "Russian Bear" Ivan Koloff.

JULY

11: Andre the Giant defeats "Big" John Studd in a Steel Cage match in the Meadowlands.

16: World Wrestling Federation World Heavyweight Champion Bob Backlund pins George "The Animal" Steele in 58 seconds.

AUGUST

29: Andre the Giant defeats "Big" John Studd in a $10,000 Bodyslam rematch at the LA Sports Arena.

SEPTEMBER

24: World Wrestling Federation World Champion Bob Backlund defeats Sgt. Slaughter in a Texas Death match.

OCTOBER

17: World Wrestling Federation Intercontinental Champion Don Muraco defeats Jimmy "Superfly" Snuka in a Steel Cage match. After the match Snuka leaps off the top of the cage onto the bloodied, fallen champion. The fans at Madison Square Garden go berserk.

NOVEMBER

23: Pedro Morales makes history once again, defeating the Magnificent Muraco to become the first two-time Intercontinental Champion.

DECEMBER

1: The first ever official World Wrestling Federation magazine, titled *Victory,* hits newsstands.

26: Iron Sheik defeats Bob Backlund when "Golden Boy" Arnold Skaaland throws in the towel to end the match. Technically, Backlund was never pinned, nor did he give up.

1984

JANUARY

7: "Mean" Gene Okerlund makes his World Wrestling Federation television debut alongside Vince McMahon on an episode of *Championship Wrestling.*
23: *Hulkamania* is born as Hulk Hogan defeats the Iron Sheik in Madison Square Garden to become the ninth World Champion in World Wrestling Federation history.

FEBRUARY

7: Dynamite Kid defeats the Cobra in the finals of World Wrestling Federation Junior Heavyweight Championship Tournament in Tokyo. This tournament is revered as one of the greatest in wrestling history.

MARCH

11: Andre the Giant wins an eighteen-man, $50,000 battle royal in East Rutherford, New Jersey. Participants include Hulk Hogan, Sgt. Slaughter, Big John Studd, Pat Patterson, Jimmy "Superfly" Snuka, Tito Santana, Mil Mascaras, and Paul Orndorff.

APRIL

6: Hulk Hogan defeats "Big" John Studd in a Steel Cage match when the Hulkster escapes through the door.
17: Adrian Adonis & Dick Murdoch defeat "Mr. USA" Tony Atlas & Rocky Johnson for World Wrestling Federation World Tag Team Championship.

MAY

25: Jimmy "Superfly" Snuka and "Rowdy" Roddy Piper fight to a countout at the Kiel Auditorium. Piper leaves the ring area when Snuka gives "Hot Rod" a taste of his own medicine and whips him with guest referee Lou Thesz's belt.

JUNE

23: Sgt. Slaughter defeats the Iron Sheik.

JULY

23: *The Brawl to End It All* airs live on MTV from Madison Square Garden to a sell-out crowd of over 22,000 fans. Wendi Richter defeats Fabulous Moolah. This puts an end to Moolah's near-thirty-year reign as champion.

AUGUST

4: Bob Backlund defeats Salvatore Bellomo at the Philadelphia Spectrum. This turns out to be Backlund's last match until his World Wrestling Federation return in 1992.

SEPTEMBER

24: Greg "The Hammer" Valentine defeats Tito Santana for the Intercontinental Championship.

25: Hulk Hogan, Wendi Richter, and Cyndi Lauper appear as guest VJs on MTV.

OCTOBER

The first World Wrestling Federation action figures slam into stores across the United States and are an instant smash. The first ones out are Hulk Hogan, Andre the Giant, "Rowdy" Roddy Piper, Jimmy "Superfly" Snuka, Junkyard Dog, Hillbilly Jim, Iron Sheik, and Nikolai Volkoff.

NOVEMBER

1: Andre the Giant defeats "The Ugandan Giant" Kamala.

22: Rocky Johnson wins a $10,000, twenty-man Steel Cage battle royal against other Superstars like Tito Santana, Big John Studd, the Moondogs, Ken Patera, Mr. Fuji, Bobby "The Brain" Heenan, Greg "The Hammer" Valentine, and many more.

DECEMBER

29: The legendary Brisco Brothers face off against World Wrestling Federation World Tag Team Champions Adrian Adonis & Dick Murdoch at the Met Center.

1985

JANUARY

21: Bret Hart makes his Madison Square Garden debut, defeating Rene Goulet with a sleeper hold. The US Express—Barry Windham and Mike Rotundo—defeat Adrian Adonis & Dick Murdoch to win the World Wrestling Federation World Tag Team Championship.

FEBRUARY

4: Andre the Giant, Junkyard Dog & Jimmy "Superfly" Snuka defeat "Big" John Studd, "Rowdy" Roddy Piper & Ken Patera

5: World Wrestling Federation World Heavyweight Champion Hulk Hogan defeats Japanese Superstar Tatsumi Fujinami in Nagoya, Japan.

18: "The War to Settle the Score" originates from Madison Square Garden and sets the stage for the historic, first ever *WrestleMania.*

MARCH

31: The inaugural *WrestleMania* originates from Madison Square Garden. The star-studded event is seen by over one million fans worldwide.

APRIL

21: Hulk Hogan faces off against "Mr. Wonderful" Paul Orndorff in the main event at the Maple Leaf Gardens, where Orndorff's momentum from a cross-body allows Hogan to roll through the move for the pin. After the match Hogan and Orndorff shake hands.

MAY

11: The first episode of *Saturday Night's Main Event* airs live on NBC from the Nassau Coliseum in Uniondale, New York. In the main event, Hulk Hogan defeats "Cowboy" Bob Orton to retain the World Wrestling Federation World Heavyweight Championship.

JUNE

13: World Wrestling Federation World Heavyweight Champion Hulk Hogan clashes with IWGP Champion Antonio Inoki in Japan.

17: Barry Windham & Mike Rotundo defeat Iron Sheik & Nikolai Volkoff for the World Wrestling Federation World Tag Team Championship.

JULY

8: The first nontelevised *King of the Ring* tournament takes place in Foxboro, Massachusetts, and is won by the Magnificent Muraco.

AUGUST

13: World Wrestling Federation arrives at the Ohio State Fair, where 50,000 fans come out to see the likes of Hulk Hogan, Junkyard Dog, "Mr. Wonderful" Paul Orndorff, "Big" John Studd, Iron Sheik, the Magnificent Muraco, and "Mr. USA" Tony Atlas.

SEPTEMBER

13: The British Bulldogs are co-winners of a twenty-man, $50,000 battle royal.

28: The first singles meeting between Hulk Hogan and Randy "Macho Man" Savage takes place.

OCTOBER

3: World Wrestling Federation World Champion Hulk Hogan pins Nikolai Volkoff with a legdrop during a Flag match on *Saturday Night's Main Event.*

26: Bruno Sammartino teams with "Mr. Wonderful" Paul Orndorff to defeat "Rowdy" Roddy Piper & "Cowboy" Bob Orton in a steel cage.

NOVEMBER

1: World Wrestling Federation World Heavyweight Champion Hulk Hogan defeats Jesse "The Body" Ventura at the Nassau Coliseum in Uniondale, New York.

2: *Saturday Night's Main Event* from Hershey Park Arena sees World Wrestling Federation Champion Hulk Hogan & Andre the Giant defeat King Kong Bundy & "Big" John Studd. Randy "Macho Man" Savage fights to a double countout with Intercontinental Champion Tito Santana. Ricky "The Dragon" Steamboat defeats Mr. Fuji in a Kung Fu Challenge.

7: *The Wrestling Classic* emanates from the Rosemont Horizon and hosts a sixteen-man single-elimination tournament that is won by the Junkyard Dog. The World Wrestling Federation Heavyweight Championship is also up for grabs as Hulk Hogan faces "Rowdy" Roddy Piper. Hogan wins via disqualification.

25: The Masked Spider Lady shocks Madison Square Garden when she defeats Wendi Richter. Jaws drop even further when the masked woman turns out to be Fabulous Moolah.

DECEMBER

5: World Wrestling Federation Champion Hulk Hogan & Intercontinental Champion Tito Santana join forces and defeat Jesse "The Body" Ventura & Randy "Macho Man" Savage.

27: A thirty-man, $75,000 battle royal takes place at the Nassau Coliseum. Superstar participants include: Chief Jay Strongbow, Terry Funk, Junkyard Dog, George "The Animal" Steele, Randy "Macho Man" Savage, Iron Sheik, Hercules, and Brutus Beefcake.

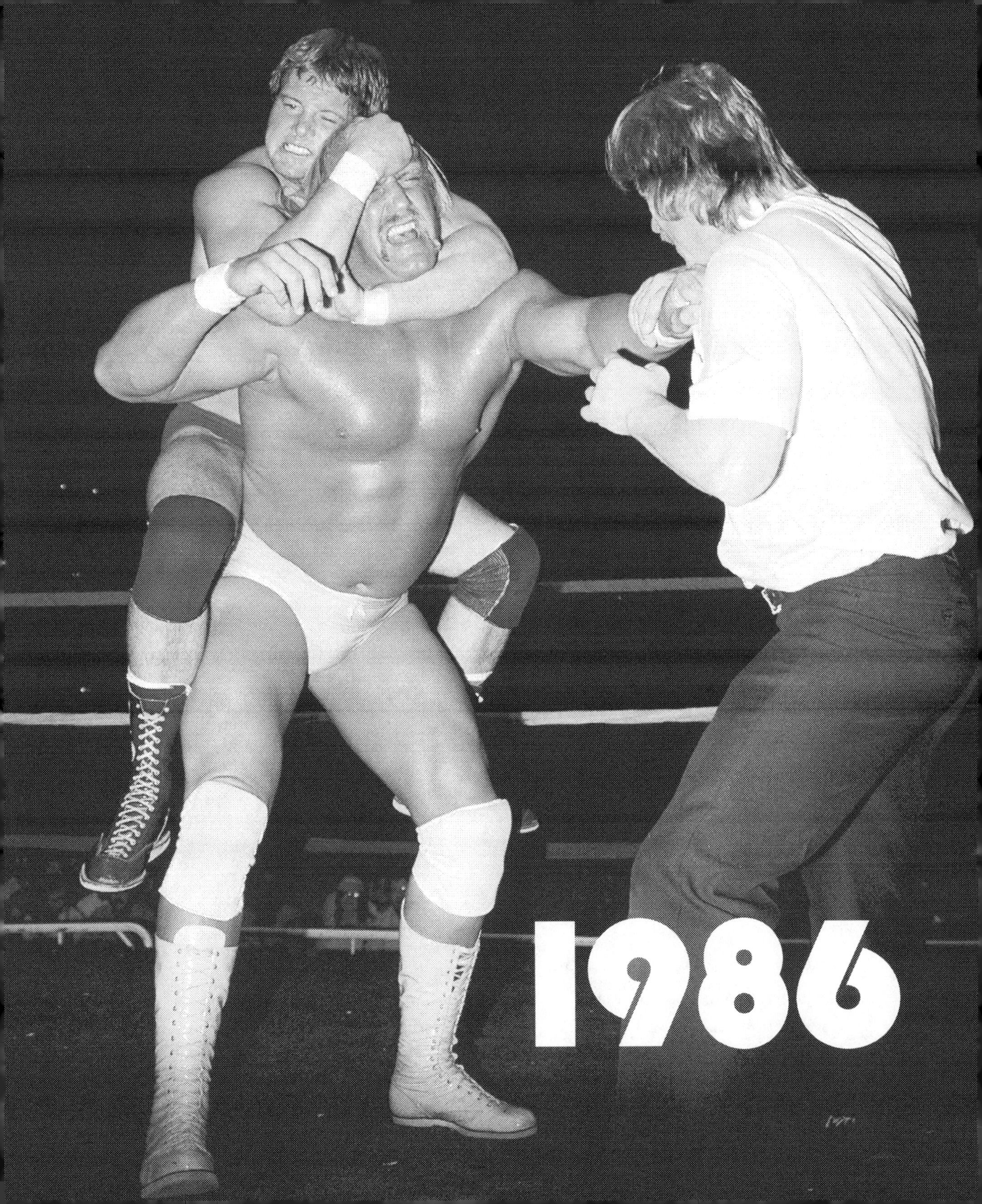

1986

JANUARY

1: World Wrestling Federation World Heavyweight Champion Hulk Hogan pins Terry Funk after he nails the man from the Double Cross Ranch with Jimmy Hart's megaphone.

11: Adrian Adonis is a guest on *Piper's Pit.* The former Brooklyn street fighter retires his leather jacket, gives it to Piper as a gift, and unveils his "Adorable" persona.

12: Andre the Giant defeats King Kong Bundy inside a fifteen-foot-high steel cage at Toronto's Maple Leaf Gardens.

FEBRUARY

8: Bruno Sammartino defeats "Rowdy" Roddy Piper in a Steel Cage match at the Boston Garden.

MARCH

1: The first ever World Wrestling Federation Slammy Awards air on MTV. During *Saturday Night's Main Event,* Hulk Hogan's "Real American" music video is premiered.

APRIL

7: *WrestleMania 2* emanates from three separate locations—Los Angeles, Chicago, and Uniondale, New York—all with their own main events.

MAY

3: World Wrestling Federation World Champion Hulk Hogan & Junkyard Dog defeat the Funk Brothers on an episode of *Saturday Night's Main Event.*

JUNE

13: Tito Santana takes on Intercontinental Champion Randy "Macho Man" Savage with Bruno Sammartino as special guest referee.

15: King Tonga defeats "Big" John Studd in the $15,000 Bodyslam Challenge.

JULY

14: Harley Race defeats Pedro Morales in the finals of the *King of the Ring* tournament held in Foxboro, Massachusetts. On the same card World Wrestling Federation World Tag Team Champions the British Bulldogs defeat the Dream Team in a Steel Cage match.

19: After a Tag Team match against "Big" John Studd & King Kong Bundy, "Mr. Wonderful" Paul Orndorff clotheslines Hulk Hogan and gives him a piledriver in the middle of the ring.

26: World Wrestling Federation President Jack Tunney announces that Andre the Giant has been suspended for missing a series of matches against members of the Heenan Family. At the Philadelphia Spectrum the Junkyard Dog defeats the Magnificent Muraco in a Dog Collar match.

28: Bruno Sammartino and Tito Santana defeat Randy "Macho Man" Savage and "Adorable" Adrian Adonis in a Steel Cage match at Madison Square Garden. Sammartino walks through the door, and Santana scales the cage wall at the same time.

AUGUST

2: "Classy" Freddie Blassie announces that he has found someone who is going to purchase 50 percent of the contracts of Iron Sheik and Nikolai Volkoff.

9: "Adorable" Adrian Adonis announces that "Cowboy" Bob Orton is his new bodyguard.

28: *The Big Event* emanates from Toronto's Exhibition Stadium. Over 74,000 fans set an outdoor attendance record to see Hulk Hogan defend his World Wrestling Federation World Heavyweight Championship against "Mr. Wonderful" Paul Orndorff.

29: The Sam Muchnick Memorial Tournament takes place at the Kiel Auditorium in St. Louis. In the tournament finals, "King" Harley Race defeats Ricky "The Dragon" Steamboat. Also on the card, World Wrestling Federation World Champion Hulk Hogan faces "Mr. Wonderful" Paul Orndorff.

30: The official coronation of "King" Harley Race; Capt. Lou Albano appears on *The Flower Shop* and introduces Giant, Super, and Big Machines to the world.

SEPTEMBER

7: The debut edition of *The Snake Pit* with host Jake "The Snake" Roberts. At the Maple Leaf Gardens, Hulk Hogan & "Rowdy" Roddy Piper join forces and battle "Mr. Wonderful" Paul Orndorff & "Adorable" Adrian Adonis.

16: Super, Big & Hulk Machines defeat King Kong Bundy, "Big" John Studd & Bobby "The Brain" Heenan.

28: Bobby "The Brain" Heenan debuts on *Wrestling Challenge* alongside Gorilla Monsoon.

OCTOBER

3: Hillbilly Jim defeats Mr. Fuji in a Tuxedo match at Nassau Coliseum in Uniondale, New York.

4: "Rowdy" Roddy Piper destroys the set of *The Flower Shop.*

9: At San Francisco's Cow Palace, Iron Sheik & Nikolai Volkoff win a twelve-tag-team battle royal.

NOVEMBER

24: After a fan from the crowd selects his partner, "Rowdy" Roddy Piper teams with Hulk Hogan and faces "Mr. Wonderful" Paul Orndorff & "King" Harley Race at Madison Square Garden. Though Piper and Hogan are victorious, Piper leaves his partner to fend for himself toward the end of the contest.

DECEMBER

3: The British Bulldogs defeat the Hart Foundation on a Best-Two-Out-of-Three Falls contest in the Tacoma Dome to retain the World Wrestling Federation World Tag Team Championship.

1987

JANUARY

3: Hulk Hogan defeats "Mr. Wonderful" during *Saturday Night's Main Event* in one of the most controversial Steel Cage matches ever.

24: Andre the Giant walks off the set of *Piper's Pit* after he receives an award for being the only undefeated Superstar in World Wrestling Federation history.

26: The Hart Foundation defeats the British Bulldogs for the World Wrestling Federation World Tag Team Championship.

FEBRUARY

6: Blackjack Mulligan wins a $50,000 Bunkhouse battle royal at Sacramento's Arena.

7: During *Piper's Pit,* Andre the Giant turns on his longtime friend and challenges the Hulkster to a match at *WrestleMania III* for the World Wrestling Federation World Heavyweight Championship.

14: Hulk Hogan appears on *Piper's Pit* and accepts the Giant's challenge.

21: "Rowdy" Roddy Piper confirms in an interview that takes place in an empty arena that *WrestleMania III* will be his last match.

23: In what is billed as his last Madison Square Garden appearance, "Rowdy" Roddy Piper teams with Ricky "The Dragon" Steamboat and Junkyard Dog to fight Randy "Macho Man" Savage, "King" Harley Race, and "Adorable" Adrian Adonis in an Elimination match.

MARCH

1: Hulk Hogan (with Billy Jack Haynes) takes on Hercules (with Bobby "The Brain" Heenan and Andre the Giant) in a Chain match at the St. Paul Civic Center.

15: The Frank Tunney Sr. Memorial Cup Tag Team Tournament takes place at the Maple Leaf Gardens in Toronto. The Killer Bees defeat Demolition in the tournament finals and earn a shot at the Hart Foundation for World Wrestling Federation Tag Team titles that same evening, but the Harts retain their title.

21: The first ever World Wrestling Entertainment event is held in Las Vegas at the Thomas & Mack Center.

29: *WrestleMania III* from the Pontiac Silverdome, with 93,173 fans, sets the all-time indoor attendance record as Hulk Hogan clashes with Andre the Giant for the World Wrestling Federation World Heavyweight Championship in the biggest match in wrestling history.

APRIL

27: World Wrestling Federation Intercontinental Champion Ricky "The Dragon" Steamboat teams with Jake "The Snake" Roberts and Billy Jack Haynes to face Randy "Macho Man" Savage, Honky Tonk Man, and Hercules.

MAY

3: At the famous Cobo Hall, Ricky "The Dragon" Steamboat defeats Randy "Macho Man" Savage in a Steel Cage match when Savage inadvertently throws "The Dragon" through the cage door for the win.
5: The Hart Foundation beat the British Bulldogs in a Lumberjack match.

JUNE

2: The Honky Tonk Man scores an upset win over Ricky "The Dragon" Steamboat to win the Intercontinental Championship. This is the start of the longest Intercontinental title reign to date.

JULY

5: The Junkyard Dog wins a $50,000 twenty-man battle royal at the Rosemont Horizon. Other participants include King Kong Bundy, Hillbilly Jim, One Man Gang, Demolition, and the Killer Bees.
24: Sensational Sherri defeats her mentor, the Fabulous Moolah, for the World Wrestling Federation Women's Championship.

AUGUST

12: Jake "The Snake" Roberts defeats World Wrestling Federation Intercontinental Champion the Honky Tonk Man by countout. "Mouth of the South" Jimmy Hart is suspended high above the ring in a locked cage to prevent him from interfering.

SEPTEMBER

25: *The Princess Bride,* starring Andre the Giant, premieres in theaters across the country.

OCTOBER

27: Strike Force defeats the Hart Foundation for the World Wrestling Federation World Tag Team Championship.

NOVEMBER

26: The first *Survivor Series* airs live on Pay-Per-View from the Richfield Coliseum in Richfield, Ohio.

DECEMBER

27: Randy "Macho Man" Savage defeats Intercontinental Champion the Honky Tonk Man by disqualification. Wrestling legend Nick Bockwinkel is special guest referee.

28: World Wrestling Federation Champion Hulk Hogan & Bam Bam Bigelow defeat Andre the Giant & King Kong Bundy.

1988

JANUARY

1: The first World Wrestling Federation video game, *WrestleMania,* is released.
3: Bam Bam Bigelow wins a Bunkhouse Stampede battle royal at Nassau Coliseum in Uniondale, New York. Other participants include Ernie Ladd, "The Rock" Don Muraco, Demolition, the British Bulldogs, Ultimate Warrior, Junkyard Dog, Hillbilly Jim, and One Man Gang.
24: The first ever *Royal Rumble* airs live on the USA Network. "Hacksaw" Jim Duggan wins the twenty-man, over-the-top-rope main event.

FEBRUARY

5: Wrestling returns to prime-time television when World Wrestling Federation and NBC debut *The Main Event.* Hulk Hogan loses World Wrestling Federation World Heavyweight Championship to Andre the Giant. One of the most controversial matches in World Wrestling Federation history, this ends Hogan's nearly four-year championship reign.

MARCH

27: *WrestleMania IV* comes from the Trump Plaza. The event hosts a record-setting fifteen matches, including a fourteen-man tournament to decide the undisputed World Wrestling Federation World Heavyweight Champion. Randy "Macho Man" Savage is victorious on four separate occasions to become the undisputed Heavyweight Champion.

MAY

8: Intercontinental Champion Honky Tonk Man defeats Brutus Beefcake by countout when Peggy Sue interferes in the match. It turns out that this Peggy Sue is none other than "The Colonel" himself Jimmy Hart incognito.

JUNE

19: The debut of *The Brother Love Show.*

JULY

11: Strike Force member Rick Martel is put out of action for eight months with various injuries after he feels the Decapitation Elbow from Demolition out on the floor.
31: The first World Wrestling Federation *Wrestlefest* takes place in front of over 25,000 fans at Milwaukee's County Stadium. The main event is a Steel Cage match, in which Hulk Hogan defeats Andre the Giant.

AUGUST

29: The first *SummerSlam* takes place at Madison Square Garden. Ultimate Warrior wins the Intercontinental title in record time. In the main event the Mega Powers take on the Mega Bucks.

SEPTEMBER

27: "Million Dollar Man" Ted DiBiase announces that he's reached an agreement with Bobby "The Brain" Heenan to purchase the contract of Hercules. Heenan agrees to sell Hercules to DiBiase as a slave in exchange for cash.

OCTOBER

7: Rockin' Robin defeats longtime World Wrestling Federation Women's Champion Sensational Sherri in Paris, France. Rockin' Robin is the last World Wrestling Federation Women's Champion of the decade.

NOVEMBER

4: *They Live,* starring "Rowdy" Roddy Piper, opens in movie theaters across the United States.

24: The second annual *Survivor Series* returns to the Richfield Coliseum and introduces team co-captains.

DECEMBER

24: On *The Brother Love Show,* a returning "Big" John Studd tells Bobby "The Brain" Heenan that he wants nothing to do with him and that Heenan is no longer his manager.

1989

JANUARY

15: The second *Royal Rumble* is the first to air live on Pay-Per-View. "Big" John Studd eliminates "Million Dollar Man" Ted DiBiase to win the battle royal.

FEBRUARY

3: *The Main Event* sees Randy Savage slap Hulk Hogan in the face and leave the ring during the Mega Powers tag match against the Twin Towers.

MARCH

10: "Big" John Studd slams "African Dream" Akeem on his way to victory at San Francisco's Cow Palace.

APRIL

2: *WrestleMania V*—for the first time in World Wrestling Federation history, *WrestleMania* is hosted in the same venue—Trump Plaza—two years in a row. The Mega Powers explode, and Hulk Hogan begins his second reign as World Wrestling Federation Champion.

MAY

12: "Rowdy" Roddy Piper's first World Wrestling Federation match in two years takes place at the Los Angeles Sports Arena, where he defeats "Million Dollar Man" Ted DiBiase.

JUNE

2: *No Holds Barred,* starring Hulk Hogan, opens in movie theaters nationwide.

JULY

18: Demolition's record-breaking sixteen-month title reign comes to an end in a Two-Out-of-Three Falls classic with Arn Anderson & Tully Blanchard, the Brain Busters.

AUGUST

28: *SummerSlam '89* airs live on Pay-Per-View from the Meadowlands Arena in East Rutherford, New Jersey.

SEPTEMBER

9: At the historic Boston Garden, Intercontinental Champion Ultimate Warrior pins the "Eighth Wonder of the World" Andre the Giant in 18 seconds.

OCTOBER

10: The first World Wrestling Federation event from the United Kingdom.

NOVEMBER

23: The third annual *Survivor Series* airs live from the Rosemont Horizon.

DECEMBER

13: The Colossal Connection duo of Andre the Giant & Haku defeats Demolition for the World Wrestling Federation World Tag Team Championship.

27: The last Pay-Per-View of the decade is a special *No Holds Barred: The Match, the Movie* event where Hulk Hogan & Brutus "The Barber" Beefcake battle Randy "Macho Man" Savage & Zeus in a steel cage.

SUPERSTAR BIOS

WILL ALWAYS

Hulk Hogan

FROM: **Venice Beach, CA**

HEIGHT: **6'7"**

WEIGHT: **303 lbs.**

FINISHING MOVE: **Atomic legdrop**

THIS NATIVE OF VENICE BEACH, CALIFORNIA, AND TWELVE-TIME WORLD HEAVYWEIGHT CHAMPION IS RECOGNIZED AROUND THE WORLD AS THE icon of professional wrestling and is credited for its transformation to sports entertainment. Before the bright lights, packed arenas, and championship gold, this former dockworker was discovered by wrestling greats Jack and Jerry Brisco playing bass guitar in Tampa, Florida. He would be trained by Japanese wrestler extraordinaire Hiro Matsuda. To gauge Hulk's toughness and dedication, Matsuda snapped Hogan's leg in half during their first training session. After a quick ten-week recovery, a motivated Hogan returned stronger than ever. Though he struggled to find success, and even took an eighteen-month hiatus from the ring, Hulk debuted in the then World Wide Wrestling Federation (WWWF) in 1978 as a villain managed by "Classy" Freddie Blassie. After competing in regional promotions throughout the southeastern United States, he moved to the American Wrestling Association, where he became a contender for their heavyweight title and threat to the reign of then-champion Nick Bockwinkel. In a harbinger of things to come, Hogan traveled to Japan and, by defeating Antonio Inoki in a tournament, was crowned the first ever IWGP Heavyweight Champion. Then, almost as unexpectedly, Hulk received a call to appear in *Rocky III* as Thunderlips alongside Sylvester Stallone. Shortly following his big-screen debut, he returned to World Wrestling Federation, where something even more amazing was about to take place.

On January 23, 1984, replacing an injured Bob Backlund, Hogan defeated the Iron Sheik for the World Wrestling Federation World Heavyweight Championship. That night, in Madison Square Garden, one of the most powerful forces in the universe was conceived as the voice of Gorilla Monsoon declared, "*Hulkamania* is here!" No statement would be more prophetic as the twenty-four-inch pythons, ripped T-shirt, and three commandments of training captured the heart of a generation. The magical ride that followed would be like no other. Hogan would go on to a near-four-year reign as World Heavyweight Champion during his first title run, the longest of any champion in twenty years, and headline every *WrestleMania* of the decade.

As the 1980s progressed, *Hulkamania* grew, and so did the list of challengers for wrestling's richest prize. Hogan's legendary feuds with the likes of "Rowdy" Roddy Piper, "Big" John Studd, King Kong Bundy, "Mr. Wonderful" Paul Orndorff, and Randy "Macho Man" Savage captured frenzied fans and brought attendance numbers to new heights. However, no other Superstar posed a greater danger to the life of *Hulkamania* than the Eighth Wonder of the World, Andre the Giant. The most recognizable athlete in the world, Andre had been undefeated throughout his storied career. During an episode of *Piper's Pit,* Andre issued a challenge to Hulk for a match at *WrestleMania III,* betraying his best friend and succumbing to the sinister influences of Bobby "The Brain" Heenan. The once gentle giant was now a monster. Hogan was accustomed to the Benedict Arnolds attempting to get close enough to him to steal the World Wrestling Federation Heavyweight Championship, but never in his wildest dreams had he thought Andre's name would be added to that list. From the opening bell to the final three-count, the match was a back-and-forth struggle. In an incredible spectacle, the Hulkster's power and mythical strength lifted the mighty five-hundred-pound giant and bodyslammed him to the canvas. Hogan then bounced off the ropes and landed his signature legdrop, and World Wrestling Federation official Joey Marella made the final three-count. The more than 90,000 fans in attendance erupted and rose to their feet, joining millions of *Hulkamaniacs* watching on Pay-Per-View around the globe. In the blink of an eye, Hulk Hogan had done the unthinkable and been catapulted to immortal icon status. His remarkable feat would indelibly carve his name in the monument of World Wrestling Entertainment history forever, and prove once and for all that *Hulkamania* is one of the most powerful forces in the universe.

As *Hulkamania* blazed into 1988, a new challenger would emerge in the form of "Million Dollar Man" Ted DiBiase, his obsession with the World Wrestling Federation Championship matched only by his unquenchable thirst for money. In an unholy alliance with Andre the Giant and Bobby "The Brain" Heenan, DiBiase devised a plot to dethrone Hogan, ending his historic reign as World Wrestling Federation World Heavyweight Champion. During a special *Friday Night's Main Event* telecast, Hogan lost the title to Andre under controversial circumstances. Despite being robbed of his title, Hogan would prove his greatness by recapturing it on April 2, 1989, at *WrestleMania V* against his former Mega Powers partner, the sinister Randy "Macho Man" Savage. Hogan remained champion and entered the 1990s with more momentum than ever. He would go on to hold the World Wrestling Federation World Heavyweight Championship another three times and win two *Royal Rumbles* before leaving the company in the spring of 1993.

In 1994, Hogan went to rival World Championship Wrestling, and on July 17 he defeated "Nature Boy" Ric Flair to become World Heavyweight Champion, a distinction he would hold on six separate occasions between 1994 and 1999. His WCW tenure is remembered best for what would be the most shocking turn in pro wrestling history. In 1996, at the *Bash at the Beach* Pay-Per-View, Hogan turned his back on the millions of *Hulkamaniacs* around the world by joining Kevin Nash and Scott Hall as their partner. This betrayal gave birth to one of the most wretched factions sports entertainment has ever seen, the nWo.

In 2002, Hogan and his nWo cohorts returned to wrestling, making their World Wrestling Federation debut at *No Way Out*. This led to the dream "Icon vs. Icon" battle at *WrestleMania X8* against The Rock. In the aftermath, Hogan heard the cries of fans around the world and returned to the ring in his classic red and yellow colors, setting his sights on a new breed of foe. Opponents included Triple H, Chris Jericho, Kurt Angle, and a renewed feud with Undertaker. Hogan claimed his sixth World Wrestling Federation Heavyweight title and added a new title to his trophy case, winning the World Wrestling Federation Tag Team Championship with Edge. Hogan even headlined *WrestleMania XIX* and locked horns with Mr. McMahon in a street fight that saw both men beat one another from pillar to post.

In April 2005, this immortal career culminated at the Hall of Fame ceremony, where Sylvester Stallone inducted Hogan in front of a capacity crowd. The next night at *WrestleMania XXI,* Hogan added another *WrestleMania* moment to his already long résumé when he came to the aid of the beaten Eugene. After a brief alliance with the Heartbreak Kid, Shawn Michaels, Hogan proved to the Showstopper at *SummerSlam* that there is no answering the question, "Whatcha gonna do when *Hulkamania* runs wild on you?"

Three decades of dominance is difficult to comprehend. Perhaps no one can describe it better than WWE Chairman Vince McMahon: "The term *Hulkamania* now is an endearing term because it means so many different things to so many different people."

Randy "Macho Man" Savage

FROM: **Sarasota, FL**

HEIGHT: **6'2"**

WEIGHT: **237 lbs.**

FINISHING MOVE: **Flying elbow drop**

A FORMER MAJOR LEAGUE BASEBALL PROSPECT, THIS SECOND-GENERATION WRESTLER HAD HIS FIRST MATCH IN 1973 AND DECIDED TO wrestle full-time. In 1979, while wrestling for his father's local International Championship Wrestling promotion, he defeated his brother, who would later become known as Leapin' Lanny Poffo, to win its heavyweight title. Savage arrived in Memphis in 1983 and would enter into a bloody feud with Jerry "The King" Lawler for the southern title. It was here Savage showed his innate mean streak by piledriving a blood-covered Lawler on a metal plate, sending him to the hospital. From that point on, Randy Savage was considered a star on the rise.

In 1985, Randy made it to the big time and entered World Wrestling Federation with the anticipation of a number-one first-round draft pick. After rejecting lucrative offers from managerial greats Bobby "The Brain" Heenan, Mr. Fuji, and "Mouth of the South" Jimmy Hart, Randy decided to go with an unknown to steer his career: the breathtaking Miss Elizabeth. It was then that he added "Macho Man" to his name and began coming to the ring in flamboyant sequinned robes, headbands, and shades. Savage immediately made his presence felt in World Wrestling Federation; in his first Pay-Per-View event, *The Wrestling Classic,* the Macho Man reached the tournament finals, taking on the Junkyard Dog. Though the Macho Man wasn't victorious that night at the Rosemont Horizon, he caught the eye of Superstars and fans everywhere.

On February 8, 1986, in an Intercontinental Championship rematch against Tito Santana, the Macho Man was unrelenting in his drive to become champion. In an effort to get Savage back in the ring, an overzealous Santana attempted to bring him from the ring apron courtesy of a belly-to-back suplex. While in midair, Savage knocked the two-time champion in the head with a foreign object, rendering him unconscious. Pinning a lifeless Santana, the Macho Man won the Intercontinental title and stunned a capacity crowd at the Boston Garden in the process. Though Savage's methods were labeled unfair, he proved to be a worthy champion, holding the Intercontinental Championship for an incredible thirteen months. With the Intercontinental title firmly wrapped around his waist, the Macho Man garnered a reputation for retaining it by any means necessary. This included everything from getting himself disqualified or counted out to

even stooping so low as to put Miss Elizabeth between himself and a charging opponent. Oddly enough, Savage's next challenge came in the form of someone who was more interested in wrapping his arms around Miss Elizabeth than getting his hands on the Macho Man. George "The Animal" Steele was one of World Wrestling Federation's most bizarre Superstars, and his infatuation with the lovely Elizabeth enraged Savage no end. The Macho Man violently lashed out when the beastly Steele was calmed by Elizabeth's stunning beauty. This resulted in a series of brutal matches around the country, with the final fight at *WrestleMania 2*. In an impressive *WrestleMania* debut, Savage's rage fueled him to victory, and he left the Nassau Coliseum with his Intercontinental Championship in hand.

Not until a title defense in November of 1986 against Ricky "The Dragon" Steamboat would we see the true wickedness of Macho Madness. Unable to pin the challenger, the champion's frustration grew, and the Macho Man took the battle to the outside, draping Steamboat's throat across the top of the steel barricade. Savage moved at the speed of light to the top rope and, in an attempt to cause permanent injury, came crashing down onto the challenger's throat with his signature double ax-handle. With the audiences in shock, Savage once again placed a dazed Steamboat onto the barricade and, like a man possessed, committed the unthinkable: he ripped the timekeeper's bell from the table and returned to the top rope. With no hesitation, the Macho Man leaped from the turnbuckle, soaring through the air, smashing the bell to the back of Steamboat's neck and crushing his larynx over the barricade, thereby disqualifying him. Steamboat would be out of action for two months, going through intense physical and speech rehabilitation. When the Dragon returned, he was driven to take the one thing the Macho Man loved more than anything: the Intercontinental Championship. This highly anticipated rematch was set for March 28, 1987, at *WrestleMania III.* The bell rang, and these two stellar athletes went hold-for-hold in a classic mano-a-mano battle. When all was said and done, the Macho Man had lost his title, but it was one of the greatest wrestling matches of all time.

In the following months the Macho Man underwent a change of heart, and during the October 2 episode of *Saturday Night's Main Event* he wrestled then Intercontinental Champion the Honky Tonk Man. During the bout, Savage was jumped by the Hart Foundation and was on the receiving end of a broken guitar over his head. Trying to protect her man, Miss Elizabeth stepped in front of Randy. A cowardly Honky Tonk Man threw her to the mat. She then went to the locker room for help and, in a shocking turn of events, returned with Hulk Hogan. Hogan and a rejuvenated Macho Man cleared the ring. Their backing into one another finally began a tense stare-down, until Miss Elizabeth explained how Hogan had come to their aid. In one of the most exciting moments in *Saturday Night's Main Event* history, a grateful Macho Man extended his hand in friendship to Hogan, forming an alliance that would later become officially known as the Mega Powers. From that point on, Savage and Hogan were inseparable. Hogan even appeared ringside during the Macho Man's *WrestleMania IV* tournament finals match against "Million Dollar Man" Ted DiBiase. Under Hogan's watchful eye, Savage would become the undisputed champion and capture his first of two World Wrestling Federation World Heavyweight Championships. These two greats fought in tandem against World Wrestling Federation's most dangerous Superstars at *SummerSlam '88*. With the controversial Jesse "The Body" Ventura as special guest referee, Savage and Hogan defied the odds by defeating the Mega Bucks team of Andre the Giant and "Million Dollar Man" Ted DiBiase. Unfortunately, a series of misunderstandings between the two heroes caused Savage to walk out on Hogan during a Tag Team match against the Twin Towers. When Hogan got the win and returned to the locker room, the Macho Man blindsided the Hulkster with the championship belt that he had helped Savage win. It was clear that the Macho Man was reverting to his ruthless ways, and on April 2, 1989, the Mega Powers exploded at *WrestleMania V.* In an intense bout, Hogan kicked out of Savage's flying elbow to emerge victorious, winning his second World Wrestling Federation World Championship.

As the 1990s began, the Macho Man would become the official voice for Slim Jim, demanding that people across the United States "snap into it." In the ring, he had a new valet at his side, Sensational Sherri. Savage would briefly be known as the Macho King, defeating "Hacksaw" Jim Duggan. It wasn't long after that Savage entered into a battle with "The American Dream" Dusty Rhodes. After losing a retirement match to Ultimate Warrior at *WrestleMania VII,* a disgusted Sherri attacked the Macho Man, and the lovely Miss Elizabeth, who was in the audience, came in to make the save. At *SummerSlam '91* they would be reunited in a tearful ceremony that was ruined when Jake "The Snake" Roberts presented the two with a gift box harboring a king cobra. After a successful campaign to be reinstated by then World Wrestling Federation president Jack Tunney, the Macho Man defeated Roberts at the *Tuesday in Texas* Pay-Per-View and once again during an episode of *Saturday Night's Main Event.* "Nature Boy" Ric Flair began making outrageous claims that he once had a romantic relationship with Miss Elizabeth. Determined to clear his wife's name, Savage defeated Flair in a fiery contest at *WrestleMania VIII* to capture his second World Wrestling Federation World Heavyweight Championship. Unfortunately, on September 1, 1992, Flair defeated an injured and outnumbered Macho Man for his second title reign. As his World Wrestling Federation in-ring career was coming to a close, Savage provided commentary and was behind the microphone for the first-ever episode of *Monday Night Raw.* He was also part of the three-man announcing team at *WrestleMania IX* alongside Bobby "The Brain" Heenan and newcomer Jim Ross. His last major match was a Falls Count Anywhere match at *WrestleMania X* against Crush. The capacity crowd at Madison Square Garden saw the Macho Man stand in the ring with his arm raised in victory. Sadly, shortly after that, Randy and World Wrestling Federation parted ways.

In 1995 Savage joined his on-again, off-again ally Hulk Hogan in World Championship Wrestling. On November 26 at the *World War III* Pay-Per-View, he earned his first of two WCW World titles by winning a sixty-man three-ring over-the-top-rope battle royal. He also reignited his feud with Ric Flair, even tagging with his father to battle the "Nature Boy." Savage crossed paths with new opponents, including Taskmaster Kevin Sullivan, Diamond Dallas Page, and Lex Luger. At one point the Macho Man even donned the black-and-white colors of the nWo. In 1999, after a brief return and feud with Kevin Nash, he left WCW for good. In 2002 he made his silver-screen debut, appearing as Bonesaw McGraw in *Spider-Man.*

Randy "Macho Man" Savage will always be fondly remembered as an incredible competitor, the epitome of intensity, and one of the most athletically gifted athletes of his time. Oooh yeah!!!!!

HULKA

Ultimate Warrior

FROM: **Parts unknown**

HEIGHT: **6'2"**

WEIGHT: **275 lbs.**

FINISHING MOVE: **Warrior press slam/splash**

TAKE SUPREME ENERGY AND COMBINE IT WITH UNMATCHED INTENSITY, INFUSE IT WITH UNPARALLELED RAW POWER, AND YOU GET—THE Ultimate Warrior. To his loyal fans around the world, he is both mystical and mythical. From his trademark face paint and his cannonlike arms to the music that fueled his sprint to the shaking of the ropes that sent crowds into a frenzy, the Warrior was a hero like no other. The pillar of strength came from the world of amateur body building. When he became interested in professional wrestling, the Warrior traveled to California to be trained by Red Bastien. Here he would not only learn the basics of pro wrestling but meet and form a tag team with the man who would later be known as Sting. The two entered the pro ranks in November 1985 as Power Team USA, then became villains and went by the name of the Blade Runners. After a brief run, the two parted ways, and the Warrior headed to World Class Championship Wrestling. While in Texas, he was one half of the WCCW Tag Team Champions as well a holder of the Texas Heavyweight Championship. But the Warrior knew his destiny lay elsewhere.

In June 1987, Warrior made his World Wrestling Federation debut, and in his first television appearance he made quick work of journeyman wrestler Terry Gibbs in 1 minute, 38 seconds. In January 1988, after being attacked with a chain, the Warrior entered into a feud with Hercules. The two would settle their differences at *WrestleMania IV,* and Warrior defeated Hercules in his *'Mania* debut. That summer the Warrior lived out the dream of many fans and Superstars by getting his hands on Bobby "The Brain" Heenan in a series of Loser Wears a Weasel Suit matches. It was not until *SummerSlam '88* that the Warrior displayed his full sense for the dramatic. Intercontinental Champion the Honky Tonk Man was taunting the crowd and wrestlers for an opponent, since Brutus "The Barber" Beefcake was injured and couldn't compete. As Honky Tonk was concluding his rant, Warrior's music hit, and out he came to the ring, answering the call to a deafening crowd in Madison Square Garden. In an unprecedented 10 seconds, the Ultimate Warrior ended Honky Tonk's fourteen-month title reign to become the new Intercontinental Champion. At *Royal Rumble 1989,* Warrior was attacked from behind by "Ravishing" Rick Rude during their posedown. The two locked horns at *WrestleMania V,* and with a little help from his manager Bobby

"The Brain" Heenan, Rude took the Intercontinental title from Warrior. The Ultimate One did not retreat, nor surrender, and he regained his title by defeating Rude at *SummerSlam '89.*

As the 1980s came to a close, Warrior's star was on the rise, and a showdown with the immortal Hulk Hogan was inevitable. As the two crossed paths at *Royal Rumble 1990,* dreams would soon become reality. Once the match was signed, both men came to the aid of the other to ensure they would be a hundred percent for their showdown. These two mega-forces clashed in a historic Champion vs. Champion match at *WrestleMania VI* dubbed "The Ultimate Challenge." In an exchange of strength and force, Warrior emerged victorious and became World Wrestling Federation World Heavyweight Champion three months into the new decade. Once the title was around his waist, he met the challenge of Superstars like Andre the Giant, Ted DiBiase, the Honky Tonk Man, Haku, and past rival "Ravishing" Rick Rude. It was not until *Royal Rumble 1991* that Warrior would once again be adversely affected by outside interference. During his title defense against newly turned Iraqi sympathizer Sgt. Slaughter, the Macho Man's valet Sensational Sherri appeared at ringside and baited Warrior to chase her. Then Savage clobbered Warrior with his scepter. Slaughter seized the opportunity and covered an unconscious Warrior to win his only World Wrestling Federation Championship. Warrior would get revenge on Savage at *WrestleMania VII,* sending him into retirement. At *SummerSlam '91* Warrior joined forces with Hulk Hogan to defeat the Triangle of Terror consisting of Sgt. Slaughter, Col. Mustafa, and General Adnan. After a hiatus, the Ultimate Warrior made a surprise return at *WrestleMania VIII* and shocked the world by coming to the aid of Hulk Hogan, fending off an attack by Papa Shango and Sid Justice. The Warrior would again battle Randy "Macho Man" Savage at *SummerSlam '92,* but would leave World Wrestling Federation in November.

Warrior resurfaced again in the mid-1990s, at *WrestleMania XII,* making quick work of an up-and-coming Hunter Hearst-Helmsley. In the coming months he defeated such names as Jerry "The King" Lawler, Goldust, and Owen Hart. Unfortunately for his fans, the Ultimate Warrior once again disappeared from the company without a trace. He did not resurface until 1998, but this time it would be in World Championship Wrestling to reignite his feud with Hulk Hogan. Many fans were curious to see how the Warrior would fare against new opponents, and if he would reunite with former tag partner Sting. Unfortunately the duo made only one appearance together as a team before the Warrior left the organization. This would be the last fans would see of the Ultimate Warrior in the squared circle.

After leaving wrestling, Warrior dedicated himself to learning American history, Western culture, and the great books of the western world. Today he travels the globe speaking on the importance of self-empowerment and living a full life. The Ultimate Warrior will always be remembered as a great champion, a defender of truth, and the founding father of ring intensity. Though he has not been seen in WWE in over a decade, the fans' infatuation with this larger-than-life hero has always been the impetus for questions regarding his whereabouts and rumors of a return to the ring.

"Rowdy" Roddy Piper

FROM: **Glasgow, Scotland**

HEIGHT: **6'2"**

WEIGHT: **230 lbs.**

FINISHING MOVE: **Sleeper hold**

ARGUABLY THE GREATEST MOUTHPIECE SPORTS ENTERTAINMENT HAS EVER known, the man who became known as "Hot Rod" had a pro wrestling debut that was far from legendary. A fifteen-year-old Roddy Piper was on the receiving end of a brutal ten-second beating in Winnipeg, Canada, courtesy of Larry "The Ax" Hennig. However, this scrappy newcomer and International Golden Gloves Boxing Champion would not be discouraged. Piper traveled up and down the West Coast for the better half of the 1970s, proving himself in the ring against names like Chavo Guerrero, Buddy Rose, and "Killer" Tim Brooks. At one point he was even known as the Masked Canadian in Los Angeles. In 1980, Roddy joined Jim Crockett's NWA Mid-Atlantic promotion, where he battled the likes of Ric Flair, Wahoo McDaniel, and Paul Jones. His storied feud with Greg "The Hammer"

Valentine, one of the most talked-about rivalries, reached its violent apex at *Starrcade '83*. Piper and Valentine met in a ferocious Dog Collar match that would be regarded as one of the most violent in pro wrestling history. Piper lost 75 percent of the hearing in his left ear, an injury that still plagues the legend today.

In 1984, "Rowdy" Roddy Piper made his riotous World Wrestling Entertainment debut, dressed in his signature kilt. Piper became one of wrestling's most hated villains. His feuds were so violent that the company added security around the ring in arenas across the country to prevent fan attacks. It reached a point where the tension became so great he had to enlist the services of "Cowboy" Bob Orton as his bodyguard. "Mean" Gene Okerlund once described Piper's ego as "simply astounding in size." During this era of mayhem, Roddy also introduced the most influential and controversial television segment in sports entertainment—*Piper's Pit*. It was here that Hot Rod expressed his offensive views, applauded deplorable behavior, and antagonized fan favorites to incite altercations. One of his more popular tactics was to ask his guest a question and, before the guest could answer, bring the microphone back to himself to continue his rant. Piper began a bloody feud with Jimmy "Superfly" Snuka when, during an episode of the *Pit,* he made disparaging remarks about Snuka and his Samoan ancestors. When Snuka bent down to pick up a banana, a shameless Piper smashed the Superfly in the head with a coconut, knocking him out. The force was so great that it sent Snuka through the show set and down to the floor. A crazed Piper added insult to injury by pummeling the fallen Superstar until he was restrained by fellow wrestlers.

Piper's revolting behavior did not reach its pinnacle until he was feuding with World Wrestling Federation World Champion Hulk Hogan. This ongoing war was so consuming that even celebrities like Cyndi Lauper and Mr. T got caught in its violent groundswell. Piper and Hogan battled during the "War to Settle the Score" that aired live on MTV. This match ended in sheer bedlam and set the stage for an incredible *WrestleMania* main event as the lines were drawn in the sand. "The Rowdy One" and "Mr. Wonderful" Paul Orndorff were set to go against Hogan and Mr. T. Both sides had men in their corner: Piper had his bodyguard Bob Orton, and Hogan called upon friend and Piper archenemy Jimmy Snuka. The match was fast and furious, and while the Piper-Hogan saga continued, a feud began between Hot Rod and Mr. T that reached a near boiling point. The match ended when Mr. Wonderful got accidentally clobbered in the head with Orton's "protective" cast and was pinned for the three-count. With the world watching, Piper once again displayed his true nature, leaving Orndorff alone in the ring.

Throughout 1986 Piper tormented Mr. T and even appeared on the set of his hit TV show *The A-Team*. The two met in a boxing match at *WrestleMania 2*. Before the event, Roddy sent a message to his opponent during an episode of *Piper's Pit*, by shaving the head of Mr. T's friend the Haiti Kid. Roddy came to the ring with legendary trainer Lou Duva in his corner. The match went three rounds, and each man knocked the other to the canvas. As the contest continued, Roddy displayed his infamous temper when he threw a stool at Mr. T and jawed derogatory remarks at his corner. Eventually, Piper was disqualified when he bodyslammed Mr. T, inciting a near riot in the ring. Toward the end of the year, the Rowdy One began to change some of his unpopular views and took aim at one-time allies. During an episode of *The Flower Shop*, show host "Adorable" Adrian Adonis took issue with Piper on his newfound attitude. Adonis attacked Piper; as he drew first blood, he had no idea of the fury that was going to be unleashed upon him. The two clashed at *WrestleMania III* in a Hair vs. Hair match in what was billed as Roddy's final bout. Though the match saw the pendulum shift on several occasions, when Hot Rod was in serious trouble, he received help from an unexpected source. When Adonis had Roddy in his "Good Night Irene" sleeper, he thought Piper was out cold. As Adonis prematurely celebrated in the ring, Brutus Beefcake ran in and revived the Hot Scot. With Piper alert and back on his feet, the former Golden Gloves Champion rallied, slapping Adonis in his own version of the sleeper. As Adorable Adrian went goodnight, Piper helped introduce fans to the new incarnation of Brutus "The Barber" Beefcake as Brutus shaved Adonis's head. When he was awakened and Piper showed him his new look, the Adorable One fled the ring in disgust and humiliation. As he promised, Piper left World Wrestling Entertainment, but he did not stay out of the spotlight for too long. On November 4, 1988, Piper made his major motion picture debut, starring in John Carpenter's *They Live*. The movie became an instant sci-fi cult hit and established Piper as a star in Tinseltown. Despite the fanfare that surrounded his new profession, "Hot Rod" couldn't stay away from the ring. At *WrestleMania V*, Roddy hosted an episode of *Piper's Pit* and squared off in a verbal brawl with two other controversial talk show hosts, Brother Love and Morton Downey Jr.

Soon Piper returned to World Wrestling Federation full-time and feuded with Bad News Brown. The two faced off at *WrestleMania VI*, and Toronto witnessed a brutal clash of fighting styles. Always the devil's advocate, Piper showed he was an equal-opportunity pugilist when he sprinted down the SkyDome aisle with his body painted half black. The two Superstars fought tooth-and-nail in a wild altercation. Though the match ended in a double countout, this marked the return of the Hot Rod. On wrestling's grandest stage, Piper showed he hadn't lost a step, or the myriad tricks that were always up his sleeve. The early and mid-1990s saw Piper exhibit his amazing versatility as a World Wrestling Federation Superstar. Roddy made his formal announcing debut when he got behind the broadcast booth. Then, on January 19, 1992, Piper won his first major championship when he defeated the Mountie for the World Wrestling Federation Intercontinental title in Albany, New York. Piper held the title for three months until he faced longtime friend and former Intercontinental Champion Bret "Hit Man" Hart at *WrestleMania VIII.* After the two traded table turns, the referee was knocked out. When Piper returned to the ring with the timekeeper's bell and raised it above his head, the capacity Hoosier Dome crowd almost collapsed in shock as Roddy stood over a bloodied Bret Hart. Piper lost the match and the Intercontinental Championship, but the two friends embraced in the middle of the ring in a show of mutual respect and admiration. At *WrestleMania X,* Piper was the special guest referee for a World Wrestling Federation Heavyweight Championship match that saw Hart defeat the mighty Yokozuna. In 1996, after Gorilla Monsoon was injured at the hands of Vader, Roddy became World Wrestling Federation's interim president. One of his greatest achievements while in office was at *WrestleMania XII,* when he defeated Goldust in a Hollywood Backlot Brawl. Shortly after his *'Mania* victory, Roddy and the company parted ways.

On October 27, 1996, Piper shocked the world when he appeared at WCW's *Halloween Havoc* Pay-Per-View and confronted his supreme nemesis, Hulk Hogan. The circumstances that surrounded their standoff were dramatically different this time. Hogan was now the loathsome Hollywood Hulk Hogan, leader of the nWo. "The Hot Rod" was the beloved figure that resonated with an entire generation of fans. The rekindled feud was to settle who was professional wrestling's true icon. Piper popped in and out of World Championship Wrestling until the fall of 2000, when he left the company. Roddy appeared at select independent events before he again surprised the wrestling world. At *WrestleMania XIX,* Hot Rod bum-rushed the ring during the Hulk Hogan vs. Mr. McMahon street fight and laid both men out before he quickly exited Safeco Field. Shortly afterward, Piper returned to WWE and resurrected *Piper's Pit.* Unfortunately, his stay was brief.

In 2005, Piper was awarded the ultimate honor. On April 2 he was inducted into the WWE Hall of Fame with fellow legends who had helped usher in the sports entertainment rebellion. The next night at *WrestleMania 21,* Hot Rod hosted a special episode of *Piper's Pit* with guest Stone Cold Steve Austin. Since then Piper has made surprise appearances at WWE live events around the world, including WWE Homecoming, when his guest in the *Pit* was hardcore legend Mick Foley. You just never know when the Hot Scot will appear, or what will happen. One thing you can be sure of is to expect the unexpected. "Rowdy" Roddy Piper is one of the WWE legends who has fomented as much hatred as a villain as he inspired love as a hero. Adored by many, hated by a few, and respected by all—no one will ever top "The Rowdy One."

Jimmy "Superfly" Snuka

FROM: **The Fiji Islands**

HEIGHT: **6'**

WEIGHT: **250 lbs.**

FINISHING MOVE: **Superfly Splash**

THIS WWE HALL OF FAMER HAD A SUCCESSFUL PROFESSIONAL BODYBUILDING CAREER BEFORE HE MADE HIS 1969 WRESTLING DEBUT IN HAWAII. Since his family roots were firmly planted in professional wrestling, it was only a matter of time before he'd reach heights in the ring that matched the scope of his vertical leap. Jimmy Snuka first made a name for himself as a fan favorite in the NWA's Pacific Northwest territory. He spent the early 1970s feuding with Jesse "The Body" Ventura in both tag team and singles competition. In 1977 he won the Texas Heavyweight and Tag Team titles and toured Japan, teaming with Bruiser Brody. Snuka then landed in Mid-Atlantic Championship Wrestling and formed a successful tag team with "Mr. Wonderful" Paul Orndorff. Here Snuka battled the likes of Ricky Steamboat, Greg Valentine, and "Nature Boy" Ric Flair for the United States Championship. He spent the remainder of the late

1970s and early 1980s touring the NWA territories. Despite having won regional singles and tag team championships, the "Superfly" had yet to have his unique abilities recognized on a national level.

Jimmy "Superfly" Snuka debuted in World Wrestling Federation in 1982 as a rule-breaker managed by Capt. Lou Albano. Snuka's wrestling and aerial prowess set a new standard, and he became an immediate contender for Bob Backlund's World Wrestling Federation World Heavyweight title. The two Superstars battled at Madison Square Garden in three consecutive main events. The last was inside a fifteen-foot-high steel cage. During this classic match, Snuka climbed to the top of the cage and jumped off. As the crowd looked on in astonishment, a resilient Backlund moved out of the way, and Snuka crashed down on the mat. Backlund crawled out of the cage door and retained the title. In September 1982 the Backlund/Snuka feud ended when Backlund defeated Snuka, and in the ultimate show of mutual respect, the two shook hands after the match. Thanks to the help of then World Wrestling Federation announcer "Nature Boy" Buddy Rogers, Snuka realized that Capt. Lou was embezzling money from him. The "Superfly" fired Albano and took the the Nature Boy on as his new manager. With Buddy Rogers in his corner and his death-defying acrobatics, Snuka became one of the most popular Superstars. "Superfly" also feuded with the Wild Samoans and recruited partners such as Andre the Giant, Chief Jay Strongbow, and Rocky Johnson to help fight the untamed Polynesian beasts. During one match at Madison Square Garden, Snuka climbed and performed his Splash from Andre's mammoth shoulders.

The next year "Superfly" became entrenched in a violent feud with Intercontinental Champion the Magnificent Muraco. These men battled in Singles matches, Tag Team matches, even a Strap match—nothing could contain the fury between these two Superstars. During a TV taping, Muraco came out and spit in Snuka's face. Acting in sheer rage, the Superfly ran across the ring and dove over the top rope onto the champion. On October 17, 1983, the Superfly and the Magnificent One met at Madison Square Garden inside a fifteen-foot-high steel cage for the Intercontinental Championship. It was pure pandemonium as the cage door was locked and both men circled one another, prepared to do battle in wrestling's most dangerous contest. The two foes exchanged blows at the onset, and Snuka was busted open after a slingshot into the cage. The Superfly fired back with offense of his own, and both men were bleeding profusely. As Snuka bounced off the ropes, he hit Muraco with a flying head-butt. Muraco called for the door in midair, and allowed the force of the aerial attack to take him through the cage door and on to victory. An enraged Superfly exited the cage and dragged Muraco back into the ring. After giving Muraco a vertical suplex, Snuka climbed to the top rope, then to the top of the cage, sending the capacity Garden crowd to their feet. As blood poured down his face, Superfly gave his "I Love You" hand sign to the 20,000 plus in attendance and leaped off the top of the cage, crashing down on the motionless champion. Snuka stood over the fallen Muraco and dropped the Intercontinental Championship belt on him in disgust. Superfly gave the crowd one last hand sign, then exited the steel structure. Muraco had to be helped back to the locker room by onsite medical staff and security. This was a turning point in Snuka's career, sending his popularity to an all-time high. His number of main event matches increased, and his likeness was featured in the hit Saturday-morning cartoon *Hulk Hogan's Rock and Wrestling.* Superfly's next opponent would later become his greatest nemesis. That World Wrestling Federation Superstar was none other than "Rowdy" Roddy Piper.

During an episode of *Piper's Pit,* the "Hot Rod" insulted Snuka's family, called him a monkey, and accused him of acting like a big shot. When Snuka wasn't looking, the dastardly Piper whaled Superfly across the head with a coconut and knocked him through the show set. While Snuka was on the floor, the Hot Rod proceeded to beat him with a belt and had to be restrained by other Superstars who came from the locker room to stop the assault. The Superfly and the Hot Scot fought tooth-and-nail, facing off in a Fijian Strap match where there's no disqualification and there must be a winner. Though Snuka won the match, Piper jumped him from behind, and the war waged on. Unfortunately for Snuka, Piper's bodyguard "Cowboy" Bob Orton was never far behind and often interfered. To neutralize these attacks, Superfly enlisted the help of Superstars like Hulk Hogan, Junkyard Dog, and "Mr. USA" Tony Atlas to face off against the villainous duo in tag team bouts. "Superfly" had the last laugh when he led the team of Hulk Hogan & Mr. T to victory against the team of "Rowdy" Roddy Piper & "Mr. Wonderful" Paul Orndorff at the first *WrestleMania.* Soon after this historic event, the Superfly vanished from World Wrestling Federation.

In 1986 Superfly resurfaced in the American Wrestling Association when he appeared as Greg Gagne's surprise tag team partner at *WrestleRock '86*. Over the next year, Snuka split time between the Minnesota-based organization and tours of Asia with All-Japan Pro Wrestling. While at an AWA event, Snuka was attacked by the ruthless South African separatist Col. DeBeers and received a piledriver on the concrete floor. The two fought in one of the bloodiest feuds in AWA history. In 1989 the Superfly returned home to World Wrestling Federation and appeared at *WrestleMania V.* During Snuka's ovation, commentator and former foe Jesse "The Body" Ventura said to Gorilla Monsoon, "I wanna see if he still got it." Superfly returned better than ever as he battled the likes of "Million Dollar Man" Ted DiBiase, the Honky Tonk Man, Greg "The Hammer" Valentine, Mr. Perfect, "Ravishing" Rick Rude, and Hercules. At *WrestleMania VII,* the Superfly faced Undertaker in the Dead Man's *WrestleMania* debut. In the early 1990s the Superfly and World Wrestling Federation parted ways. Snuka toured the U.S. independents before he landed in the upstart Eastern Championship Wrestling. On April 25, 1992, Snuka became the first ECW World Heavyweight Champion. While champion, Snuka battled former rival Don Muraco for the title and appeared in events along with Tito Santana and legend Terry Funk. Snuka was instrumental in generating early excitement for the Philadelphia-based group of renegades, who later evolved into the underground outlaws known as Extreme Championship Wrestling. In November of 1996, Superfly's pioneering four-decade career was celebrated by his induction into WWE Hall of Fame. The next night at Madison Square Garden, the Superfly returned for his last WWE match to date at the *Survivor Series.* Snuka was the mystery partner of Savio Vega, Flash Funk, and Yokozuna as they battled Faarooq, Vader, Diesel, and Razor Ramon. To the delight of the capacity Garden crowd, Superfly once again took flight. Snuka continued to tour the U.S. independent scene for the remainder of the decade.

On the August 26, 2002 episode of *Raw,* Snuka once again surprised fans at Madison Square Garden when he accepted a Lifetime Achievement Award. In April of 2003 Superfly crashed an episode of *Piper's Pit,* and in 2005 he appeared at the WWE Homecoming, where fans saw him soar again as WWE legends put Superstar Rob Conway in his place. That same evening, "Superfly" also chased after a provocatively dressed Mae Young with some spending money in hand courtesy of "Million Dollar Man" Ted DiBiase. At *Taboo Tuesday 2005* fans voted Snuka as Eugene's partner against Rob Conway and Tyson Tomko. In vintage Superfly fashion, he won the match for his team when he flew from the top rope and landed on a beaten Conway.

Perhaps no WWE legend in history has been more popular or influential on future generations than this wrestling phenom from the Fiji Islands. His revolutionary blend of aerial attacks, strength, mat wrestling, and martial arts was the precursor to the versatile Superstars fans see today. Due to fans' eternal love for this iconic figure, you never know when the "Superfly" will return.

Andre the Giant

FROM: **Grenoble, France**

HEIGHT: **7'4"**

WEIGHT: **540 lbs.**

FINISHING MOVE: **Headbutt / splash**

AS A BOY GROWING UP IN GRENOBLE, FRANCE, ANDRE ROUSIMOFF NEVER DREAMED OF BECOMING THE WORLD'S LARGEST PROFESSIONAL ATHLETE. Andre suffered from acromegaly, commonly known as "giantism," an endocrinological disorder that causes an accelerated growth rate, continuing beyond the age of physical maturity. Though self-conscious about his size, Andre was determined to use it to his advantage. While working at a furniture store in Paris, the seventeen-year-old Andre was discovered by wrestler and former World Wrestling Federation commentator Lord Alfred Hayes and made his first pro appearance in 1971. Andre left crowds awestruck with his incredible size, strength, and agility. His moves were so devastating to opponents that he could end a match with any maneuver he pleased. When competing in French-speaking regions, he went by the name Jean Ferre. In Japan, he was known as "Monster" Rousimoff. Andre's mentor Frank Valois arranged a meeting with the head of the WWWF, Vince McMahon Sr. This marked the beginning of a twenty-year relationship with the McMahon family, and in 1973 a young Rousimoff debuted in Madison Square Garden as Andre the Giant.

At the time the wrestling world was divided into territories, but Andre quickly became professional wrestling's premier attraction wherever he competed. Standing at seven-foot-four and weighing over 500 pounds, he was dubbed, "The Eighth Wonder of the World." Andre rode a wave of mainstream popularity through the 1970s that saw him appear on *The Tonight Show,* make cameos as Bigfoot on the hit program *The Six Million Dollar Man,* and become the first wrestler featured on the cover of *Sports Illustrated.* During this time Andre had violent confrontations with the likes of the Sheik, Abdullah the Butcher, Stan Hansen, Don Leo Jonathan, "Big Cat" Ernie Ladd, and Blackjack Mulligan. During a 1976 boxer-vs.-wrestler bout at Shea Stadium, Andre faced the "Bayonne Bleeder," Chuck Wepner. In an incredible show of strength, he hurled Wepner into the third-row seats. Four years later Andre returned to Shea and squared off against a rule-breaking Hulk Hogan, who at the time was under the tutelage of "Classy" Freddie Blassie.

The 1980s marked the beginning of what would be a turbulent decade for "The Eighth Wonder of the World." Andre briefly formed a successful tag team with "The American Dream" Dusty Rhodes and captured regional NWA tag team titles. He returned to World Wrestling Federation and during a match with Mongolian terror Killer Khan, broke his ankle when Khan jumped from the top rope, landing on the Giant. In November of 1981 Andre came back, seeking revenge. The two met at the Philadelphia Spectrum in a Mongolian Stretcher match, in which the loser had to be carried on a stretcher back to the locker room. Andre destroyed Khan, launching him into wrestling obscurity. By the mid-1980s Andre had fended off villains such as "Rowdy" Roddy Piper, the Wild Samoans, Ken Patera, King Kong Bundy, and "Big" John Studd. His toughest opponent up to this point was Studd, who claimed to be wrestling's true giant, bragging that he could not be bodyslammed. At one point Studd recruited fellow Heenan Family member Ken Patera, and the two knocked Andre unconscious during a televised event and cut his famous long locks in an attempt to humiliate Andre in front of his adoring fans. This established the $15,000 Bodyslam Challenge at *WrestleMania.* Andre emerged victorious, but after he tried to throw his cash winnings to the Madison Square Garden crowd, an enraged Bobby "The Brain" Heenan jumped into the ring and took the bag of money from Andre. The Giant continued his amazing undefeated streak, and fans referred to him as wrestling's "Uncrowned World Champion."

At *WrestleMania 2* Andre won the twenty-man World Wrestling Federation/NFL Battle Royal and added to his record-setting number of battle royal victories. In 1986, Andre was at the center of controversy when then World Wrestling Federation

President Jack Tunney suspended him for not appearing at matches against members of the Heenan Family. Andre was forbidden to appear on World Wrestling Federation television or at live events. While he was serving his suspension, a team from the Orient called "The Machines" debuted with the goal of becoming the number-one tag team in the world. Their largest member, Giant Machine, became the target of a witch hunt orchestrated by Bobby "The Brain" Heenan. "The Brain" insisted that the man underneath the mask was Andre, and would stop at nothing to reveal the masked man's identity. After feuding with the Heenan Family, the Machines left World Wrestling Federation, and their identities remain a mystery to this day.

In 1987, Andre costarred in Rob Reiner's hit film *The Princess Bride* as the gentle giant Fezzik. He returned to World Wrestling Federation, shocking the world when he appeared on *Piper's Pit* alongside his former nemesis Bobby "The Brain" Heenan. Andre then challenged longtime blood brother Hulk Hogan to a Heavyweight Championship match at *WrestleMania III*. Showing his true turn to evil, Andre tore Hogan's shirt off his chest and the gold cross off his neck. In that swift movement, best friends became sworn enemies, and the biggest match in pro wrestling history was set. With 93,173 fans in attendance at the Pontiac Silverdome, Andre clashed with Hogan in a battle of the irresistible force meeting the immovable object. In the end, the power of *Hulkamania* was too much for the Giant. Though Andre did not fulfill his goal of becoming World Wrestling Federation Champion, he continued decimating opponents in hopes of defeating Hogan. During a February 5, 1988, episode of *The Main Event,* Andre's plot with Heenan and financial backer "Million Dollar Man" Ted DiBiase came to fruition. Toward the end of the match, Andre administered a suplex to the Hulkster and went for the pin. When the official reached two, Hogan raised his right shoulder. However, the referee continued and made the three-count. In that moment, the Hulkster's near-four-year title reign was over. As Hogan argued the call, referee Dave Hebner ran out from the back, and all of a sudden two referees who looked exactly alike stood in the ring arguing. Hogan then press-slammed the evil twin and tossed him over the top rope and into the group of Andre, DiBiase, Virgil, and Heenan. Andre forfeited the belt moments later when he sold it to DiBiase.

In order to crown a new world champion, a tournament was created for *WrestleMania IV.* Though Andre had a first-round bye, his second-round match with Hogan ended in a double countout, and both men were disqualified.

Andre teamed with Haku to form the Colossal Connection, and on December 13, 1989, they defeated Demolition to capture the World Wrestling Federation World Tag Team Championship. Demolition would regain their titles at *WrestleMania VI* when a botched double-team move sent Andre tangled into the ropes. Demolition saw this opportunity to attack Haku and set him up for their Decapitation Elbow Drop. After the match Heenan berated Andre and slapped him in the face. This sent Andre over the edge, and the Giant grabbed "The Brain" by his neck, shook him, and cleared the ring in the process, to the pleasure of the capacity SkyDome crowd. Andre continued to appear at World Wrestling Federation events around the world, and on April 13, 1990, he made a special appearance at the Wrestling Summit in Japan. Here Andre teamed with Japanese *puroresu* legend Shohei Baba to take on Demolition. His last wrestling appearance would be in 1992 during a tour of Japan.

Sadly, on January 27, 1993, this remarkable life came to an end. While in France for his father's funeral, Andre passed away in his sleep, the result of a heart attack. He was forty-six years old. Andre the Giant will forever be remembered as one of wrestling's most beloved and recognizable figures. He was adored by fans and peers around the world not only because of his famed career, but for his gentle nature and golden heart. Shortly after his death, Andre was paid the ultimate honor and became the first person inducted into the WWE Hall of Fame. This was an accolade commensurate with the stature of the man who was wrestling's first and arguably most famous global icon.

Iron Sheik

FROM: **Tehran, Iran**

HEIGHT: **6'**

WEIGHT: **265 lbs.**

FINISHING MOVE: **The camel clutch**

Before his days of inciting U.S. audiences, the Iron Sheik was an amateur wrestler in his home country of Iran and became an expert in Greco-Roman-style wrestling. In the early 1970s he arrived in the United States and began his pro training under Verne Gagne. The Sheik first appeared in the AWA in late 1972 and had a hand in training future stars like Ricky "The Dragon" Steamboat, "Jumping" Jim Brunzell, Greg Gagne, and even a young Bret Hart. Sheik spent the rest of the 1970s touring regional promotions until a brief stay in the WWWF as "Hussein Arab." In the early 1980s he wrestled in the southeastern part of the country until his 1983 World Wrestling Federation debut.

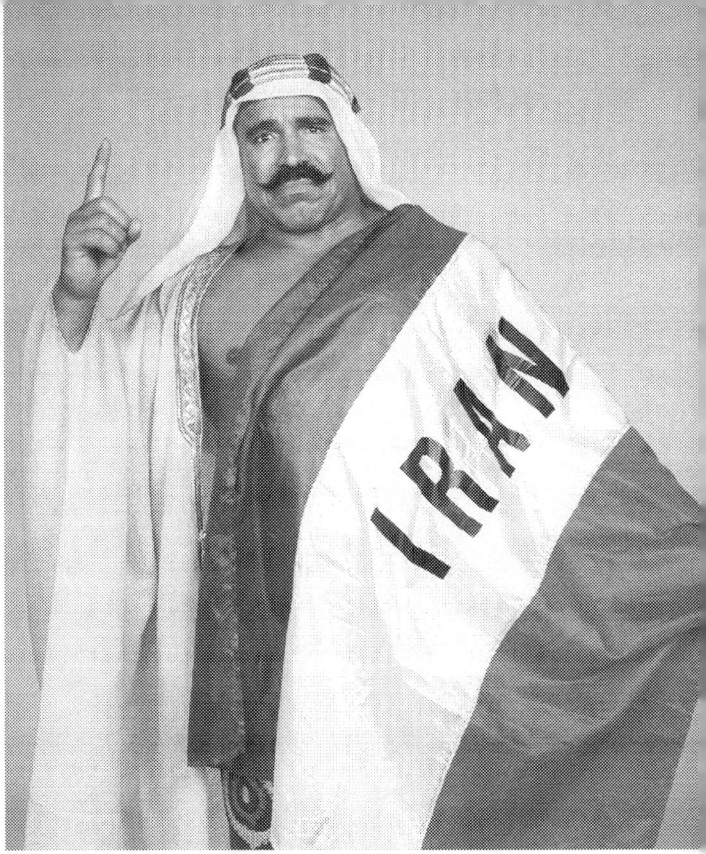

The Sheik racked up an impressive list of victories and was recognized for his superb technical ring abilities. He quickly became known as "The Master of the Suplex," using a myriad of variations of this classic wrestling maneuver. This earned him a shot at then World Wrestling Federation Champion Bob Backlund. In the antithesis of the perfect holiday gift for wrestling fans, the Sheik defeated Backlund at Madison Square Garden the day after Christmas, 1983. The win was a controversial one; Backlund's manager, Arnold Skaaland, threw in the towel while the champ was locked in the Sheik's dreaded camel clutch. Backlund refused to submit, so technically, he never gave up. It appeared the Sheik would enjoy a long title reign, defeating Chief Jay Strongbow, Pat Patterson, and Tito Santana. As fate would have it, on January 23, 1984, his championship days came to an end when rising star Hulk Hogan substituted for an injured Backlund. The Sheik lost, and it is this match that is credited with giving birth to *Hulkamania*.

The Sheik then started to feud with another American hero, Sgt. Slaughter. This bloody war spanned across the United States and culminated on June 16, 1984, at Madison Square Garden when Slaughter defeated Sheik in a Boot Camp match. Shortly after, the Sheik entered the tag team ranks with Russian force Nikolai Volkoff. Along with manager "Classy" Freddie Blassie, the team not only rose to fame at *WrestleMania*, defeating the US Express for the World Wrestling Federation World Tag Team Championship, but became public enemy number one in the eyes of wrestling fans everywhere. After a disappointing loss that saw Barry Windham and Mike Rotundo regain their titles, the Sheik returned to singles competition, and in July of 1985 he even reached the finals of the first *King of the Ring* tournament against the Magnificent Muraco. Then, reunited with Volkoff, he took on the Killer Bees at *WrestleMania III*. In 1988, the Sheik left World Wrestling Federation. He briefly appeared in WCW in 1989 and challenged Sting for the Television title.

In 1991, Sheik returned to World Wrestling Federation, but this time under the name Col. Mustafa and as a member of the Triangle of Terror. He was joined by Gen. Adnan and new Iraqi sympathizer and former archenemy Sgt. Slaughter. The trio feuded with Hulk Hogan and Ultimate Warrior and battled the two superpowers at *SummerSlam '91*. After the match, Mustafa and Adnan turned on Slaughter, spawning a rebirth of his American patriotism. Shortly thereafter, Sheik disappeared from World Wrestling Federation until 1997, when he returned as manager of the Sultan. This was the Sheik's last World Wrestling Federation run. At *WrestleMania X-Seven,* he returned for one night only to participate in the over-the-top-rope Gimmick battle royal. The Sheik emerged victorious and reopened old battle scars with Sgt. Slaughter.

At the 2005 WWE Hall of Fame induction, the Iron Sheik's thirty-year professional career was recognized, along with those of WWE fellow greats Hulk Hogan, "Rowdy" Roddy Piper, "Mr. Wonderful" Paul Orndoff, "Mouth of the South" Jimmy Hart, "Cowboy" Bob Orton, and of course his partner in political upheaval, Nikolai Volkoff. The Sheik will always be remembered as one of the greatest rule-breakers pro wrestling has ever known, and set the standard for future anti-American villains who enter the squared circle.

Nikolai Volkoff

FROM: **Moscow, Russia**

HEIGHT: **6'4"**

WEIGHT: **313 lbs.**

FINISHING MOVE: **Russian bear hug**

NIKOLAI VOLKOFF WAS AN AMATEUR WRESTLER AND BODYBUILDER IN HIS NATIVE RUSSIA. IN 1968, VOLKOFF HAD HIS FIRST EVER PRO MATCH against WWWF Champion Bruno Sammartino. In the early 1970s, under the name Beppo, Nikolai, along with his partner Geeto, were known as the Mongols. Under the guidance of Capt. Lou Albano, the Mongols defeated Victor Rivera and Tony Marino on June 15, 1971, for the WWWF International Tag Team titles. They exchanged title reigns with the team of Bruno Sammartino and Dominic DeNucci until they were defeated by Luke Graham and Tarzan Tyler on November 12, 1971. This match would unify the WWWF International and World Tag Team Championships. After the Mongols split, Nikolai entered singles competition and had memorable matches with

Sammartino for the WWWF Heavyweight crown. These two powerhouses were so evenly matched that the contests ended in time limit draws. During the mid-1970s Nikolai donned a mask and became the third member of the Executioners, along with "Big" John Studd and Killer Kowalski. On October 26, 1976, the Executioners were stripped of their titles when the masked men were caught using Volkoff as the third member of the team during a championship match. Nikolai spent the rest of the 1970s in the WWWF and toured the southeastern United States and Japan.

After a brief hiatus, Volkoff returned to World Wrestling Federation in 1984 as the Soviet nationalist who proudly waved the hammer and sickle and did anything to produce a victory in the name of Mother Russia. Early into his return he formed one of the most hated tag teams in wrestling history with former World Wrestling Federation Heavyweight Champion the Iron Sheik. Managed by "Classy" Freddie Blassie, the pair defeated the US Express for the World Wrestling Federation World Tag Team Championship at the first *WrestleMania.* At this time, Volkoff developed his trademark of insisting the audience rise to their feet out of respect during his rendition of the Russian national anthem. This infuriated fans around the United States, and Volkoff was met with boos and objects thrown from the crowd. Volkoff and Sheik's successful title reign ended on June 17, 1985, when former champions Barry Windham and Mike Rotundo took back their titles at a World Wrestling Federation live event in Poughkeepsie, New York.

Nikolai returned to singles competition and engaged in a heated politically driven rivalry with former U.S. paratrooper Corp. Kirschner. These two Superstars battled across the country and fought in the first ever series of Flag matches. They met at *WrestleMania 2* in their final encounter. In late 1986, "Classy" Freddie Blassie retired and sold the contracts of Volkoff and Sheik to new manager Slick, the self-proclaimed Doctor of Style. Nikolai then briefly reunited with his former partner, and at *WrestleMania III,* the two defeated the Killer Bees by disqualification when a fired-up

"Hacksaw" Jim Duggan interfered and attacked the Sheik. Later that year Nikolai and the Sheik went their separate ways, and Volkoff joined forces with fellow Russian extremist Boris Zukhov. The two would be known as the Bolsheviks, with the conniving Slick in their corner. Though they never won World Wrestling Federation Tag Team titles, the Bolsheviks antagonized fans with their anti-American rhetoric and singing of the Russian national anthem. After an embarrassing nineteen-second loss to the Hart Foundation at *WrestleMania VI,* the Bolsheviks imploded.

With a new decade came a new attitude, and in mid-1990 Nikolai shocked wrestling fans around the world and began supporting the United States. He formed a tag team with former foe "Hacksaw" Jim Duggan to take on then Iraqi sympathizer Sgt. Slaughter. Volkoff and Duggan displayed excellent teamwork, and at *SummerSlam '90* they triumphed over the veteran duo of Tanaka & Kato, the Orient Express. Nikolai was also part of the winning team at *Survivor Series 1991* and along with "Hacksaw" Jim Duggan, Tito Santana, and the Texas Tornado bested the team of Hercules, Col. Mustafa, Skinner, and the Berzerker. Shortly after, Nikolai left World Wrestling Federation but would return for the last time in 1995 as part of Ted DiBiase's Million Dollar Corporation. Throughout the rest of the 1990s Volkoff made appearances on the independent scene, and in 2001 he participated in the *WrestleMania X-Seven* Gimmick battle royal along with the likes of Iron Sheik, Sgt. Slaughter, Earthquake, the Bushwackers, One Man Gang, Kamala, Hillbilly Jim, Repo Man, and Tugboat.

In 2005 Nikolai's four-decade career was officially recognized, and he was inducted into the WWE Hall of Fame. It was only fitting that he entered the Hall in the same class as his partner in chaos, the Iron Sheik. Nikolai's brute power and deceptive agility made him a serious threat to any champion's title reign. Though the Cold War is long over, Nikolai Volkoff will forever be remembered as one of the greatest villains in professional wrestling history.

Bobby "The Brain" Heenan

FROM: **Beverly Hills, CA**

HEIGHT: **6'**

WEIGHT: **190 lbs.**

THIS MASTERMIND'S ASSOCIATION WITH PROFESSIONAL WRESTLING GOES BACK TO THE DAYS WHEN HE SOLD PROGRAMS IN ARENAS DURING live shows. When he made his professional debut in 1965, he was known as "The Pretty Boy." In the early 1970s Bobby "The Brain" Heenan debuted in the AWA and founded a stable of rule-breakers collectively known as the Heenan Family. Original members consisted of Nick Bockwinkel, Ray Stevens, Bobby Duncum Sr., Blackjack Lanza, and Dick Warren. The Heenan Family saw several incarnations over his twenty-year managerial career, each more dastardly than the next. His numerous protégés included a virtual who's who of legendary figures: AWA Champion Nick Bockwinkel, "Crippler" Ray Stevens, "Killer" Karl Kox, Baron Von Raschke, Olympic strongman Ken Patera, "Nature Boy" Ric Flair, Mr. Perfect, King Kong Bundy, Hercules, the Islanders, Masked Superstar, "Ravishing" Rick Rude, Brooklyn Brawler, Arn Anderson., Tully Blanchard, Andre the Giant, "Big Cat" Ernie Ladd, "Big" John Studd, Harley Race, "Mr. Wonderful" Paul Orndorff, and the Blackjacks. When he was suspended by the AWA for one year, Heenan appeared in Georgia Championship Wrestling before returning to Minnesota in late 1979. Heenan remained in the AWA through the early 1980s.

In 1984, the Brain debuted in World Wrestling Federation. Though his original client was to be Jesse "The Body" Ventura, Heenan became the manager of the massive "Big" John Studd. Almost immediately a feud with Andre the Giant was ignited. As Heenan's Family expanded, so did the number of Superstars that fell victim to their attacks. Superstars and fans began to refer to Heenan as "The Weasel" because of his constant suspicious and unsavory activities. In typically Heenan fashion, he retorted by referring to fans as "humanoids." In 1986, "The Brain" lengthened his résumé and became a broadcast journalist alongside Gorilla Monsoon, appearing on World Wrestling Federation programs like *Wrestling Challenge, Prime Time Wrestling,* and later on World Wrestling Federation Pay-Per-Views. The Heenan-Monsoon duo was among the favorites of television audiences around the world. Another individual Heenan was obsessed with eliminating at all costs was then World Wrestling Federation World Heavyweight Champion Hulk Hogan. "The Brain" closely aligned himself with anyone who appeared to have the ability to eradicate Hogan. Heenan's greatest chance of destroying *Hulkamania* came when he coaxed former adversary Andre the Giant to betray his best friend and challenge him to a championship match at *WrestleMania III.* At *WrestleMania V* Heenan won his first piece of World Wrestling Federation Championship gold when his man "Ravishing" Rick Rude defeated the Ultimate Warrior for the Intercontinental title. This was only the beginning of "The Brain's" collection of precious metals. In 1989, he guided two tandems to the World Wrestling Federation World Tag Team Championship over Demolition. The first was the Brainbusters in July, followed by the Colossal Connection team of Andre the Giant & Haku in December. In 1990 Heenan led Mr. Perfect to the Intercontinental Championship and served as an adviser to two-time World Heavyweight Champion "Nature Boy" Ric Flair. Shortly after, Heenan was physically removed from the broadcast booth by Gorilla Monsoon during a broadcast. That was the last World Wrestling Federation fans saw of "The Brain."

Throughout his wrestling career Heenan also made his presence felt on other television programs like *Good Morning with Regis & Kathy Lee, The Jerry Lewis Telethon, Nickelodeon Kids Choice Awards, Family Feud, Arsenio Hall,* and *The Dennis Miller Show.* In 1995, the Brain made his acting debut in the film *Timemaster.* As the mid-1990s evolved, so did his appeal with the younger generation; Heenan was behind the mic during *Nitro's* greatest days. In April 1997, Indianapolis mayor Steve Goldberg proclaimed April 3 to be "Bobby Heenan Day." In the fall of 2000, "The Brain's" time in the broadcast booth ended as he parted ways with World Championship Wrestling. Just when fans thought Heenan had disappeared from wrestling, he returned to World Wrestling Federation in 2001 at *WrestleMania X-Seven.* To the pleasure of fans everywhere, Heenan and "Mean" Gene Okerlund called the action during the Gimmick battle royal.

In March of 2004, Heenan's unprecedented five-decade career was celebrated when "The Brain" was inducted into the WWE Hall of Fame. He occasionally appears on WWE programming and is on the board of directors of the nationally recognized

Cauliflower Alley Club, but fans hope that one day "The Brain" will return to ringside. Heenan was indispensable as a manager and brilliant as a broadcast journalist. According to many he is the greatest manager of all time and one of the most significant figures in professional wrestling history. If you ask him, he would wholeheartedly agree.

Junkyard Dog

FROM: **Charlotte, NC**

HEIGHT: **6'3"**

WEIGHT: **280 lbs.**

FINISHING MOVE: **THUMP powerslam**

SYLVESTER RITTER WAS AN ALL-AMERICAN FROM NORTH CAROLINA'S FAYETTEVILLE STATE UNIVERSITY. AN UP-AND-COMER WITH THE GREEN Bay Packers, his pro hopes were cut short by knee and back injuries. After surgery, Ritter trained for a new "full contact" sport: wrestling. In 1977 he debuted in Tennessee for longtime promoter Jerry Jarrett. After a year, Ritter left the region and briefly toured Europe. His next stop was Calgary and Stu Hart's Stampede Wrestling. Appearing as "Big Daddy" Ritter, he won the North American Heavyweight title and faced the area's top talent, including a young Jake Roberts. Sylvester returned to the United States and competed in that wrestling territory hotbed, Mid-South Wrestling. Thanks to Ritter's ruffian, hard-hitting style and a line from the Jim Croce song, the one-time college All-American was now known as the Junkyard Dog.

The Dog, or JYD as he was also called, became the territory's top star and battled the likes of "Hacksaw" Jim Duggan, Butch Reed, Tully Blanchard, and One Man Gang. In the 1980s he began a battle with "Big Cat" Ernie Ladd. None of his Mid-South brawls were as violent as his 1980 feud with the Fabulous Freebirds. During this time JYD held both the Louisiana and Mississippi championships. After a brutal sneak attack by the dastardly Terry "Bam Bam" Gordy and Michael "P. S." Hayes, JYD lost his sight when they threw an abrasive powder in his eyes. He was forced to relinquish both titles. Although the Dog was blind, he returned and faced his attackers in a series of Blind Dog Collar matches. This led to a Steel Cage Dog Collar match between the Dog and Hayes at the New Orleans Superdome. JYD continued his regional tour of the NWA and went through Georgia Championship Wrestling and Championship Wrestling from Florida. In 1984 he traveled to World Class Championship Wrestling and defeated the peculiar Missing Link at the David Von Erich Memorial Parade of Champions, held at Texas Stadium.

In 1984 the Junkyard Dog made his World Wrestling Federation debut. With his near-300-pound frame, deceptive speed, and incredible resistance to pain, JYD immediately showed that the squared circles were his yard. Walking to the ring to Queen's "Another One Bites the Dust," JYD skyrocketed to fame, second in popularity only to his friend Hulk Hogan. His fame reached such remarkable heights that in 1986 he was featured on the CBS Saturday morning cartoon *Hulk Hogan's Rock and Wrestling* and sang lead vocals on his own entrance theme, the timeless classic "Grab Them Cakes." The Dog leveled opponents with every power move imaginable and with signature maneuvers like the rolling headbutt, where he got down on all fours and charged foes, often sending them to the arena floor; a high-legged clothesline that when he bounced off the ropes practically knocked the head off his opponents; and his THUMP powerslam, which had such force that JYD's challengers sprang high off the mat on impact. Despite his rough and tough demeanor, this grizzly grappler had a soft side. After his victories, the Dog pulled young fans from the crowd to dance with him in the ring. He never captured a World Wrestling Federation Championship, but JYD was a top contender for World Wrestling Federation World Heavyweight and Intercontinental titles. At the 1985 *Wrestling Classic,* he beat future Intercontinental Champion Randy "Macho Man" Savage in the tournament finals. At the first *WrestleMania,* he scored a victory via countout over then Intercontinental Champion Greg "The Hammer" Valentine. His singles success crossed over into tag team competition with partners like Hulk Hogan, Andre the Giant, Jimmy "Superfly" Snuka, Ricky "The Dragon" Steamboat, and George "The Animal" Steele. The Dog took a bite out World Wrestling Federation's principal evil forces, like "Rowdy" Roddy Piper, "Cowboy" Bob Orton, the Heenan Family, the Magnificent Muraco, Mr. Fuji, and "Adorable" Adrian Adonis. With friend

Tito Santana, JYD faced the legendary Funk Brothers at *WrestleMania 2*. Soon after his chaotic bout with the two Texans, JYD feuded with Harley Race. This war culminated at *WrestleMania III* in a Loser Bows match. Though he was defeated, JYD got in the last word when he nailed Race with a chair and left the Silverdome wearing Race's robe and crown.

After being one of the last three Superstars in the *WrestleMania IV* battle royal, JYD locked up with "Ravishing" Rick Rude at *SummerSlam '88*. Unfortunately the Dog was disqualified when Jake "The Snake" Roberts attacked Rude, who moments before had pulled his tights down while perched on the top rope and revealed another pair that had the image of Jake's wife, Cheryl Roberts, on the front. Regrettably for his fans, World Wrestling Federation's first *SummerSlam* marked Junkyard Dog's last appearance with World Wrestling Entertainment.

Soon after, JYD arrived in the National Wrestling Alliance and battled "Nature Boy" Ric Flair for the NWA World Heavyweight Championship. At *Starrcade '88* the Dog pulled double duty when he first won a Bunkhouse Stampede battle royal and outlasted greats like Abdullah the Butcher, "Hot Stuff" Eddie Gilbert, Dick Murdoch, and "Dr. Death" Steve Williams. Then he teamed with former World Wrestling Federation World Heavyweight Champion Ivan Koloff and faced the masked Russian Assassins. After a brief hiatus Dog returned to the newly named World Championship Wrestling in 1990 and joined Sting's "Dudes with Attitudes" group, alongside members Lex Luger, "Mr. Wonderful" Paul Orndorff, and the Steiner Bros. This collection of fan favorites battled against the Four Horsemen across the country in a series of singles and tag team matches. JYD wrestled in various independent organizations for the better portion of the early and mid-1990s. In May of 1998 he was honored as a hardcore legend at ECW's *Wrestlepalooza*. The rabid ECW fan faithful broke out in deafening chants of "JYD" when the Dog was introduced. Sadly, a few weeks later Sylvester died in a one-car accident while returning from his daughter's high school graduation in North Carolina. He was forty-five years old.

On March 14, 2004, Junkyard Dog's career saw the perfect ending as he was posthumously inducted into the WWE Hall of Fame at *WrestleMania XX*. JYD entered the hall with former rivals Greg "The Hammer" Valentine, "Big" John Studd, the Magnificent Muraco, and Harley Race as well as former friend Tito Santana. On hand to receive the award was JYD's daughter, LaToya Ritter. Whether it was Madison Square Garden, the Omni in Atlanta, or the Superdome, the Dog brought fans of all ages to their feet. The Junkyard Dog will be remembered as one of the most charismatic and popular wrestlers of all time, and a beloved legend.

Greg "The Hammer" Valentine

FROM: **Seattle, WA**

HEIGHT: **6'**

WEIGHT: **243 lbs.**

FINISHING MOVE: **Figure-four leglock**

A SECOND-GENERATION WRESTLER, THIS GRAPPLER WOULD GO ON TO COMPETE IN SOME OF THE MOST FEROCIOUS MATCHES IN THE HISTORY of the sport. His teachers—the great Johnny Valentine, the rugged Stu Hart, and the unpredictable Original Sheik—would not accept anything less. Greg Valentine would debut in 1968 and spend the early part of the 1970s developing one of the most crippling versions of the figure-four leglock. In 1976 he arrived in Mid-Atlantic Championship Wrestling and formed a successful tag team with "Nature Boy" Ric Flair. The two soon defeated the Minnesota Wrecking Crew for the NWA World Tag Team titles. It was here that Valentine also feuded with Wahoo McDaniel over the Mid-Atlantic Heavyweight title, breaking the Chief's leg. Adding insult to injury, Valentine began taunting his injured opponent by wearing a shirt that read, "I Broke Wahoo's Leg." Valentine eventually turned on Flair, and in 1980 he defeated him for the U.S. Championship. In 1981 Greg briefly appeared in the WWWF, guided by the Grand Wizard, to battle then Champion Bob Backlund, as well as feud with Chief Jay Strongbow. Returning to the NWA, Valentine renewed his feuds with Wahoo McDaniel and "Rowdy" Roddy Piper over the U.S. title. It was at the first *Starrcade* that Valentine and Piper would fight in a Dog Collar match, participating in one of the most violent contests wrestling has ever seen.

Now known as "The Hammer," Valentine made his World Wrestling Federation debut in 1984 and began dropping a crushing elbow across the throat of his opponents. On September 24, Valentine defeated Tito Santana to win the coveted Intercontinental Championship. As a result, "The Hammer" engaged in a brutal near-one-year feud with Santana over the belt. The battles were so fierce that Santana was forced to have knee surgery after sustaining injuries courtesy of Valentine's figure-four leglock. On July 6, 1985, the two collided in a Steel Cage match where Santana got his revenge. After the loss, an irate Valentine took the title belt and smashed it against the cage, resulting in a new championship belt being created.

"The Hammer" then moved to the tag team division and formed a tandem with newcomer Brutus Beefcake, the Dream Team. The two showed great teamwork, and with Johnny Valiant as their manager, it was only a matter of time before they would wear tag team gold. On August 24, 1985, the duo defeated the US Express—Barry Windham and Mike Rotundo. The Dream Team enjoyed a near-seven-month title reign until they came up against a hungry British Bulldogs team at *WrestleMania 2*. Making the most of their last title shot, the Bulldogs defeated Valentine and Beefcake in front of a capacity Rosemont Horizon crowd. In April 1987, the two split, and Beefcake was replaced by Canadian strongman Dino Bravo. As a slap in the face to Beefcake, the team was called "The New Dream Team." After a short run the two parted, and Valentine returned to singles competition as a contender for both the Intercontinental and World Heavyweight Championships. As the 1980s came to an end, Valentine returned to the tag ranks with another former famous Intercontinental Champion, the Honky Tonk Man. The two, managed by "Mouth of the South" Jimmy Hart, went by the name Rhythm and Blues. While they were contenders for World Wrestling Federation Tag Team titles, Valentine did not see the success he had known with past partners, and the team was disbanded.

Continuing into the 1990s, Valentine remained a thorn in the side of the World Wrestling Federation Superstars participating in *Survivor Series* and *Royal Rumbles*. In 1993 he traveled to WCW, winning the United States Tag Team Championship with partner Terry Taylor. In the late 1990s Valentine appeared frequently on *Nitro*.

On March 14, 2004, at *WrestleMania XX*, the Hammer's three-decade career was honored as he was inducted into the WWE Hall of Fame. An emotional Valentine dedicated the tribute to his late, great father, Johnny Valentine. He still appears on the independent wrestling circuit, but Greg "The Hammer" Valentine will always be remembered as one of wrestling's toughest, the man who helped make the figure-four leglock one of the most feared holds in professional wrestling history.

Ricky Steamboat

FROM: **Honolulu, HI**

HEIGHT: **5'10"**

WEIGHT: **235 lbs.**

FINISHING MOVE: **Flying cross-body**

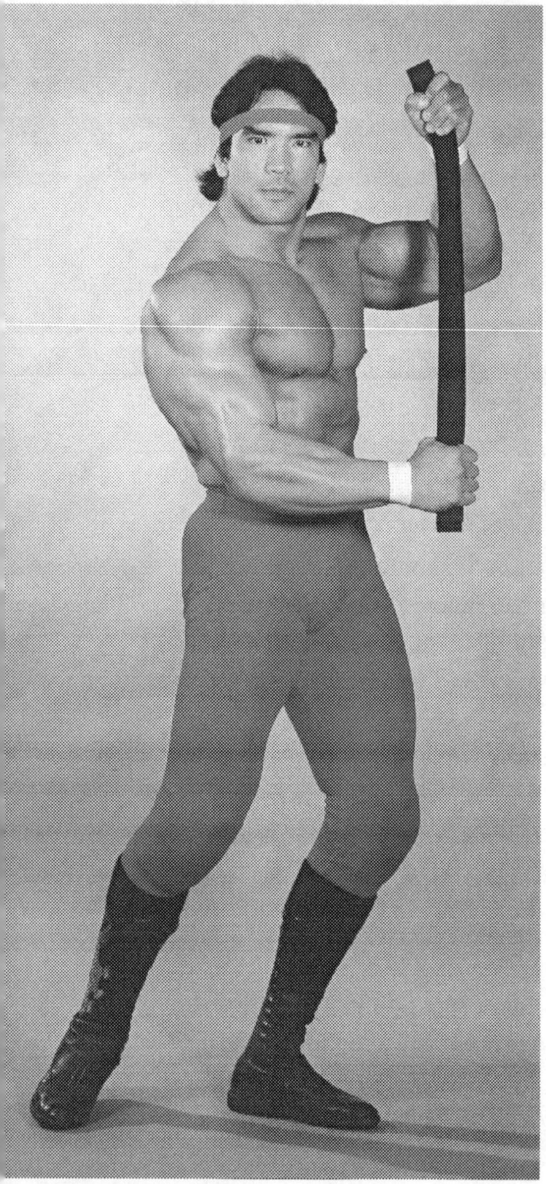

TRAINED BY VERNE GAGNE AND IRON SHEIK, THIS GIFTED ATHLETE IS A FORMER FLORIDA State amateur wrestling champion. Ricky Steamboat made his wrestling debut in the AWA in 1976 and after one month moved to NWA Mid-Atlantic Championship Wrestling. Steamboat immediately got people's attention by defeating "Nature Boy" Ric Flair for the TV title in June 1977 and was voted the *Pro Wrestling Illustrated* Rookie of the Year. As the 1970s progressed, so did Steamboat's list of achievements. He feuded with Flair over the prestigious United States Championship. He garnered tag team gold with partners Paul Jones, Dino Bravo, and Jay Youngblood. Steamboat's winning ways continued, and in 1981 he defeated Ivan Koloff for the Mid-Atlantic Heavyweight title as well as regaining the Mid-Atlantic and NWA World Tag Team championships with Jay Youngblood. In 1983, Ricky announced his retirement from professional wrestling. As fate would have it, this was a personal sabbatical, and Steamboat soon resurfaced.

In 1985 Steamboat made his World Wrestling Federation debut, adding the moniker "The Dragon" to his name. He immediately wowed audiences around the country with his innovative wrestling style, which saw high-flying maneuvers perfectly blended with sound mat wrestling and expert martial arts techniques. The Dragon became quickly acquainted with World Wrestling Federation's most dangerous Superstars, with his first challenger being the diabolical Magnificent Muraco. His next opponent was the dangerous Jake

"The Snake" Roberts. These battles were so fierce, fans saw "The Snake" administer a DDT to Steamboat on the concrete, knocking him unconscious on a May 1986 episode of *Saturday Night's Main Event*. To settle the score, they met in a Snake Pit match where the victor puts their reptile of choice on their fallen opponent. Steamboat came to the ring with a Komodo dragon and, after his victory, put Roberts up close and personal with the endangered species, sending "The Snake" to higher ground.

Steamboat's next foe would come in the form of Intercontinental Champion Randy "Macho Man" Savage. During their meeting an aggravated Macho Man brought the fight to the outside and put Steamboat's throat across the steel barricade. In total brutality, Savage jumped from the top rope and landed his double ax-handle on the back of Steamboat's neck. Then, in a blatant attempt to end Steamboat's career, Savage tore the timekeeper's bell from the table and returned to the top turnbuckle. The Macho Man flew through the air and crashed down on "The Dragon," crushing his larynx. Audiences were shocked as their hero was carried out on a stretcher, unable to talk and gasping for air. Incapacitated for several weeks, Steamboat was forced to undergo intense physical and voice therapy sessions. In the meantime, Savage was gloating over his actions and boasting how he put the Dragon out of wrestling.

Steamboat made his heroic return at *WrestleMania III* in one of the most anticipated rematches in wrestling history. As a psychological edge, Steamboat brought former Savage nemesis George "The Animal" Steele to ringside, sending the Macho Man into a state of uncontrollable anger. This contest was a struggle for control from the opening bell, with twenty-two near pinfalls. The turning point of the match came when Savage attempted to repeat his barbarism and climbed to the top rope with the timekeeper's bell in hand. George "The Animal" Steele suddenly appeared on the apron and sent the Macho Man crashing to the canvas. Steamboat regrouped and rolled Savage in a small package for the three-count. The Silverdome crowd jumped to their feet to celebrate Steamboat's victory. This marked the beginning of his Intercontinental title reign. Unfortunately, the Dragon's reign abruptly ended on the June 2, 1987, when Steamboat faced the fast-rising Honky Tonk Man. For the remainder of the year and into 1988 Steamboat remained a championship contender and competed in the first *Survivor Series* and *Royal Rumble*. His last appearance would be at *WrestleMania IV*, when he lost a first-round match in the World Title tournament to fellow former Intercontinental Champion Greg "The Hammer" Valentine.

After another brief hiatus from the ring, the Dragon shockingly returned to the NWA as the masked mystery partner of "Hot Stuff" Eddie Gilbert against the duo of "Nature Boy" Ric Flair & Barry Windham. After he pinned Flair with his trademark flying cross-body, the classic feud was reignited as the Dragon and the Nature Boy once again were at war. Fans would see the two exchange victories in classic matches for the NWA World Heavyweight Championship. At the outset of the 1990s, Steamboat briefly returned to World Wrestling Federation before rejoining World Championship Wrestling in November 1991. Here Steamboat won the WCW Tag Team titles with then-rising stars Dustin Rhodes and Shane Douglas. The Dragon spent the rest of the early 1990s in feuds with the likes of "Ravishing" Rick Rude and "Mr. Wonderful" Paul Orndorff for the Television and U.S. titles. He would also help Sting in his battles against the Dangerous Alliance. A series of matches against a young "Stunning" Steve Austin would end up being the Dragon's final bouts.

Sadly, in 1994 a recurring back injury forced the Dragon to retire. For the rest of the 1990s Ricky remained out of the public eye, concentrating on business ventures. In 2001 he began making select appearances on the independent wrestling scene and returned to World Wrestling Federation as a road agent in 2004. He appears on World Wrestling Federation programming on occasion and still receives as big a roar from the crowd as if he'd just captured the Intercontinental title at *WrestleMania III*. Ricky "The Dragon" Steamboat will always be remembered as a true hero and wrestling innovator whose immeasurable influence in professional wrestling will be felt for decades to come.

Brutus "The Barber" Beefcake

FROM: **San Francisco, CA**

HEIGHT: **6'4"**

WEIGHT: **271 lbs.**

FINISHING MOVE: **The sleeper hold**

WAY BEFORE THE DAYS OF GIVING "FREE" HAIRCUTS TO UNCONSCIOUS OPPONENTS, BEEFCAKE TRAVELED THROUGH THE SOUTHEASTERN TERRITORIES alongside friend Hulk Hogan trying to break into professional wrestling. When he debuted in 1976, he appeared under the names Ed Boulder, Eddie Golden, and Dizzy Hogan. Through the late 1970s and early 1980s he continued to compete in the regions of the NWA, AWA, and Mid-South Wrestling until his World Wrestling Federation debut in 1984.

When Brutus Beefcake arrived in World Wrestling Federation, he sought a manager to steer his career. After entertaining offers from World Wrestling Federation's top managers, he selected "Luscious" Johnny Valiant. With Beefcake's power and Valiant's penchant for dishonorable deeds, Brutus became a threat to the prosperity of every Superstar. At *WrestleMania,* Beefcake battled the son of a living legend, David Sammartino. With Valiant in Brutus's corner and Bruno in his son's corner, the match was guaranteed mayhem and ended in a no contest. Soon after, Valiant paired Beefcake with fellow rule-breaker and former two-time World Wrestling Federation Intercontinental Champion Greg "The Hammer" Valentine. Together they went by the name "The Dream Team" and contained the perfect blend of strength, teamwork, and technical ability. As a result, the pair became World Wrestling Federation World Tag Team Champions on August 24, 1985. Two-time champions Barry Windham and Mike Rotundo—The US Express—lost to them in Philadelphia.

Riding the momentum from their impressive championship victory, Beefcake and Valentine successfully defended their titles for seven months. At *WrestleMania 2* Beefcake and Valentine lost the titles to the British Bulldogs when "The Hammer" met the famous hard head of Dynamite Kid. After the loss the Dream Team continued to wrestle but had started to drift apart when "Luscious" Johnny Valiant brought in Canadian strongman Dino Bravo as an associate. After their *WrestleMania III* victory over the Rougeau Brothers, the group turned on Beefcake. Later that day "The Barber" was born when Beefcake entered the ring and cut "Adorable" Adrian Adonis's hair in celebration of the Hot Rod's victory. This marked a new chapter in Brutus's career. As a result, he came to the ring with a new attitude, new attire, and giant scissors. His former finishing move, the high knee, was now used as a setup for a sleeper hold. Once that was slapped on an opponent, it meant nighty-night, and a fresh haircut soon followed. Beefcake spent the following months in a feud with Intercontinental Champion Honky Tonk Man. The two met face-to-face at *WrestleMania IV,* with "The Barber" picking up the win via DQ. Unfortunately Brutus didn't win the Intercontinental title or give Honky Tonk a trim. They continued their brawl through 1988, and a championship rematch was set for *SummerSlam.* Days before the event, Brutus was mercilessly attacked by "Outlaw" Ron Bass in a scene that had to be edited for the television audience. As a result of the serious injuries sustained during the attack, the Barber was unable to compete in the inaugural *SummerSlam.* Upon his return, Brutus was motivated to get back into the title hunt and met "Million Dollar Man" Ted DiBiase at *WrestleMania V.* This match was a brawl from the start, and the two Superstars fought to a double countout. In the aftermath of the Mega Powers explosion, Beefcake joined the fight and along with Hulk Hogan faced the team of Randy "Macho Man" Savage and the monstrous Zeus at *SummerSlam '89.*

Unfortunately for the Barber and his fans, the 1990s began in tragedy as Beefcake was involved in a terrible parasailing accident. Brutus required emergency medical treatment and had to undergo facial reconstructive surgery. He returned in 1991 and introduced his talk show segment, appropriately named *The Barber Shop.* In 1993 Brutus fell victim to an unprovoked attack with a metal briefcase courtesy of Money Inc. Hulk Hogan saved him, and the duo formed the Mega Maniacs. They battled Money Inc.—"Million Dollar Man" Ted DiBiase & Irwin R. Schyster—for the World Wrestling Federation World Tag Team Championship at *WrestleMania IX.* Shortly after, Beefcake left World Wrestling Federation.

In 1994, Brutus debuted in World Championship Wrestling under myriad monikers, none of them earning the popularity of Brutus "The Barber" Beefcake. His last major television appearance was in May of 2003 when he appeared on Nickelodeon's *Slime Time Live.* Beefcake can still be seen today on the independent circuit and occasionally reunites with Dream Team partner Greg "The Hammer" Valentine. Though it has been over thirteen years since WWE fans have seen the Barber cut and strut, Brutus Beefcake will always be remembered as one of the most entertaining and beloved wrestlers.

Tito Santana

FROM: **Tocula, Mexico**

HEIGHT: **6'2"**

WEIGHT: **234 lbs.**

FINISHING MOVE: **The flying forearm**

TITO SANTANA HAD DREAMS OF RULING THE GRIDIRON, AS A TIGHT END AT WEST TEXAS UNIVERSITY. (IRONICALLY, THE QUARTERBACK OF THAT squad was future World Wrestling Federation Superstar Tully Blanchard.) After he graduated, Santana had a tryout with the NFL's Kansas City Chiefs. He landed in the Canadian Football League and played a season for the BC Lions. Then in 1976 Tito turned his attention to the squared circle and began wrestling in local promotions throughout Texas. Santana then moved to the AWA and had several matches with then Heavyweight Champion Nick Bockwinkel. After winning the NWA Western States Tag Team titles with a young Ted DiBiase, Santana appeared in World Wrestling Federation in 1979. Tito soon formed a tag team with "Polish Power" Ivan Putski. On October 22 they defeated the Valiant Brothers for the World Wrestling Federation World Tag Team Championship. After Santana and Putski dropped the title to the Wild Samoans, Santana went back to the AWA and briefly appeared in Georgia Championship Wrestling.

In 1983, Tito Santana returned to World Wrestling Federation, ready to make an impact. On February 11, 1984, he ended the Magnificent Muraco's one-year reign as World Wrestling Federation Intercontinental Champion. Santana then engaged in one of the most brutal feuds in pro wrestling history with Greg "The Hammer" Valentine. Valentine wanted the Intercontinental Championship, but decided he also wanted to end Santana's career. On September 24

Valentine defeated Santana, and after the match he attacked Tito's already injured leg. After "The Hammer" slapped on the figure-four leglock, Santana had to be carried from the ring on a stretcher. Tito was out of action for several months and required knee surgery, which was televised.

Returning in time for *WrestleMania,* Santana was victorious in the opening match against the Masked Executioner. On July 7, 1985, Tito defeated his attacker Greg "The Hammer" Valentine for the Intercontinental title inside a steel cage. In the aftermath of winning his second Intercontinental title, an irate Valentine destroyed the title belt against the cage, and Santana was awarded a new championship title. Tito's second reign as Intercontinental Champion lasted seven months, until he tangled with rising star Randy "Macho Man" Savage, on February 8, 1986, in the historic Boston Garden. Anxious to get Savage back in the ring, Tito attempted a belly-to-back suplex, and while he had the challenger in midair, Savage clocked Santana in the head with a pair of brass knuckles. An unconscious Santana was pinned.

Santana spent time in tag team matches with allies Junkyard Dog and the British Bulldogs before he united with another former World Wrestling Federation World Tag Team Champion, the energy-personified Rick Martel. These two Superstars formed Strike Force and shot up World Wrestling Federation Tag Team ranks. On October 27, 1987, Santana and Martel defeated the Hart Foundation and became the World Wrestling Federation World Tag Team Champions. At the first *Survivor Series* their team was victorious, and the duo's winning ways continued until they faced Demolition at *WrestleMania IV* in Atlantic City, New Jersey. The team returned the next year at *WrestleMania V.* Unfortunately for Santana, after a mistake he made during the match, his longtime partner Rick Martel left him stranded in the ring. The former friends feuded for almost the next year. Rick "The Model" Martel had a new, self-involved outlook on life and soon retained the managerial services of Slick. Tito showed he was still a threat when he won the *King of the Ring 1989* tournament. He made his presence felt each time he competed in *Royal Rumble* and *Survivor Series.* At *Survivor Series 1990,* Santana was the sole survivor on his team and ended up alongside Hulk Hogan and Ultimate Warrior in the final *Survivor* match against "Million Dollar Man" Ted DiBiase, "The Model," the Warlord, and Power and Glory. That April, he competed against Mr. Perfect in the finals of the Intercontinental Championship tournament.

In late 1991, Santana took on a new persona: "El Matador." Battling World Wrestling Federation's top Superstars, El Matador's team was victorious at the *Survivor Series 1991* over the team of General Adnan, the Berzerker, Hercules, and Skinner. El Matador also saw action versus "Million Dollar Man" Ted DiBiase and wrestled a young

Shawn Michaels at *WrestleMania VIII*. In 1993, Santana's tenure with World Wrestling Federation came to an end. Tito continued to wrestle, and in 1996 he started his own promotion, the American Wrestling Federation. In 1997, Tito returned to World Wrestling Federation as part of the Spanish announcing team.

In March 2004 Tito Santana was inducted into the WWE Hall of Fame. This was the perfect ending to a career that spanned three decades, eight *WrestleManias*, two reigns as a coholder of World Wrestling Federation World Tag Team Championship, a King of the Ring win, and two World Wrestling Federation Intercontinental Championships. Throughout his career, Santana brought prestige and distinction to any championship he held.

"Mr. Wonderful" Paul Orndorff

FROM: **Tampa, FL**

HEIGHT: **6'**

WEIGHT: **252 lbs.**

FINISHING MOVE: **The piledriver**

WHEN WRESTLING HISTORIANS TALK ABOUT TENACITY, EXCELLENT TECHNICAL skills, and chiseled physiques, one of the first names mentioned is "Mr. Wonderful" Paul Orndorff. He debuted in 1976, and one of his first bouts was with current *Raw* announcer Jerry "The King" Lawler. Orndorff then went to Mid-South Wrestling and battled "Big Cat" Ernie Ladd. During the late 1970s Orndorff also teamed with Jimmy "Superfly" Snuka, and the two held regional NWA Championships. In the early 1980s "Mr. Wonderful" became known as an athletically versatile mat wrestler who possessed great strength and quickness plus a mean streak second to none. Paul Orndorff did whatever was necessary to win, and whoever stood in his way was going to get steamrolled. His finishing move, the piledriver, also began to receive attention as one of the most feared maneuvers in all of wrestling. Paul's time in the Southeast was spent in battles with the likes of Jake Roberts, Junkyard Dog, Ted DiBiase, Dusty Rhodes, Dick Murdoch, and Ivan Koloff. After he fought the Masked Superstar, Orndorff left the regional surroundings of the National Wrestling Alliance. When World Wrestling Federation made him an offer, Orndorff jumped at the chance to compete against the world's best.

On January 14, 1984, "Mr. Wonderful" Paul Orndorff entered World Wrestling Federation. He joined with fellow rule-breaker Roddy Piper, interjecting himself in the Piper-Hogan saga. Paul became one of the first challengers to Hogan's World Wrestling Federation World Heavyweight Championship. In 1985 Orndorff fulfilled every wrestler's dream and competed in the first-ever *WrestleMania* main event, teaming with the "Hot Rod" to take on the duo of Hulk Hogan & Mr. T. This bout set the standard for *WrestleMania* headliners and put "Mr. Wonderful" on a new path. When "Cowboy" Bob Orton mistakenly nailed Orndorff from the top rope with his cast, Orndorff was knocked cold and pinned. Piper and Orton blamed him for the loss and then attacked their former ally on an episode of *Saturday Night's Main Event.* Bobby "The Brain" Heenan then placed a $50,000 bounty on Orndorff's head. This led to Mr. Wonderful teaming with Hogan through the middle of 1986 and battling World Wrestling Federation's most mischievous Superstars. As the duo reached their peak, "Adorable" Adrian Adonis caused trouble between them, and Orndorff turned on Hogan during a match against "Big" John Studd and King Kong Bundy. Mr. Wonderful made his plans crystal clear when he gave an already worn Hogan his trademark piledriver. Adding insult to injury, Orndorff cupped his ear, mocking Hogan, who was twitching on the mat, to intense boos from the crowd.

Orndorff, now an official member of the Heenan Family, set his sights on dethroning World Wrestling Federation's greatest hero. To further anger Hogan, Orndorff stole his "Real American" theme song and used it on his way out to his matches. Hogan and Orndorff collided in violent bouts across the country for the next six months. At World Wrestling Federation's outdoor "Big Event," their match drew a record-setting 76,000 fans in Toronto and led to one of the greatest Steel Cage matches of all time. During the episode of *Saturday Night's Main Event,* while both men simultaneously climbed out and down opposite sides of the cage, it appeared they touched down on the arena floor at the same time. Senior Referee Joey Marella decided that the match should restart. This resulted in Hogan's defeat of Mr. Wonderful, and one of the greatest feuds in pro wrestling history was laid to rest. After taking time off to heal, Mr. Wonderful returned as a fan favorite, led to the ring by Sir Oliver Humperdink. Their feud resolved, Orndorff appeared on Hogan's team at *Survivor Series 1987.*

Shortly after, the Master of the Piledriver disappeared from World Wrestling Federation without a trace. This sudden exit spawned rumors about his whereabouts and well-being. A rumor spread through the wrestling world that Orndorff had died. He remained dormant for the rest of the decade. In 1990 he appeared on the independent scene in bouts against Kerry Von Erich. That spring, Orndorff appeared in World Championship Wrestling as part of Sting's Dudes with Attitudes faction and fought the Four Horsemen. Orndorff left WCW and returned to the independents. After a brief tenure in Smoky Mountain Wrestling—where he feuded with Hector Guerrero and "Rugged" Ronnie Garvin—Orndorff reappeared in WCW in 1993. Paul wasted no time in making his presence felt and fought Cactus Jack in a Falls Count Anywhere match at *SuperBrawl III*.

Orndorff captured the first major championship of his famed career when he defeated Erik Watts in the finals of a sixteen-man tournament for the WCW World Television Championship. Here "Mr. Wonderful" also feuded with Ricky Steamboat, Ron Simmons, and Dustin Rhodes. In late 1993 Orndorff joined forces with Paul Roma and formed the self-involved duo appropriately named "Pretty Wonderful." The two won the WCW World Tag Team Championship on two separate occasions after victories over Stars-N-Stripes and Cactus Jack & Kevin Sullivan. When the team split, Orndorff returned to singles competition and squared off against Brad Armstrong, Johnny B. Badd, and Japan's Great Muta.

Mr. Wonderful's last feud was with Four Horsemen member Brian Pillman in 1996. Reenergized with positive encouragement, Orndorff came to the ring looking at himself in a mirror. Pillman insulted Orndorff's new attitude, and the Horsemen attacked him and administered a spike piledriver. Sadly, this marked the end of Mr. Wonderful's career. Once he had fully recovered, Orndorff became a trainer for WCW's Power Plant, molding many of wrestling's top stars with the toughness that was instilled in him by his teacher, Hiro Matsuda. Superstars that were trained by Mr. Wonderful include Stacy Keibler, Chuck Palumbo, and Goldberg. In 2000 he briefly returned to WCW television and showed that his piledriver was still the most devastating one in wrestling.

On April 2, 2005, Orndorff's storied twenty-five-year career was celebrated at the WWE Hall of Fame induction ceremony in the Universal Ampitheatre in Los Angeles. Ironically, Mr. Wonderful took his place among World Wrestling Federation's elite, along with former allies and enemies Hulk Hogan, Roddy Piper, and "Cowboy" Bob Orton. Orndorff is credited with making the piledriver the feared maneuver it is today. Mr. Wonderful's unyielding desire to be the best and unquenchable thirst to win set him apart.

King Kong Bundy

FROM: Atlantic City, NJ

HEIGHT: 6'4"

WEIGHT: 446 lbs.

FINISHING MOVE: The Avalanche

THIS BEHEMOTH BEGAN ANNIHILATING OPPONENTS IN THE 1980S. IN 1982 HE ENTERED WORLD CLASS CHAMPIONSHIP WRESTLING, FEUDING with the legendary Fritz Von Erich. Bundy made his World Wrestling Federation debut in February 1985 with the "Mouth of the South" Jimmy Hart by his side. At the first *WrestleMania,* King Kong Bundy showed how devastating he could be by pulverizing S. D. "Special Delivery" Jones with his Avalanche in 10 seconds. The Avalanche was so crushing that Bundy demanded the referee count to five. He would soon become known as the "Master of the Five Count." His size was so great, Gorilla Monsoon called him "the walking condominium."

On the September 10, 1985, episode of *Piper's Pit,* Bobby "The Brain" Heenan announced Bundy as the newest member of his Heenan Family. Bundy now seemed unstoppable with "The Brain" in his corner. He immediately went on a tear through World Wrestling Federation, displaying his talents in a series of two-on-one handicap matches and forming one of the largest tag teams in wrestling history with "Big" John Studd. Andre the Giant was soon in his sights, although these matches often ended in disqualifications due to Heenan Family interference. In August 1985, this strategy reached new lows when Bundy interfered in a match that pitted Andre against "Big" John Studd. These two monsters double-teamed Andre, and while Studd held Andre down, Bundy landed on him with a big splash, breaking the Eighth Wonder of the World's sternum. These appalling displays became customary, reaching their peak of brutality on a

December episode of *Saturday Night's Main Event*. While receiving assistance from his manager Bobby "The Brain" Heenan and the Magnificent Muraco, Bundy repeatedly Avalanched World Wrestling Federation Champion Hulk Hogan, nearly compressing his entire ribcage. This put Hogan out of action for almost four months. Against doctor's orders, Hogan faced his attacker in the main event of *WrestleMania 2* inside a fifteen-foot-high steel cage. That night Bundy and his manager would see their dreams shattered as Hogan overcame the odds by scaling the cage and retaining his title.

King Kong Bundy's desire to end careers didn't waver, though, and at *WrestleMania III,* Bundy once again showed his distain for the rules and his opponents. During his Mixed Tag Team match with partners Lord Littlebrook and Little Tokyo, Bundy grew frustrated at the antics of his opponents and match stipulations that he couldn't be in the ring with the midgets. It was then he flattened Little Beaver with an elbow drop, shocking and horrifying the record-breaking Silverdome crowd. This resulted in Bundy's team's disqualification, and Little Beaver had to be carried back to the locker room and receive emergency medical attention.

The last major World Wrestling Federation event of the 1980s Bundy competed in was the first *Survivor Series* in November 1987. Here he was a member of former enemy turned Heenan Family member Andre the Giant's team alongside "Natural" Butch Reed, One Man Gang, and "Ravishing" Rick Rude. They were victorious over Hulk Hogan's team of Bam Bam Bigelow, Don Muraco, Ken Patera, and "Mr. Wonderful" Paul Orndorff. Bundy spent the remainder of the decade out of the ring but not out of the spotlight. He made appearances on Fox's hit comedy *Married with Children* as Uncle Irwin and in computer system ads, and in 1988 he made his silver screen debut in *Moving*.

After an almost-seven-year absence, Bundy returned to World Wrestling Federation in 1994. As a member of Ted DiBiase's Million Dollar Corporation, Bundy planned to eliminate Undertaker. The two collided at *WrestleMania XI,* and the Dead Man came out with the victory. Shortly after this, Bundy left the company.

Though it's been over a decade since he has been inside a WWE ring, King Kong Bundy will always be remembered for crushing the hopes of fans and the body parts of his opponents with his amazing size and strength. He can still be seen across the country on the independent circuit as well as promoting wrestling shows in his home state of New Jersey. Bundy also runs his own wrestling school, training future sports entertainment hopefuls. Let's hope Midget Flattening 101 is not part of the core curriculum.

George "The Animal" Steele

FROM: **Parts unknown**

HEIGHT: **6'1"**

WEIGHT: **245 lbs.**

FINISHING MOVE: **Flying hammerlock**

THE TRADEMARK GREEN TONGUE, FUR-LIKE BODY HAIR, AND INSATIABLE APPETITE FOR TURNBUCKLES MEANS IT CAN ONLY BE ONE MAN: GEORGE "The Animal" Steele. Before this unorthodox wrestler became a fan favorite, he was one of the sport's most bizarre and hated figures. His animal behavior in the ring was first recognized in Detroit's Big Time Wrestling, when he was involved in a bloody feud with the Sheik. "The Animal" began shocking World Wrestling Federation Superstars in the 1970s with behavior as unpredictable as it was uncontrollable. Steele's finishing move, the flying hammerlock, could break an opponent's arm or separate a shoulder within seconds. Steele became a contender for Bruno Sammartino's World Wrestling Federation Heavyweight Championship. These matches often ended in disqualification due to Steele's outlandish ring tactics and disregard for the rules. "The Animal's" normal ring habits were a myriad of illegal maneuvers, including blatant chokes, incessant biting, eye-rakes, and clawing at his opponents. Steele also feuded with Gorilla Monsoon, Pedro Morales, and Bob Backlund. During this time of terror, Steele was managed by the likes of "Classy" Freddie Blassie, Johnny Valentine, the Grand Wizard, Mr. Fuji, and "Luscious" Johnny Valiant.

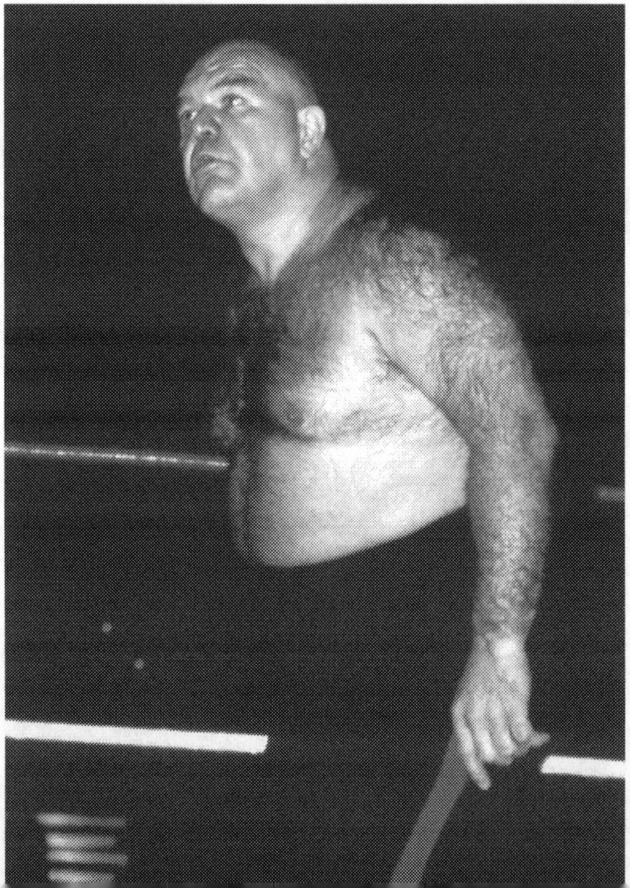

After disappearing from professional wrestling, "The Animal" returned to World Wrestling Federation in 1984. Capt. Lou Albano managed him in hopes of ending his villainous ways. Though Steele still could not be contained in most instances, he quickly became one of wrestling's most beloved figures. In 1986 he feuded with Intercontinental Champion Randy Savage in a series of violent contests. Despite losing their match at *WrestleMania 2,* Steele would not be discouraged, as he was more interested in holding Savage's beautiful manager Miss Elizabeth than the Intercontinental title. The Animal would remain a thorn in the Macho Man's side, helping Ricky Steamboat to defeat him at *WrestleMania III.* Throughout the remainder of the late 1980s, Steele would appear at World Wrestling Federation events tearing turnbuckles and opponents apart while bringing a puppet mascot with him to the ring that he would converse with in an unknown tongue named "Mine."

As the 1990s began, George made occasional appearances inside the squared circle. In 1994 he made his movie debut in Tim Burton's Oscar Award–winning film *Ed Wood.* In 1995 his forty-year career was celebrated as he was inducted into the WWE Hall of Fame in New York City. Then, to the delight of fans everywhere, the Animal returned to WWE for one last run during the "Attitude" era of the late 1990s as part of the one group where he blended in: the Human Oddities.

Though it has been over eight years since he has been on WWE programming, the legend of George "The Animal" Steele continues to grow. His talents are perhaps appreciated today more than ever; although he never uttered a word of intelligible speech or won a major championship during his career, he remains one of the most recognizable figures in sports entertainment history.

The British Bulldogs (Dynamite Kid & Davey Boy Smith)

FROM: **United Kingdom**

COMBINED WEIGHT: **488 lbs.**

FINISHING MOVE: **The Rocket Launcher headbutt**

THE DYNAMITE KID AND DAVEY BOY SMITH WERE TWO OF THE BRIGHTEST STARS EVER TO COME OUT OF STU HART'S FAMOUS STAMPEDE TERRITORY. Early in their careers the two feuded over the Stampede British Commonwealth Mid-Heavyweight Championship, and their matches raised eyebrows. Before their World Wrestling Federation debut, Smith gained a reputation for his incredible blend of power, speed, and ring presence. Though Dynamite Kid possessed similar attributes, he received global attention for his classic battles with Japanese legend Tiger Mask.

In 1985 the British Bulldogs made their World Wrestling Entertainment debut and were an instant hit with fans all over the world. With their combined strengths in the

ring and "manager of champions" Capt. Lou Albano in their corner, the Bulldogs were practically unbeatable. Their lightning-quick tags and sound strategy made for some of the greatest continuity ever seen in the squared circle. After many matches with then champions the Dream Team—Valentine & Beefcake—the Bulldogs would receive one last shot at the titles. At *WrestleMania 2,* Dynamite & Davey Boy brought added insurance with them in the form of Ozzy Osbourne. During the match both teams traded the upper hand, but in the end a hardheaded Dynamite Kid proved to be the deciding factor. Once Davey Boy Smith pinned Valentine, the Rosemont Horizon crowd jumped to their feet as the Bulldogs' dream came true. As champions, Dynamite & Davey Boy defeated all challengers, including the Dream Team, Iron Sheik & Nikolai Volkoff, "Big" John Studd & King Kong Bundy, and the Hart Foundation. The Harts and Bulldogs were archrivals. These matches were so highly contested that a victory could be decided in the blink of an eye. The Bulldogs' ten-month title reign ended on January 26, 1987, when, after Dynamite Kid was attacked before the match, Davey Boy had to face the Harts by himself. The Hit Man and Anvil took full advantage of the outnumbered Bulldog and received an enormous amount of latitude from the official, Danny Davis.

After Dynamite recovered from his attack, the Bulldogs returned hungrier than ever to reclaim what they felt was rightfully theirs. During the May 2, 1987, episode of *Saturday Night's Main Event* they defeated the Harts in a Best-Two-Out-of-Three Falls.

Since the first fall victory was the result of a disqualification, the title did not change hands. The Bulldogs soon entered into a feud with Bobby "The Brain" Heenan's Islanders. Heenan and company stole their bulldog, Matilda, from ringside during a Bulldogs Tag Team match and refused to return her to her owners. At *WrestleMania IV*, the Bulldogs and "Birdman" Koko B. Ware faced the three marauders in six-man action. Matilda took a bite out of her abductor when she caught up to "The Brain" in the Trump Plaza aisle. Dynamite & Davey Boy remained title contenders for the remainder of the decade and feuded with the likes of Demolition, the Dream Team, and the Bolsheviks.

At *SummerSlam '88*, they fought to a time limit draw with rivals the Fabulous Rougeau Brothers. Shortly after that match, Dynamite and Davey Boy left World Wrestling Federation. That December they returned to their wrestling roots: Canada's Stampede Wrestling. Almost immediately they captured the Stampede International Tag Team Championship. As a result of outside interference, the Bulldogs lost the titles days later. A furious Dynamite Kid blamed Smith for the loss, and a feud between the longtime partners was ignited. In the aftermath the two permanently parted ways.

In the early 1990s, Davey Boy Smith toured Europe and Japan as a singles wrestler before he returned to World Wrestling Federation. Smith wrestled in one of the greatest matches of all time in the main event of *SummerSlam '92* against brother-in-law Bret "Hit Man" Hart for the Intercontinental Championship, holding the title until that November, when he lost it to Shawn Michaels. Shortly afterward, Smith left. After a brief tenure in World Championship Wrestling, he returned to World Wrestling Federation and was once again one of its premier Superstars. During a hiatus from the ring, Davey Boy Smith tragically passed away on May 18, 2002, while on vacation. His wrestling legacy lives on through his son Harry, who appropriately holds the moniker of "Bulldog."

The Dynamite Kid toured Japan, but as the decade continued, he took on a lighter schedule. His last in-ring appearance was in a 1996 Six-man Tag Team match for Giant Baba's All-Japan Pro Wrestling promotion. Sadly, his years of physical brilliance in the ring caught up to him, and he was forced to retire. In 2001 he released his autobiography, *Pure Dynamite*.

The Bulldogs changed the face of tag team wrestling and are revered as WWE legends. Their classic bouts with the Hart Foundation helped establish the World Wrestling Federation World Tag Team Championship as the most prestigious prize for teams to strive for. Their influence is seen today throughout the world and is a testament to their radically innovative style. No one had a bigger bite than Dynamite Kid and Davey Boy Smith, the British Bulldogs.

Fabulous Moolah

FROM: **Columbia, SC**

HEIGHT: **5'5"**

WEIGHT: **138 lbs.**

FINISHING MOVE: **Schoolgirl roll-up**

WHEN WRESTLING HISTORIANS SIT AT THEIR ROUND TABLE AND DISCUSS THE IRREFUTABLE GREATEST WOMEN'S WRESTLER OF ALL TIME, ONE NAME is said in unison: the Fabulous Moolah. She debuted in 1949 as the provocatively dressed valet "Slave Girl Moolah," leading wrestlers like the ghastly Elephant Boy and "Nature Boy" Buddy Rogers to the ring. As she was trained by the most famous female wrestler of the era, Mildred Burke, being a valet was a mere steppingstone. During the mid-1950s she made a name for herself in the ring under the name Fabulous Moolah. In 1956, Moolah started an astounding thirty-year championship dynasty when she defeated Judy Grable in a finals tournament match to crown the Women's Champion. A championship reign of this magnitude has never been seen again. One of Moolah's crowning achievements was in 1972, when she and Vincent McMahon Sr. successfully beat the ban against women's wrestling at Madison Square Garden. Moolah spent the rest of the 1970s as the sole holder of the World Wrestling Federation Women's Championship and the dominant force in women's wrestling. She traveled across the United States and soundly defeated the competition in Canada, Mexico, Japan, and across Europe.

As a new decade began, Moolah's squared-circle supremacy continued until she met World Wrestling Federation fan favorite Wendi Richter at "The Brawl to End It All" on July 23, 1984. Richter's title reign lasted six months until she lost to Moolah protégée Leilani Kai. With Kai as champion, Moolah lightened her in-ring schedule to manage the Hawaiian Superstar. Under Moolah's guidance, Kai went into the first *WrestleMania* as the Women's Champion. That night Richter regained the title as the Rock-N-Wrestling Connection took Madison Square Garden by storm. However, Moolah later returned to the ring to take her championship back, defeating Richter as the "Masked Spider Lady." During a tour of the land Down Under in the summer of 1986, Moolah exchanged victories with Irish grappler Velvet McIntyre. Moolah made sure she returned to the States with the Women's Championship title firmly around her waist. After another lengthy title reign, Moolah's championship days officially came to an end on July 24, 1987, when she was defeated by the woman she trained, Sensational Sherri. One of Moolah's last major appearances in the ring came at the *Survivor Series 1987* when her team of Rockin' Robin, Velvet McIntyre, and Japan's Jumping Bomb Angels defeated Sherri Martel, Leilani Kai, Judy Martin, Donna Christanello, and Dawn Marie. Moolah then disappeared from the World Wrestling Federation scene.

Moolah appeared sporadically during the early 1990s in video packages and at live World Wrestling Federation events. In 1995 she took her rightful place among wrestling's immortals in the WWE Hall of Fame. Then, during the height of the Attitude era at *No Mercy '99,* Moolah returned with long-time friend Mae Young in her corner and showed she could still battle with the best of them. The Fabulous One once again made wrestling history when she caught then champion Ivory in a roll-up. This marked Moolah's fourth World Wrestling Federation Women's title, forty-three years after she won her first Women's Championship. This amazing achievement made her the oldest champion in the history of professional wrestling. Though she didn't enjoy one of her lengthy title reigns, the victory was a testament to Moolah's eternal greatness within the squared circle. In years since, Moolah and Mae Young have appeared at many major World Wrestling Federation events, including *WrestleMania XVI* and many episodes of *Raw* and *SmackDown.* In 2002 Moolah expanded her résumé and authored her autobiography, *The Fabulous Moolah: First Goddess of the Squared Circle.*

The Fabulous Moolah is an icon of women's wrestling and a pioneer like no other. No champion, male or female, enjoyed a longer period of domination, and no woman has done more for her sport. The Fabulous One has stated that she will wrestle when she's one hundred years old. Knowing this WWE Hall of Famer, not only is this likely to happen, but she could win a fifth World Wrestling Federation Women's Championship in the process.

The Magnificent Muraco

FROM: **Sunset Beach, HI**

HEIGHT: **6'3"**

WEIGHT: **270 lbs.**

FINISHING MOVE: **Reverse piledriver**

DON MURACO BUILT A NAME FOR HIMSELF WHILE TRAVELING THROUGH THE TERRITORIES OF THE NATIONAL WRESTLING ALLIANCE. IN MARCH 1980 he defeated "Raging Bull" Manny Fernandez for the Florida Heavyweight title. After a five-month reign as champion, Muraco sought national exposure, making his World Wrestling Federation debut later that year with manager Capt. Lou Albano. Muraco was arrogant, brash, and fierce in the squared circle. During his walk to the ring, angry fans yelled, "Beach bum," a derogatory term that infuriated him. He immediately became a force to be reckoned with, on June 20, 1981, defeating Pedro Morales to capture his first World Wrestling Federation Intercontinental Championship. Though Muraco lost the title to Morales five months later, the Magnificent One returned to World Wrestling Federation, and on January 22, 1983, he regained the championship from the beloved Morales. Muraco mowed down every opponent in his path, battling World Wrestling Federation Champion Bob Backlund in classic sixty-minute matches that ended in draws and doing whatever it took to hold on to his cherished title.

On October 17, 1983, he had arguably his toughest title defense at Madison Square Garden, in a rematch against Jimmy Snuka, in a fifteen-foot-high steel cage. Muraco stepped into the steel enclosure with hate pumping through his veins and threw running forearms at the cage in anticipation of his opponent. The bell rang, and the match was a dog fight from the onset, with both men bleeding profusely. Snuka bounced off the ropes and nailed Muraco with a flying headbutt. In midair Muraco called for the door to be opened and fell through it, winning the match. Snuka's shock turned to rage, and the blood-soaked Superfly brought the battered champion back into the ring. After giving Muraco a vertical suplex, Snuka did the amazing and climbed to the top of the cage. After giving the crowd his trademark "I Love You" sign, Snuka leaped off the top and crashed down onto the bloody champion. Muraco enjoyed one of the longest championship reigns in World Wrestling Federation history, finally losing the Intercontinental Championship to Tito Santana on February 11, 1984.

In 1985 Muraco's vanity reached its zenith when he and Mr. Fuji debuted the soap opera *Fuji Vice* on an episode of *Tuesday Night Titans.* At one point Muraco brought a sandwich to the ring and vowed to eat it while defeating his opponent. Unfortunately

for fans, Muraco made good on his guarantee, displaying the scope of his ego and his innate wrestling ability simultaneously. Acquiring the services of the devious Mr. Fuji, he then entered into battle with Ricky Steamboat. These bouts were ferocious. During one match Muraco wrapped a leather belt around Steamboat's neck and hung him from the top rope, bringing the Dragon inches away from asphyxiation. In July 1985 Muraco once again proved his dominance by winning the first ever *King of the Ring* tournament, defeating the Iron Sheik in the finals.

One of the most despicable acts of Muraco's storied career took place during the March 1, 1986, episode of *Saturday Night's Main Event* After his match with World Wrestling Federation Champion Hulk Hogan was thrown out due to outside interference, he held Hogan chest first in the corner while Hogan's assailant, King Kong Bundy, Avalanched the champion and broke his ribs. During that year the Magnificent One also formed a dangerous tag team with ring strategist "Cowboy" Bob Orton. The tandem wreaked havoc in the tag team division against opponents like the British Bulldogs, the Killer Bees, and the Young Stallions. At *WrestleMania III* Muraco & Orton met the short-lived team of Rick Martel & Tom Zenk, the Can-Am Connection. Muraco and Orton severed all ties, and in the fall of 1987 Muraco vowed to be his own man.

On television, when Superstar Billy Graham fell victim to a Pearl Harbor attack by One Man Gang and Butch Reed, Muraco came to his aid. With Graham as his inspiration, Muraco turned over a new leaf and became the first World Wrestling Federation Superstar to be called "The Rock." He was now known as Don "The Rock" Muraco. Later that year he appeared at the first ever *Survivor Series* as a substitute for the injured

Graham as part of Hulk Hogan's team. At *WrestleMania IV,* the Rock made it to the second round of the World Title tournament before losing to eventual finalist "Million Dollar Man" Ted DiBiase. In August 1988 Muraco left World Wrestling Federation and split his time between the AWA and Stu Hart's Stampede Wrestling. While in Calgary, Muraco defended his Stampede North American title in 1989 against Davey Boy Smith.

As a new decade dawned, Muraco spent the 1990s traveling to independent promotions across the United States, wrestling the likes of Cactus Jack, B. Brian Blair, and "Dr. Death" Steve Williams. In 1992 Muraco signed with the Philadelphia-based Eastern Championship Wrestling and rekindled feuds with longtime adversaries Jimmy Snuka and Tito Santana over its Heavyweight title. This organization later became known as Extreme Championship Wrestling. In 1993 Muraco left ECW and continued to travel the independents.

In June 2003, Muraco launched his own promotion, Hawaiian Championship Wrestling. Soon he entered into a talent exchange program with New Japan Pro Wrestling that brought the Orient's top stars to the Islands of Aloha. On March 13, 2004, at *WrestleMania XX,* Don Muraco's magnificent career was celebrated as he was inducted into the WWE Hall of Fame.

Mr. Fuji

FROM: **Tokyo, Japan**
HEIGHT: **5'10"**
WEIGHT: **235 lbs.**
FINISHING MOVE: **Banzai drop**

BEFORE HE WAS KNOWN AS WRESTLING'S MOST DEVIOUS MANAGER, MR. FUJI WAS A FIVE-TIME CO-HOLDER OF THE WORLD WRESTLING Federation World Tag Team Championship and a threat to the World Wrestling Federation World Heavyweight Championship reigns of Bruno Sammartino, Pedro Morales, and Bob Backlund. From Tokyo, he made his wrestling debut in 1966 and traveled through the NWA territories. When he landed in Hawaii, he was closely associated with the iniquitous Tor Kamata and ran rampant through the islands. In 1972 Mr. Fuji debuted with World Wide Wrestling Federation for Vince McMahon Sr. He soon formed a tag team with Professor Toru Tanaka, and the duo was managed by the

Grand Wizard. While both were experts in the martial arts, Tanaka was the power man of the team, and Fuji provided the technical skills and ring psychology needed for success in World Wrestling Federation. Fuji also carried ceremonial salt; despite his claims that it symbolized ancient Japanese traditions, it usually found its way into the eyes of his opponents. On June 27, 1972, Fuji & Tanaka captured their first World Wrestling Federation World Tag Team Championship, besting Sonny King and Chief Jay Strongbow. At a Madison Square Garden event that October, the two Japanese stars took on the team Pedro Morales & Bruno Sammartino in an awesome main event. In 1973, Fuji & Tanaka battled the team of Tony Garea & Haystacks Calhoun for the World Wrestling Federation World Tag Team titles.

In the mid-1970s the ruthless pair ripped through the NWA with relative ease, returning to World Wrestling Federation in 1977 with manager "Classy" Freddie Blassie. On September 27 they defeated Tony Garea & Larry Zbyszko in a tournament final for their third World Wrestling Federation World Tag Team Championship. Fuji & Tanaka's final title reign ended on March 14, 1978, courtesy of Dominic DeNucci & Dino Bravo. The team remained one of World Wrestling Federation's most hated tandems, and in May of 1978 they recruited fellow villain Ken Patera to take on the mega-team of Andre the Giant, "The American Dream" Dusty Rhodes, and Mil Mascaras in a Two-Out-of-Three Falls.

In 1981 Fuji returned to World Wrestling Federation with a new partner, the cunning and shrewd Mr. Saito. They were managed by Capt. Lou Albano. On October 13 Fuji & Saito defeated Tony Garea & Rick Martel for their first of two World Wrestling Federation World Tag Team Championships. The Japanese terrors held the titles for eight months until they faced Native American heroes Chief Jay & Jules Strongbow. Fuji & Saito regained the titles on July 13 for their second and final championship reign.

As the 1980s continued, Mr. Fuji made the transition to a full-time manager, coming to the ring in an instantly recognizable tuxedo, black top hat, and cane. His first client was the unpredictable and equally dangerous George "The Animal" Steele. In one of the most infamous moments in World Wrestling Federation history, Fuji and Steele took on the team of Hulk Hogan and Gene Okerlund in a special challenge match that saw *Hulkamania* and Gene-O-Mania run wild in Minneapolis. Steele soon left Fuji and became a fan favorite. The Devious One then built his stable around the Magnificent Muraco, managing him in the opening match of *WrestleMania 2* against Paul Orndorff. The Moondogs were added to Fuji's collection of Superstars, and he briefly managed Kamala. Fuji took "The Ugandan Giant" on to *Tuesday Night Titans* and showed him eating a live chicken, to the disgust of the audience.

Rounding out his group of villains, Fuji added "Cowboy" Bob Orton, Killer Khan, and Wild Samoan Sika. Mr. Fuji brought Muraco and Orton together as tag team contenders while Killer Khan feuded with Hulk Hogan over the World Wrestling Federation World Championship. After Muraco & Orton split and Killer Khan left, Mr. Fuji obtained the contracts for Ax & Smash—Demolition. At *WrestleMania IV,* he led the Demos to the World Wrestling Federation World Tag Team Championship over Strike Force. This was Fuji's first championship as a manager. At *Survivor Series 1988,* Mr. Fuji turned against Demolition and aligned himself with the Barbarian & Warlord—the Powers of Pain. He helped them become the sole survivors when he tripped one of Los Conquistadors with his cane. However, Demolition got their revenge on the Powers of Pain and Mr. Fuji at *WrestleMania V,* when they defeated the trio in a Handicap match.

In February 1990, Mr. Fuji introduced another team, Tanaka & Sato—The Orient Express. Soon afterward, he sold the contracts of Warlord and Barbarian to Bobby "The Brain" Heenan. He reunited with Demolition, who now had a third member, Crush. After a feud with the Legion of Doom, Demolition disbanded. In 1992 Mr. Fuji introduced the six-four, six-hundred-pound Yokozuna to World Wrestling Federation. At that year's *Survivor Series,* this mammoth obliterated Virgil. Yokozuna's list of victims grew, and he earned a shot at the World Wrestling Federation World Heavyweight Championship when he won the *Royal Rumble 1993.* At *WrestleMania IX,* the Japanese star defeated then champion Bret "Hit Man" Hart when Fuji threw his ceremonial salt in the Hit Man's eyes as he applied the Sharpshooter. Though he lost the title after the match in an open challenge to Hulk Hogan, Yokozuna regained the title at the *King of the Ring 1993.* Fuji and Yokozuna hired Jim Cornette as their U.S. spokesperson and feuded with Lex Luger, Bret Hart, and Undertaker throughout 1994.

Fuji showed he was never short of surprises when at *WrestleMania XI* he led Yokozuna to the ring as the mystery partner for Owen Hart, and the unlikely pair defeated the Smokin' Gunns for the World Wrestling Federation World Tag Team

Championship. The Diabolical One left World Wrestling Federation late in 1995. However, Fuji showed that he could show up at any time when he made his final World Wrestling Federation appearance at *WrestleMania XII,* accompanying Yokozuna to the ring for the event's opening six-man bout.

Mr. Fuji will forever be remembered as one of the fiercest and most successful figures in the history of World Wrestling Entertainment. Whether as a wrestler or as a manager leading wrestling's most brutal rule-breakers to the ring, Mr. Fuji repeatedly showed he was capable of some of the most despicable acts fans have ever witnessed.

Jake "The Snake" Roberts

FROM: **Stone Mountain, GA**

HEIGHT: **6'6"**

WEIGHT: **260 lbs.**

FINISHING MOVE: **DDT**

TO ATTEMPT TO UNDERSTAND THE DARK, COLD WORLD OF THIS WRESTLER, YOU need to dig deep into the pits of despair. The journey of the man who has walked the earth for the past twenty-five years as Jake "The Snake" Roberts is not for the weak or timid. He has instilled terror and panic in the hearts and minds of all World Wrestling Federation Superstars. A second-generation wrestler, Jake Roberts began his career in the Mid-South territory and learned his first finishing move, the kneelift, from legendary masked man Mr. Wrestling II. Though his father, Grizzly Smith, discouraged him from entering the sport of kings, and even told him he'd never make it, Jake Roberts was determined to eclipse his father's career achievements and prove him wrong. Roberts toured the wrestling territories of North America and became known as an elite strategist. He had early feuds with the likes of the Grappler and Paul Orndorff before he landed in Georgia Championship Wrestling as one of the original members of Paul Ellering's Legion of Doom with cohorts the Road Warriors and the Spoiler. Roberts engaged in a feud with Ronnie Garvin over the Television title before he moved on to World Class Championship Wrestling and feuded with the Von Erichs. He briefly returned to Georgia and became the first ever NWA Television Champion.

In 1986, the mysterious Jake "The Snake" Roberts slithered into World Wrestling Federation and came to the ring with a green bag over his shoulder; in it was his thirty-foot, seventy-pound boa constrictor Damien. During his matches the bag slowly moved in the corner like a predator stalking its prey. After Roberts planted his opponents head-first into the canvas with his devastating DDT, he draped Damien across them as they foamed at the mouth. Jake was World Wrestling Federation's silent assassin as he methodically dissected his opponents and horrified fans with his cryptic, bone-chilling interviews. More times than not, Roberts's sick prophecies came to fruition. The Snake's first feud was with Ricky Steamboat; he dropped Steamboat on his head with a DDT on the cement floor and rendered him unconscious. The two then squared off in a Snake Pit match at *The Big Event.* Soon after, Roberts's attitude began to change. During an episode of *The Snake Pit,* Roberts was attacked by the Honky Tonk Man and knocked out when Honky broke a guitar over his head. This started a feud, and the two men met at *WrestleMania III.* Roberts also clashed with King Kong Bundy, Kamala, Killer Khan, and Wild Samoan Sika. At *SummerSlam '88* he defeated Hercules.

The Snake then clashed with "Ravishing" Rick Rude after Rude tried to kiss his wife, Cheryl Roberts, during an event. Rude later taunted Jake by wearing tights with Cheryl's image on them. After the Snake warned Rude to never wear the tights again and Rude continued, Roberts ran into the ring, ripped them off, and left him in the ring naked. Jake's next feud was with another member of the Heenan Family, the "Eighth Wonder of the World," Andre the Giant. Discovering that Andre's only possible vulnerability was a fear of snakes, Jake unleashed Damien on Andre and sent the Giant into cardiac arrest inside the ring. At *Royal Rumble 1989* Jake was eliminated by Andre, but when he returned to the ring moments later with Damien, Andre ran from the ring and eliminated himself from the *Rumble.* The Snake and the Giant had their last bout at *WrestleMania V,* where the special guest referee was Big John Studd.

Roberts then faced off against the "Million Dollar Man" Ted DiBiase, Greg Valentine, Bad News Brown, and Mr. Perfect. The Snake had a long battle with "The Model" Rick Martel when Martel sprayed his fragrance, "Arrogance," in Roberts's eye, blinding him. The two met at *WrestleMania VII* in the famous Blindfold match. Roberts defeated "The Model" with the DDT, and after the match sent Martel running for his life when he unveiled Damien. Jake then crossed paths with the mighty Earthquake. During their match, the monster killed Damien with his Earthquake Splash. Shortly afterward, Roberts introduced his new pet, Lucifer.

In 1991, after a brief feud with the Ultimate Warrior, Jake crashed Randy Savage and Miss Elizabeth's wedding reception at *SummerSlam*. The Snake wanted Savage out of World Wrestling Federation so badly that he unleashed his pet cobra on "The Macho Man," who was bitten on the bicep. After a confrontation with Undertaker on an episode of Paul Bearer's *Funeral Parlor,* Jake and the Dead Man met at *WrestleMania VIII.* Immediately after, Jake "The Snake" Roberts vanished from World Wrestling Entertainment. Later that year he surfaced in WCW and feuded with Sting. At *Halloween Havoc 1992,* Roberts lost a Coal Miner's Glove match to the Stinger and left the organization. For most of the early and mid-1990s Jake traveled the independents of the United States and Mexico before a surprise return to World Wrestling Federation at *Royal Rumble 1996.*

World Wrestling Federation was a different place than it was when Roberts left. He faced new opponents—Vader, Tatanka, and Owen Hart, and up-and-coming Superstars Justin "Hawk" Bradshaw and Hunter Hearst-Helmsley. Roberts made it to the finals of the *King of the Ring* tournament, where he faced Stone Cold Steve Austin and was defeated by the Texas Rattlesnake. His bout with Austin helped give birth to World Wrestling Federation's "Attitude" era.

The Snake then entered a personal war with Jerry "The King" Lawler, when Lawler began to make light of Jake's past personal problems outside the ring. In early 1997 Jake once again left World Wrestling Federation without a trace. After a brief stint in Extreme Championship Wrestling, Jake returned to the American independent circuit for the remainder of the late 1990s.

In 2002, Jake relocated to England, where he opened his own wrestling school and began promoting live shows. Then, on the March 14, 2005, episode of *Raw,* Roberts made a surprise appearance. The raucous crowd chants of "DDT, DDT" made for a surreal moment as "The Snake" got into it with Randy Orton and showed the youngster what it means to make an impact. The ovation Roberts received that evening was a testament to his undying popularity with fans of all ages. His superior technical and psychological skills within the squared circle are without equal. His signature DDT is one of the most feared and imitated maneuvers in wrestling history.

"Adorable" Adrian Adonis

FROM: **New York, NY**

HEIGHT: **5'10"**

WEIGHT: **310 lbs.**

FINISHING MOVE: **Good Night Irene sleeper hold**

THIS BIG APPLE NATIVE BEGAN HIS PROFESSIONAL CAREER IN 1974, TOURING THE PACIFIC NORTHWEST AND THE NATIONAL WRESTLING Alliance. He then appeared in Verne Gagne's American Wrestling Association in 1978. In 1980 Adrian Adonis formed a successful tag team with Jesse "The Body" Ventura. The duo was known as the East-West Connection and held the AWA World Tag Team Championship. On June 14, 1981, the two villains lost the title to the exciting team of Greg Gagne & Jim Brunzell—the High Flyers. Adonis spent a good portion of the early 1980s touring the Orient as part of New Japan Pro Wrestling and tagging with future partner Dick Murdoch. In 1984 Adonis debuted with World Wrestling Federation and along with Murdoch formed the North-South Connection. Adonis & Murdoch battled all of World Wrestling Federation's top teams and on April 17, 1984, defeated "Mr. USA" Tony Atlas & Rocky Johnson for the World Wrestling Federation World Tag Team Championship. Adonis & Murdoch held the titles for an impressive eight months before losing them on January 21, 1985, to the US Express—Barry Windham & Mike Rotundo. After dropping the titles, Adonis and Murdoch left World Wrestling Federation and returned to the Land of the Rising Sun. Here they rekindled feuds with *puroresu* greats Antonio Inoki and Tatsumi Fujinami in both singles and tag team action.

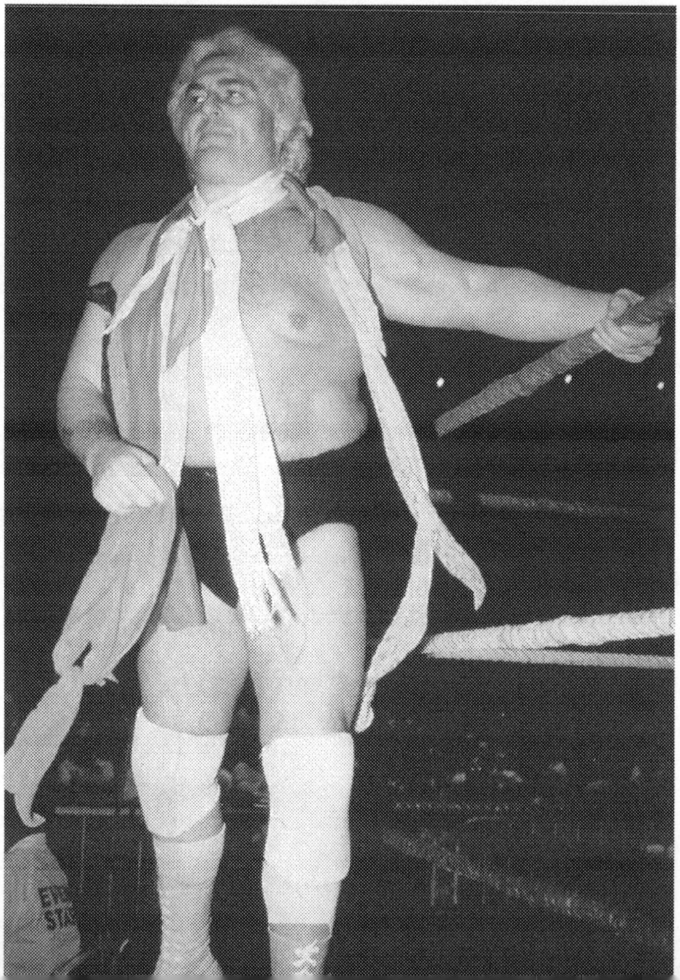

Later that year Adonis returned to World Wrestling Federation as a singles competitor. This time he was sporting a new, flamboyant look with a manager whose voice was as loud as Adonis's ensembles, "Mouth of the South" Jimmy Hart. Now known as "Adorable" Adrian Adonis, he showed the wrestling world he possessed both a brash and rugged side as well as an extravagant, ostentatious side with a mean streak. Adonis faced Cpl. Kirschner, Junkyard Dog, and George "The Animal" Steele and was a contender for the World Wrestling Federation World Championship.

Adonis made his *WrestleMania* debut at *WrestleMania 2,* defeating the mountainous Uncle Elmer. During that summer, Adonis joined forces with Randy Savage in tag team bouts to face the team of Bruno Sammartino & Tito Santana. Now one of World Wrestling Federation's most hated Superstars, Adonis soon launched his own television segment, *The Flower Shop.* To the disgust of fans across the country, Adonis often ended his show by rhetorically asking how you spell relief, then slowly spelling his last name letter by letter and walking off the show set. The Adorable One's greatest World Wrestling Federation feud was with former ally "Rowdy" Roddy Piper. The two got into a heated war of words, and Adonis hit an injured Piper with a cheap shot, sending him down to the floor. When Piper came to, he went berserk and destroyed the *Flower Shop* set. Their match at the Pontiac Silverdome was personal. The "Hot Rod" couldn't wait for the motorized cart to take him to the ring, but ran down the hundred-yard aisle in a fury. In the end, Piper defeated the Adorable One in this battle of the sleeper holds. Roddy then brought out Brutus Beefcake to cut off all Adonis's hair in one of the most humiliating acts in wrestling history. When Adonis was revived and saw his image in a mirror held up by Piper, he fled the ring.

After his unexpected trip to the barber at *WrestleMania III,* Adonis left the company and returned to the AWA. Here he feuded with "Wildfire" Tommy Rich and Greg Gagne for the International TV title. Sadly, on July 4, 1988, this gifted athlete's life was cut short when Adrian was killed in an automotive accident in Lewisporte, Newfoundland. The Adorable One will be forever in the hearts and minds of wrestling fans everywhere as a great villain and talented performer who could beat an opponent just as fast as he could incite a crowd. If you ever need to know how to spell relief: A-D-O-N-I-S.

Jesse "The Body" Ventura

FROM: Brooklyn Park, MN
HEIGHT: 6'2"
WEIGHT: 270 lbs.
FINISHING MOVE: The body breaker

A FORMER NAVY SEAL AND VIETNAM VETERAN, THIS WWE HALL OF FAMER BECAME ACCUSTOMED TO MEMBERSHIP IN ELITE GROUPS. DURING his days as a bodybuilder, Jesse Ventura had dreams of ruling the world of professional wrestling. After he fought in one of the most violent feuds the Pacific Northwest territory ever saw with Jimmy Snuka, "The Body" returned home to Minnesota, joining the American Wrestling Association. While in the AWA, Ventura became one of the promotion's most successful and hated figures. It was here that he made his motto, "Win if you can, lose if you must, but always cheat," famous. He soon formed a tag team, the East-West Connection, with Adrian Adonis. On July 20, 1980, the two villains were awarded the AWA World Tag Team Championship when the High Flyer team of Gagne & Brunzell were unable to compete. Ventura & Adonis defended the titles for almost a year before Gagne & Brunzell regained them on June 14, 1981.

When Ventura and Adonis landed in World Wrestling Federation, they were led to the ring by "Classy" Freddie Blassie. Almost instantly, they became contenders for the World Wrestling Federation World Tag Team Championship. The pair parted, and while Adonis continued in tag team competition with Dick Murdoch, "The Body" attacked the singles ranks. Ventura had several matches with then World Wrestling Federation Champion Bob Backlund and came within milliseconds of becoming the champion. Ventura also had feuds with Ivan Putski and "Mr. USA" Tony Atlas. In 1984 Ventura was slated to challenge

Hulk Hogan for the World Wrestling Federation crown. Unfortunately, an injury stemming from his tour of duty in Vietnam prevented him from doing so. Although he competed in various tag team matches after he recovered, Ventura soon retired from the ring.

In 1985 Jesse "The Body" Ventura debuted on World Wrestling Federation television as an announcer. He co-hosted *Saturday Night's Main Event* with Vince McMahon, and the major events and Pay-Per-Views with Gorilla Monsoon. Within minutes of his first broadcast, "The Body" became the most controversial commentator in wrestling. Ventura adamantly claimed to be the *only* announcer to tell it like it is. Ventura was like nothing ever seen before on World Wrestling Federation broadcasts. He had the insight of a wrestler, the convictions of a filibuster on Capitol Hill, and the biceps of a Mr. Universe winner.

In 1987 Ventura made his silver screen debut in the Arnold Schwarzenegger ultra-smash *Predator.* In typical "Body" fashion, he turned a simple one-liner into a global catchphrase when he said, "I ain't got time to bleed." When World Wrestling Federation needed an enforcer for the Mega Powers vs. Mega Bucks main event at *SummerSlam '88,* Ventura got the nod as special guest referee. Ventura's acting career also continued as he appeared in another Schwarzenegger hit, *Running Man,* and in Hulk Hogan's *No Holds Barred.* A new decade brought "The Body" new opportunities.

After a brief stint as an announcer in WCW, he left the broadcast booth and entered a new battlefield. In 1990 he won his first political election and became the mayor of his hometown, Brooklyn Park, Minnesota. Ventura also expanded his acting résumé with roles in television shows, including *Hunter, X-Files,* and *Zorro.* In 1991 "The Body" returned to Hollywood in *Ricochet,* starring Denzel Washington and John Lithgow. He also appeared in 1993's *Demolition Man,* starring Sylvester Stallone and Wesley Snipes, and 1997's *Batman & Robin,* starring George Clooney. His entertainment tour de force continued as he entered the world of team sports and called games on the radio for the NFL's Minnesota Vikings and Tampa Bay Buccaneers.

In the late 1990s Ventura's political aspirations grew, and he announced he was going to run for governor. Though his opponents initially mocked the former SEAL, on November 3, 1998, "The Body" pulled off the political upset of the decade. As an independent, Ventura beat St. Paul mayor Norm Coleman and Hubert Humphrey III, son of the former U.S. vice president. The former authority on handing out beat-downs was now referred to as Jesse "The Mind" Ventura. Though it was close to a decade from the last time he had been on World Wrestling Federation television, his services were required for the epic *SummerSlam '99* main event. "The Mind" was special guest referee for the Triple Threat match that saw Stone Cold Steve Austin, Triple H, and Mankind tear each other apart for the World Wrestling Federation World Heavyweight Championship. Ventura's schedule didn't lighten when he penned his best-seller autobiography, *I Ain't Got Time to Bleed.* From 1999 to 2002 Ventura was one of the most talked-about public figures in the country.

On March 13, 2004, this storied career came full circle when Ventura was inducted in the WWE Hall of Fame. His shameful acts as a World Wrestling Federation Superstar in the ring, his broadcasts with Vince McMahon, and his legendary war of words with Gorilla Monsoon are fondly remembered to this day. His remarkable charisma, ever-colorful appearance, and eclectic eloquence make Jesse "The Body" Ventura one of the greatest figures in World Wrestling Federation history.

The Hart Foundation (Bret "Hit Man" Hart & Jim "The Anvil" Neidhart)

FROM: **Calvary, Canada & Tampa, FL**

COMBINED WEIGHT: **515 lbs.**

FINISHING MOVE: **The Hart Attack**

WHEN THE GREATEST TAG TEAMS OF ALL TIME ARE MENTIONED, THE HART FOUNDATION IS AT THE TOP OF THE LIST. BROUGHT TOGETHER BY "Mouth of the South" Jimmy Hart, the Hit Man and the Anvil were a duo like no other. Bret Hart was known as the "Excellence of Execution," the ultimate ring technician. Jim Neidhart was one of the most powerful men in all of wrestling, his strength matched only by his tenacity. With their manager Jimmy Hart at ringside, anything was possible.

When the Hart Foundation invaded the World Wrestling Federation tag team scene in 1985, few realized the impact these Superstars would have. The world got a glimpse of what to expect when Bret and Jim were the last participants, along with Andre the Giant, in the World Wrestling Federation/NFL battle royal at *WrestleMania 2*. Their first major feud was with a team that would be their greatest opponents, the British Bulldogs. As both teams climbed up the World Wrestling Federation tag team ladder, their ring wars became tantamount to global conflicts. The Harts beat the best and in turn became the best. Before their title shot at the Bulldogs, the Foundation took matters into their own hands when they attacked Dynamite Kid and left him unconscious on the arena floor. Davey Boy Smith had to defend the titles on his own.

The Hart Foundation went on to hold the World Wrestling Federation Tag Team Championship for close to ten months, setting a new standard of tag team excellence. They were stalked by the new duo of Tito Santana & Rick Martel—Strike Force. The Hart Foundation's championship reign officially ended when the Anvil submitted to Rick Martel's Boston Crab. At *WrestleMania IV,* the Foundation participated in another battle royal. While the Anvil saw an early exit, Hit Man was once again one of the final remaining Superstars. When he collaborated with Bad News Brown to eliminate the Junkyard Dog, it appeared that Hart and Brown had made an agreement to split the winnings, but after a joint celebration in the middle of the ring, Brown gave Hit Man a ghetto blaster. The shot sent Hart over the top rope and out on the Trump Plaza floor. Hit Man was out of the battle royal. When he regrouped, Hart entered the ring and destroyed the trophy. This began Bret's first feud as a singles wrestler. Soon after rejoining his partner, Hit Man & Anvil had a falling out with their manager Jimmy. The team learned that the "Mouth of the South" had given a percentage of their earnings to his new tag team, the Fabulous Rougeaus. The Hart Foundation fired their manager.

At *SummerSlam '88* they faced Demolition for the World Wrestling Federation World Tag Team Championship. Using a legal loophole, Jimmy Hart appeared at ringside, but in the corner of the champions. Just when it seemed the Harts were on their way to a second title reign, Ax clobbered Bret with the Mouth's megaphone. Over the next two years the the Hart Foundation split time between wrestling in tag team and singles matches. At *SummerSlam '89* they had a nontitle match against then newly crowned champions the Brain Busters, losing for the second year in a row due to outside interference. The Hart Foundation captured their second World Wrestling Federation Tag Team Championship at *SummerSlam '90* when they defeated Demolition. A nearly seven-month title reign ended when they lost the titles at *WrestleMania VII* to their former manager's new team, the Nasty Boys. Once again, the Mouth of the South's extracurricular activities played a major factor in the outcome of the match.

Shortly after *WrestleMania,* the Hart Foundation went their separate ways. They feuded for a brief time when the Anvil aligned himself with Bret's brother Owen. Throughout the early and mid-1990s the Hit Man went on to become a singles mega star. Jim "The Anvil" Neidhart continued to be regarded as one of the most dangerous men in all of wrestling. In 1997, Bret re-formed the Hart Foundation and made it one of the most hated collections of Superstars in pro wrestling. Of course, his cornerstone was the Anvil. The group also included Owen Hart, British Bulldog, and Brian Pillman. The new Hart Foundation took aim at Superstars like Stone Cold Steve Austin, Undertaker, and Legion of Doom.

The Hart Foundation's legacy is a long and famed one. Few duos have enjoyed championship reigns in two different decades and earned victories over so many various types of opponents. The Foundation's continuity, ring psychology, and peak performance helped brand the 1980s as the golden era of tag team wrestling.

Honky Tonk Man

FROM: **Memphis, TN**

HEIGHT: **6'1"**

WEIGHT: **235 lbs.**

FINISHING MOVE: **The Shake, Rattle & Roll**

BEFORE HE BECAME THE "GREATEST INTERCONTINENTAL CHAMPION OF ALL TIME," THIS WORLD WRESTLING FEDERATION SUPERSTAR CUT HIS teeth in Memphis, Tennessee, and the southeastern United States during the late 1970s. As one half of the Blonde Bombers, he captured many regional tag team championships right through the early 1980s before he headed north to Stu Hart's Stampede Wrestling.

After his 1987 World Wrestling Federation debut, the company created "A Vote of Confidence" write-in program for fans to express their opinion on what direction Honky should take his career. Honky Tonk did not wait for the fan response, appearing on television with "Mouth of the South" Jimmy Hart as his manager. The Mouth was dubbed "The Colonel," and Honky Tonk was officially a rule-breaker. He came to the ring singing his theme song, "I'm a Honky Tonk Man" in sequinned body suits and played his trusty acoustic guitar to the disgust of fans all over the globe. During an episode of *The Snake Pit,* host Jake Roberts questioned Honky Tonk's singing ability. Honky Tonk responded with a song of his own in the form of a guitar smashed over the Snake's head. This knocked Roberts unconscious and prompted Honky and the Colonel to begin a spirited campaign called "Ban the DDT." They picketed at arenas all over the country and complained to World Wrestling Federation President Jack Tunney, asking him to outlaw the move.

The stage was set for *WrestleMania III.* From the opening bell, this match was the classic cat-and-mouse game, and both Superstars fought for the psychological edge. In the end, Honky Tonk got the pinfall in his

WrestleMania debut after he used the ropes for leverage, unbeknownst to the referee. This victory was the first of many big wins for the newcomer. Soon everyone saw that the description "Cool, Cocky and Bad" was more than just a line from his entrance theme. Honky Tonk was now a contender for Ricky Steamboat's Intercontinental title. In an upset, Honky Tonk shook, rattled, and rolled his way past the Dragon on July 2, 1987, to win the World Wrestling Federation Intercontinental Championship.

Honky quickly proved he was not an overnight sensation, defending the title an unbelievable fourteen months. The only thing he had more of than gold records were broken guitars and victories. One of his most intense battles was with former Intercontinental Champion Randy Savage. Honky called himself the greatest Intercontinental Champion *ever,* and belittled all who preceded him. Savage took this as a slap in the face, and during the October 2, 1987, *Saturday Night's Main Event* the two faced off. After interference from the Hart Foundation, Honky Tonk threw Miss Elizabeth down, played his favorite tune for the beaten "Macho Man," and broke a guitar over his head. This led to Elizabeth going to the back to get Hulk Hogan, and Honky Tonk and his associates fled the ring.

At *SummerSlam '88,* Brutus Beefcake was unable to wrestle due to injury. Honky Tonk made an open challenge to Superstars in either locker room, and Ultimate Warrior ran to the ring and ended Honky Tonk Man's reign. In late 1991, Honky tagged with Greg Valentine and formed the Rhythm & Blues with manager Jimmy Hart. The team saw respectable success, but never captured the World Wrestling Federation World Tag Team Championship and split shortly thereafter.

After leaving the company Honky Tonk Man engaged in a feud across the independent circuit with "Ravishing" Rick Rude to decide who was the greatest Intercontinental Champion of all time. In 1994 Honky Tonk briefly appeared in World Championship Wrestling and challenged Johnny B. Badd for the Television title. In 1997 Honky returned to World Wrestling Federation in a managerial capacity, searching for a protégé to continue the tradition of the Shake, Rattle & Roll. His search was unsuccessful, and soon after, he parted ways with World Wrestling Federation. At *Royal Rumble 2001* Honky Tonk crossed paths with Kane.

Often imitated, the Honky Tonk Man will never be duplicated. His unprecedented fourteen-month Intercontinental Championship reign made history. In 2002, wwe.com hosted a poll for fans to cast their votes for the greatest Intercontinental Champion of all time. Of all the legendary names, the hands-down winner was the Honky Tonk Man.

Wendi Richter

FROM: **Dallas, TX**

HEIGHT: **5'8"**

WEIGHT: **140 lbs.**

FINISHING MOVE: **The swinging arm wrench facebuster**

THIS TWO-TIME WORLD WRESTLING FEDERATION WOMEN'S CHAMPION MADE HER IN-RING DEBUT IN 1979. A GRADUATE OF THE LILLIAN ELLISON School of Professional Wrestling, Wendi Richter learned early that being a top women's wrestler is no stroll down the catwalk. She showed great promise early on, wrestling in the southern United States and Japan, and had a successful tag team with the legendary Joyce Grable. Wendi was sexy, charismatic, and tough, all in one explosive package, and with her size and strength, she was able to deliver powerful moves to her opponents like no female competitor before.

On July 23, 1984, Wendi used all her tools to end the near-three-decade-long title reign of the Fabulous Moolah, setting the women's wrestling scene on fire. Wendi would go on to hold the title for close to seven months before losing it under questionable circumstances at "The War to Settle the Score" to Moolah protégée Leilani Kai. However, at *WrestleMania* Richter returned, and this time she and her Rock-N-Wrestling Connection manager Cyndi Lauper were ready for anything. In a seesaw battle, Leilani connected with a high cross-body, but the ring-savvy Richter let the champion's weight and momentum work against her, rolling her up for the pin and winning her second World Wrestling Federation Women's Championship. Unfortunately, on November 25, 1985, Wendi would lose the title in a shocking turn of events in the same building where she had regained the title, Madison Square Garden. During a title defense against an unknown opponent named the Masked Spider Lady, Richter would be put in a small package and pinned for the three-count. However, after the match was over and the title was awarded to the victor, the mysterious Spider Lady removed her mask to reveal she was none other than Richter's archnemesis, the Fabulous Moolah. Some speculate that because Lauper was not present at ringside, Richter was susceptible to foul play. Unfortunately fans would never know, because this match would be Wendi's last in World Wrestling Federation.

Shortly after her departure, Wendi moved on to the American Wrestling Association, and in December of 1987 she defeated Madusa Miceli for their version of the Women's title. Wendi was also a two-time WWC Women's Champion in Puerto Rico. Some would argue that her greatest heights were reached as part of the famed Rock-N-Wrestling Connection. While her time was brief, Wendi Richter was a pioneer for women's wrestling, paving the way for the WWE Divas of today.

Bob Backlund

FROM: **Princeton, MN**
HEIGHT: **6'1"**
WEIGHT: **241 lbs.**
FINISHING MOVE: **The crossface chicken wing**

REVERED AS ONE OF THE GREATEST TECHNICAL WRESTLERS OF ALL TIME, BOB BACKLUND ACHIEVED CHAMPIONSHIP STATUS IN 1971 WITHIN THE amateur ranks as a NCAA Division II Champion at North Dakota State University. Two years later he debuted in the American Wrestling Association and became a hit with audiences thanks to his fan-friendly demeanor and razor-sharp ring skills. Backlund spent the mid-1970s touring the Georgia, Florida, and midwestern territories of the National Wrestling Alliance. While in the NWA, Backlund captured the Georgia Tag Team Championship with the legendary Gerry Brisco, earned the Florida Tag Team titles with Steve Keirn, and in 1976 won the Missouri Heavyweight title. After he had accomplished all he could in the NWA, Backlund's desire to compete against wrestling's elite led him to World Wrestling Federation.

In 1978 Bob Backlund debuted in World Wrestling Federation and was led to the ring by Arnold Skaaland. On February 20, Backlund used his superior mat skills to end the ten-month World Wrestling Federation World Championship reign of Superstar Billy Graham in Madison Square Garden. Ironically for wrestling's rule-breaking "Tower of Power," this was one instance where he did not benefit from something taking place in the ring outside the referee's field of vision. Backlund had Graham pinned, and when Graham put his foot on the ropes, the referee did not see it, and his hand hit the mat for the three-count. In that instant, Bob Backlund captured his first World Wrestling Federation Heavyweight Championship.

Now in possession of wrestling's most prestigious championship, Backlund was determined to travel the world and show he was indeed the best of the best. Backlund faced off against AWA Champion Nick Bockwinkel and NWA Champion Harley Race in heated Title vs. Title bouts. In 1980, Backlund captured the World Wrestling Federation World Tag Team Championship with Pedro Morales, defeating the Wild Samoans at Shea Stadium. Backlund beat Pat Patterson, Jesse "The Body" Ventura, the Magnificent Muraco, Jimmy Snuka, Greg Valentine, and "Big" John Studd. On July 4, 1982, a historic meeting of two distinguished ring generals took place. Backlund brought his World Wrestling Federation World Heavyweight Championship to Atlanta's Omni and clashed with NWA World Heavyweight Champion Ric Flair.

As 1983 progressed, the wear and tear of a five-year championship reign began to take its toll on World Wrestling Federation's ambassador. In his December 26 title defense against world-renowned mat technician the Iron Sheik, Backlund was nursing a severely injured back. The Sheik, a master of the suplex, focused his offense on the champion's injured area. He had Backlund locked in to the Camel Clutch. Though he refused to submit, in one of wrestling's most controversial moments, Backlund's manager threw in his white towel, ending Bob Backlund's tenure as World Wrestling Federation World Heavyweight Champion. The fact that Backlund was never defeated via pinfall or submission left many feeling that the title was still his. This caused a rift between Backlund and his manager, and the two did not speak for many years. Backlund disappeared from the company in mid-1984, as the era of sports entertainment emerged.

To the joy of wrestling fans everywhere, Backlund returned to World Wrestling Federation in 1992. He was the number-two contestant in *Royal Rumble 1993,* lasting over an hour. Later that year Backlund made his *WrestleMania* debut and tangled with Razor Ramon. Backlund also fought Doink the Clown, Rick Martel, and Shawn Michaels, collecting victories over all of them. After losing a special challenge match to then World Wrestling Federation Heavyweight Champion Bret Hart, Backlund lost it, slapping Hart in the face and locking him in his crossface chicken wing while laughing uncontrollably. The World Wrestling Federation Champion that generations had loved vanished. Bob Backlund now demanded he be referred to as "Mr. Backlund" and insisted that the World Wrestling Federation Championship was still his, since the Iron Sheik had never truly beaten him, and that the golden days of wrestling were gone.

Bob Backlund was a maniac on the loose. At *Survivor Series 1994,* Backlund and Bret Hart squared off in an I Quit match for the World Wrestling Federation World Heavyweight Championship. Backlund had Owen Hart in his corner, and Bret had his brother-in-law, British Bulldog, in his. From the opening bell this was a classic struggle, but it also saw its share of extracurricular interference. When Bulldog chased Owen around the ring, he knocked himself out on the steel steps. Then Backlund cinched Bret in the chicken wing. With Bulldog down, Owen tricked his mother, Helen—who was sitting at ringside—into throwing in the towel. Despite the efforts of the legendary Stu Hart, Helen took the towel and threw it in the ring. This gave Backlund his first World Wrestling Federation Championship in eleven years. Though he lost the championship three days later to Diesel, Backlund's feud with Bret Hart continued in *WrestleMania XI* in an I Quit rematch. That same year Backlund announced that he would run for president of the United States. "Psycho Bob," as some called him, took a break from the ring, returning briefly in 1996 to co-manage the Sultan with former archenemy the Iron Sheik. Mr. Backlund popped up again in 2000 as a participant in the *Royal Rumble,* and for a brief period was a mentor to Olympic gold medalist Kurt Angle. The year of the new millennium also saw Mr. Backlund run for a seat in the Connecticut Congress as a Republican.

Though he's not been seen in World Wrestling Entertainment in some time, you never know when Backlund will appear at a WWE event, berating fans and telling them to read their dictionaries. His first title reign as World Wrestling Federation World Heavyweight Champion was the second longest in WWE history. With his superior wrestling ability and numerous classic matches, many believe that Bob Backlund was the last of the true "wrestling" champions.

"Ravishing" Rick Rude

FROM: **Robbinsdale, MN**

HEIGHT: **6'3"**

WEIGHT: **251 lbs.**

FINISHING MOVE: **The Rude Awakening**

RUDE WORKED IN HIS HOME STATE OF MINNESOTA AS A BAR BOUNCER ON THE SAME STAFF AS THE ROAD WARRIORS, HAWK AND ANIMAL. HE also was a national arm-wrestling champion before his 1983 ring debut in local promotions across Minnesota, Canada, and Georgia. Moving to Memphis, he then joined Jimmy Hart's "First Family" stable, forming a successful tag team with future fellow Heenan Family member King Kong Bundy and briefly feuding with Jerry Lawler. In 1985 Rick Rude moved to World Class Championship Wrestling and battled the legendary Von Erichs. He was the first WCCW Heavyweight Champion after the organization seceded from the National Wrestling Alliance. After he lost the title in July 1986, Rude moved to the NWA and, with his first manager, Paul Jones, feuded with "Chief" Wahoo McDaniel. He also captured the Tag Team Championship with Ragin' Bull Manny Fernandez.

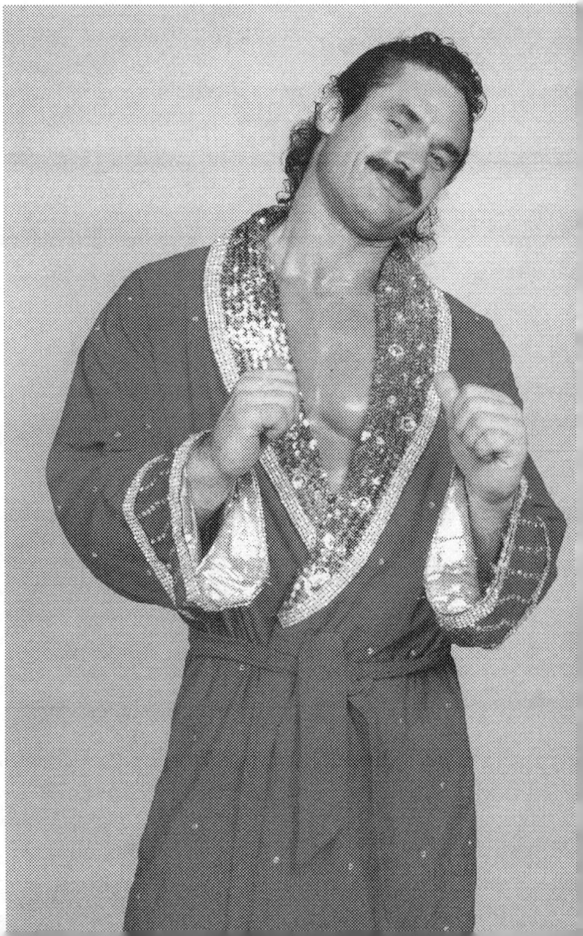

In July 1987 "Ravishing" Rick Rude made his World Wrestling Federation debut, and with manager Bobby Heenan started a long-term hate affair with fans all over the United States. His first feud was with former Heenan Family member Paul Orndorff. Before his matches, Rude grabbed the microphone and belittled audiences, calling them fat, out-of-shape sweathogs. After his matches, Heenan and Rude selected a woman from the crowd to enter the ring and receive a kiss from "The Ravishing One," which he called "The Rude Awakening." After one match he propositioned a beautiful woman in the front row. As his overtures became more aggressive, the woman identified herself as Cheryl Roberts, wife of Jake Roberts. To taunt Roberts, Rude wrestled in tights that had an imprint of Cheryl's face on them. Rude often gyrated over his fallen opponents, thus mocking Jake's marriage. The two fought to a fifteen-minute draw in the first round of the World Wrestling Federation World Heavyweight Tournament at *WrestleMania IV.*

Rude was not just all physique and attitude. He was a versatile, well-trained ring technician who knew how to gain that ever-crucial psychological edge against opponents. Rude also won the prestigious Jesse "The Body" award at the 1987 Slammy Awards. As he moved up the ranks, Rude started a feud with Ultimate Warrior at *Royal Rumble 1988* when he attacked Warrior from behind during their posedown. In the Intercontinental Championship match at *WrestleMania V,* Rude defeated Warrior with a little help from "The Brain," to the shock of the capacity Trump Plaza crowd. The Ravishing One feuded with Warrior for the entire year, and at *SummerSlam '89* Warrior regained the Intercontinental Championship. Far from being over, Rude's battles with the Warrior carried into the new decade. The two met inside a fifteen-foot-high steel cage in the main event of *SummerSlam '90* for the World Wrestling Federation World Heavyweight Championship, but in the fall of 1990 Rude left the company.

Rude returned to World Championship Wrestling at *Halloween Havoc 1991* and was revealed as the masked Halloween Phantom. He soon became the cornerstone of Paul E. Dangerously's "Dangerous Alliance" with fellow members Arn Anderson, Larry Zbyszko, Bobby Eaton, and Steve Austin. Rude feuded with Ricky Steamboat over the United States Heavyweight Championship, which was settled in 1993 in an Iron Man Challenge at the *Beach Blast* Pay-Per-View. Rude's championship battles continued into the year as he defeated Ric Flair for the WCW World Heavyweight Championship on September 19 at *Fall Brawl.* When WCW withdrew from the National Wrestling Alliance, the title was renamed the WCW International Title. Rude held the championship until March 16, 1994, when he lost to Japanese star Hiroshi Hase in Tokyo. However, Rude regained it from Hase eight days later in Kyoko, Japan, and held it until April 17, when he was defeated by Sting. The Ravishing One pinned Sting on May 1 but was later stripped of the title when it was discovered that he'd used the title belt as a weapon during the bout. In a rematch with Sting in Japan, Rude suffered a severe back injury and was forced to retire from active competition.

After heavy conjecture that he had disappeared from wrestling forever, Rude arrived in Extreme Championship Wrestling in 1996. During the ECW/World Wrestling Federation intercompany feud, Rude aided Jerry Lawler in defeating ECW icons Tommy Dreamer and the Sandman. In September 1997, Rude reappeared in World Wrestling Federation as the insurance policy for the mayhem-causing group D-Generation X.

In November of that year Rude became an infamous figure in the Monday-night TV wars between World Wrestling Federation and WCW when he appeared on both *Raw* and *Monday Nitro* on the same night. As part of World Championship Wrestling, Rude debuted as a member of the nWo and corner man for close friend Curt Hennig. Rude remained aligned with Hennig until he departed from WCW in late 1998.

On April 20, 1999, Rick Rude passed away of an apparent heart attack in his home in Alpharetta, Georgia, at the age of forty-one. "Ravishing" Rick Rude is regarded as one of the greatest villains in wrestling history, who possessed one of the most impressive physiques seen in any professional sport.

Demolition (Ax & Smash)

FROM: **parts unknown**

COMBINED WEIGHT: **594 lbs.**

FINISHING MOVE: **The Decapitation Elbow**

THESE WALKING DISASTERS ARRIVED IN WORLD WRESTLING FEDERATION IN 1987. IN THE RING, AX AND SMASH HAD A SIMPLE, SINGULAR OBJECTIVE—destroy! They obliterated the competition and, within their first year, were number-one contenders for the World Wrestling Federation World Tag Team Championship. At *WrestleMania IV,* they beat Strike Force for their first of three World Wrestling Federation World Tag Team titles. With tag team wrestling's most prestigious

championship in their possession, along with their manager the devious Mr. Fuji, the Demos were unstoppable. Ax and Smash held the belts for an astonishing sixteen months, breaking the previous record of one year and one week held by the Valiant Brothers. Backing down from no one, Demolition defeated teams like the Hart Foundation, the British Bulldogs, and the Powers of Pain. After a split with Mr. Fuji at *Survivor Series 1988,* Demolition began hearing cheers from fans around the world as they continued to defend the titles against all challengers. Both members of Demolition were so focused on destroying opponents that at *Royal Rumble 1989* they went toe-to-toe in the middle of the ring after drawing the first two entry numbers. Their show was soon ended when the horn sounded and the third entrant was Andre the Giant.

On the July 18, 1989, episode of *Saturday Night's Main Event* they fought in a Two-Out-of-Three Falls classic with Arn Anderson & Tully Blanchard, the Brain Busters. Ax and Smash lost the titles that evening, but they displayed their perseverance and regained the championship nearly three months later. As they rampaged through World Wrestling Federation's top teams, two months into their second title reign they crossed paths with the team of Andre the Giant & Haku, aptly named the Colossal Connection. This was the first time Demolition did not have a size and power advantage over their opponents. In the end, Ax & Smash could not overcome an elbow drop from Andre, and they lost the titles on December 13, 1989.

As a new decade dawned, Demolition focused anew on taking back what they felt was theirs. At *WrestleMania VI,* when Haku miscued and nailed his partner with a thrust kick, Ax and Smash hit him with their finishing move for the win. After winning the World Wrestling Federation World Tag Team Championship, Demolition reverted to their rule-breaking ways and added a third member to the team—the six-seven, 315-pound Crush. This triad of destruction defended the titles using any two of the members, swapped one another in and out of the ring so the fresher man was in at all times. At *SummerSlam '90* their new title retention method backfired when they lost to former champions the Hart Foundation. Later that year Demolition feuded with World Wrestling Federation newcomers the Legion of Doom to see which team was professional wrestling's toughest. In the definitive war of pain, all three members of Demolition feuded with the Legion of Doom and Ultimate Warrior in six-man tag action. A few months later Demolition disappeared from the company, and they have not been heard from since.

With their intimidating appearance, body-breaking double-team moves, cunning tag team tactics, and obsession with creating carnage, Demolition will go down in World Wrestling Federation history as one of the greatest tag teams of all time.

Koko B. Ware

FROM: **Union City, TN**

HEIGHT: **5'9"**

WEIGHT: **228 lbs.**

FINISHING MOVE: **The Ghostbuster**

THIS FAN FAVORITE BEGAN HIS CAREER IN 1978 AS A RULE-BREAKER, GOING BY NAMES LIKE "SWEET BROWN SUGAR" AND "STAGGER LEE." He saw regional success as both a singles and tag team competitor, being one half of the team called the Pretty Young Things. Koko spent the late 1970s and early 1980s traveling through the southeastern territories of the NWA. Then the bright lights and packed arenas of World Wrestling Federation came calling.

In 1986 "The Birdman" Koko B. Ware burst onto the scene, energizing fans with his high-flying wrestling style and captivating charisma. Accompanied to the ring by his pet macaw Frankie, Koko became an instant sensation with fans around the world. His flying dropkick knocked opponents' teeth out, and his finishing move, the Ghostbuster, was a skull-crusher. In November of 1986 he made his *Saturday Night's Main Event* debut, defeating Nikolai Volkoff and facing Butch Reed at *WrestleMania III*. Koko quickly showed that he could go toe-to-toe with any Superstar, regardless of size or strength.

As the 1980s rolled into the '90s, Koko battled the likes of Greg Valentine, Rick Rude, Mr. Perfect, Big Boss Man, Rick Martel, and Sgt. Slaughter. In 1993 Koko faced Yokozuna in the opening match of the first *Raw*.

He also briefly formed a tag team known as High Energy with Owen Hart, and the two were contenders for the World Wrestling Federation World Tag Team Championship. When the two parted, Koko briefly feuded with Doink the Clown. Shortly after, the Birdman disappeared from World Wrestling Federation programming. For the remainder of the decade, Koko traveled the world, bringing audiences to their feet to do his signature Bird Dance and watch him take to the air. In one of 2005's biggest surprises, the Birdman returned to World Wrestling Federation television on the October 3 Homecoming as part of the Legends Ceremony. Three weeks later he stepped into the ring in a special challenge match on *Heat* against Rob Conway.

It has been over thirteen years since his last full-time run with WWE, but the Birdman is still active on the U.S. independent circuit, flapping his arms and throwing his trademark dropkicks. Koko B. Ware will be fondly remembered as an exciting high flyer, adored by fans and respected by opponents.

Killer Bees (B. Brian Blair & Jim Brunzell)

FROM: **Gary, IN & White Bear Lake, MN**

COMBINED WEIGHT: **465 lbs.**

FINISHING MOVE: **The Lethal Dropkick**

ONE WAS A TECHNICAL WRESTLER SCHOOLED BY FAMED JAPANESE TRAINER HIRO MATSUDA; THE OTHER A HIGH FLYER AND TAG TEAM VETERAN TRAINED by Verne Gagne. B. Brian Blair held many regional titles within the territories of the National Wrestling Alliance as well as in Japan. Jim Brunzell was a two-time AWA World Tag Team Champion and a well-traveled ring veteran who may have possessed the greatest dropkick in the history of professional wrestling.

In June 1985, these two combined their strength and debuted in World Wrestling Federation as the Killer Bees. Displaying great speed, teamwork, and endurance, B. Brian Blair and "Jumping" Jim Brunzell became instant contenders for the World Wrestling Federation World Tag Team Championship. During this time the World Wrestling Federation Tag Team division was approaching its pinnacle. Each win could take a team one step closer to a title shot, and one loss could wipe them from the championship picture. Within their first year, the Bees battled the Moondogs and Nikolai Volkoff & the Iron Sheik, and exchanged victories with the Hart Foundation. In 1986 the Bees continued their feud with the Harts and bested them on the November 15

episode of *Saturday Night's Main Event.* Blair and Brunzell tackled new opponents like the Dream Team, King Kong Bundy & "Big" John Studd, the American Express, and the Magnificent Muraco & "Cowboy" Bob Orton. On August 28, 1986, they scored another big win at *The Big Event* against the Funks. Blair & Brunzell even wrestled then champions the British Bulldogs to a time-limit draw.

The Bees introduced their version of masked confusion. During their matches they put on matching masks that allowed them to switch places in the ring without making tags. World Wrestling Federation referees, their opponents, and fans couldn't tell who was who. Blair & Brunzell continued to challenge for the tag titles. In February 1987 they defeated then champions the Hart Foundation in a nontitle match. Unfortunately for the Bees, they were unable to beat the Hart Foundation when the championship was on the line. At *WrestleMania III,* the Bees lost to old foes Nikolai Volkoff &

Iron Sheik by disqualification when "Hacksaw" Jim Duggan unexpectedly charged into the ring and whaled Sheik in the back with his two-by-four.

A slew of new tandems emerged in 1987 onto the already competitive tag team scene: Demolition, Strike Force, the Fabulous Rougeau Brothers, the Islanders, the Young Stallions, the New Dream Team, the Bolsheviks, and Los Conquistadors. The Bees returned to their winning ways at the first *Survivor Series.* Along with teammates the Young Stallions, Blair & Brunzell were the sole survivors of their Tag Team Elimination match. The fan favorites also competed in their share of six-man tags with partners like Koko B. Ware, Hillbilly Jim, Junkyard Dog, Tito Santana, and George "The Animal" Steele. In 1988, the team split when Blair abruptly left World Wrestling Federation. Brunzell briefly remained as a singles competitor, but then also left. The Killer Bees were never seen again on World Wrestling Entertainment programming.

In 1991 the Bees briefly reunited on the independent scene, winning the World Tag Team titles in the short-lived UWF promotion before a permanent split. Brunzell made an appearance at WCW's *Slamboree '93* Pay-Per-View in a Six-Man Tag match with Dick Murdoch, Wahoo McDaniel, Jimmy Snuka, Don Muraco, and Blackjack Mulligan. He continued to wrestle locally through the late 1990s. Blair went on to become an expert franchiser and operated Gold's Gym Fitness Centers across Tampa, Florida.

Though their WWE career ended unexpectedly, their blinding speed, fluid teamwork, and thrilling matches made the Killer Bees fan favorites. When Wrestling historians talk about the best tag teams of the 1980s, the Killer Bees are on the list.

Bad News Brown

FROM: **Harlem, NY**
HEIGHT: **6'2"**
WEIGHT: **255 lbs.**
FINISHING MOVE: **The ghetto blaster**

BROWN WAS A NAME BEFORE HE ENTERED THE WORLD OF PROFESSIONAL WRESTLING. BAD NEWS BROWN COMPETED AT THE 1976 MONTREAL Olympics and won the bronze medal in judo. He also won two gold medals at the Pan-Am Games. In 1977 Bad News began the transition from judo to pro wrestling and was trained by Japanese great Antonio Inoki. He soon made his New Japan Pro Wrestling debut under the name "Buffalo Allen Coage." For the next few years

Bad News traveled the world, perfecting his hard-hitting wrestling style. He even made a stop in World Wrestling Federation in 1978.

In 1982 Bad News arrived in Stu Hart's Stampede Wrestling and feuded with up-and-comers Bret Hart, Dynamite Kid, and Davey Boy Smith. Brown also beat up the young son of local legend Archie "Stomper" Gouldie during a Stampede television broadcast, to the disgust of fans all over Canada. He captured the Stampede North American title on many occasions and became the territory's most hated villain while vying for Stampede gold with a young Owen Hart. For the next four years Bad News split time between Japan, Australia, and Calgary. In 1986 News took two years off from active competition and soon returned to the ring meaner than ever.

In 1988 Bad News debuted with World Wrestling Federation and made an immediate impact. His "lone wolf" mentality and fierce grappling style did not win him any admirers or allies. At *WrestleMania IV* he took part in the battle royal, and when he and Bret Hart eliminated the Junkyard Dog, the two Superstars raised their arms in victory and it appeared that they had an agreement to split the battle royal prize. In typical Bad News fashion, after he raised Hart's arm, Bad News tagged him with his ghetto blaster kick. This sent Hart over the top rope and onto the Trump Plaza floor. At that moment the world witnessed Bad News Brown's "by any means necessary" attitude. This ideology was reinforced during his *Survivor Series 1988* debut, when Brown walked out on his teammates in the middle of their match. That year News became entangled with the likes of Bret Hart, Junkyard Dog, and Ken Patera. He also battled Randy Savage for his World Wrestling Federation World Heavyweight Championship. In 1989, Brown battled Hulk Hogan on an edition of *Saturday Night's Main Event* and fought "Hacksaw" Jim Duggan to a no contest at *WrestleMania V.*

Bad News repeated his *Survivor Series* performance and again left his teammates to fend for themselves.

After Bad News was eliminated from *Royal Rumble 1990* by Roddy Piper, the two feuded and met at *WrestleMania VI*. The bout was such a crazed street fight that it ended in a no contest, and both men fought one another to the back of the SkyDome. At *SummerSlam '90* he locked up with Jake Roberts and was defeated after Roberts received help from the Big Boss Man. After he physically attacked World Wrestling Federation President Jack Tunney on *The Brother Love Show*, Bad News disappeared from World Wrestling Federation television.

Bad News spent the 1990s competing in Japan and independent events throughout the world. In 1999 he was forced to retire due to a recurring knee injury. Despite hanging up his boots, he still travels back to Japan and appears at regional Canadian shows in Calgary, Winnipeg, and Vancouver. In 2005, he opened his own wrestling school in his home of Calgary. Bad News Brown is regarded as one of the most malicious and hard-hitting Superstars.

Hillbilly Jim

FROM: **Mudlick, KY**
HEIGHT: **6'7"**
WEIGHT: **320 lbs.**
FINISHING MOVE: **Bear hug**

THIS COUNTRY BOY MADE ONE OF THE MOST IMPROMPTU DEBUTS IN WORLD WRESTLING FEDERATION HISTORY. DURING AN EPISODE OF *Piper's Pit*, "Rowdy" Roddy called to a fan in the crowd and offered to train him for a career in professional wrestling. The offer was declined, as the fan told Piper he wanted to be trained by Hulk Hogan. The "Hot Rod" almost went through the arena roof in a fury. Training sessions soon aired with Hogan and his protégé, Hillbilly Jim. In 1985 he made his World Wrestling Federation debut, wearing a pair of wrestling boots given to him by Hogan. Hillbilly's jovial demeanor, unmistakable overalls, and bushy beard made him an instant hit with fans around the world. Audiences were taken aback by his size, strength, and speed. During his matches Hillbilly performed cartwheels in the ring, often frustrating opponents. World Wrestling Federation Superstars quickly learned that his entrance theme, "Don't Go Messin' with a Country Boy," was more

than a catchy southern knee-slapper. Early in his World Wrestling Federation tenure, Hillbilly stood across the ring from opponents like "Rowdy" Roddy Piper, Big John Studd, and King Kong Bundy.

His most heated feud was with the Magnificent Muraco and Mr. Fuji. This battle was settled in a Tuxedo match at Madison Square Garden, in which the man who got his tuxedo ripped off lost the contest. Hillbilly also brought in family members Uncle Elmer and Cousin Luke, and the three often battled World Wrestling Federation villains in six-man tag team action. He made his *WrestleMania* debut as part of a World Wrestling Federation/NFL battle royal at *WrestleMania 2*. His *WrestleMania III* appearance was even more unusual but had a very scary ending. During his six-man tag team match with partners Little Beaver & the Haiti Kid, the monstrous King Kong Bundy suddenly squashed Little Beaver, causing him to be carried away from the ring. At the second *Survivor Series,* Hillbilly helped his mentor, Hulk Hogan, as part of the Mega-Powers team—along with Randy Savage, Koko B. Ware, and Hercules—battling "Million Dollar Man" Ted DiBiase, King Haku, the Red Rooster, and the Twin Towers.

In the early 1990s, Hillbilly split time between the squared circle and the television studio. He had the honor of working alongside announcing greats like Gorilla Monsoon, Bobby "The Brain" Heenan, and "Mean" Gene Okerlund. In 1995 he made his *Raw* debut as manager of the Godwinns, and to the delight of fans, he returned to *WrestleMania* as part of the Gimmick battle royal at *WrestleMania X-Seven*. Hillbilly also appeared on the October 3, 2005, World Wrestling Entertainment Homecoming as part of the Legends Ceremony.

Though his days of applying bear hugs and headlocks are behind him, Hillbilly Jim can be seen traveling the country as part of the annual *Road to WrestleMania* tour. Fans of country music can also hear his show *Moonshine Matinee* on satellite radio. Hillbilly Jim will always be remembered as one of the most popular figures in the WWE.

Capt. Lou Albano

FROM: **Carmel, NY**
HEIGHT: **5'10"**
WEIGHT: **350 lbs.**

WHEN WRESTLING FANS HEAR THE PHRASE "OFTEN IMITATED, NEVER DUPLICATED," ONLY ONE MAN COMES TO MIND: THE "GUIDING LIGHT OF Professional Wrestling," Capt. Lou Albano. Never known for his subtlety, the captain was unmistakable, with his bushy beard, Hawaiian shirts, and rubber bands pierced to his face.

Albano first received national attention with partner Tony Altimore in the late 1950s as the tag team the Sicilians. With their Italian gangster image, the team was one of the most hated and controversial in all of wrestling. Fans' disdain for the two *paisons* grew on July 10, 1967, when they defeated the team of Spiros Arion & Arnold Skaaland for the World Wrestling Federation U.S. Tag Team Championship. After their title reign ended, the two split and Albano divided his time between competition and managing.

Albano had an uncontrollable affinity for interfering in matches, whether as a tag partner standing on the apron or as a manager circling the ring. In the early 1970s Albano started managing full-time. He guided his first tag team, the Mongols, to World Wrestling Federation Tag Team gold on June 15, 1970. Driven by greed and delusions of wrestling dominance, Albano set his sights on dethroning World Wrestling Federation World Champion Bruno Sammartino. On January 18, 1971, Albano's dream came true when Ivan Koloff ended Sammartino's unparalleled seven-year title reign. Both Superstars were masters of the bear hug, but Koloff used a knee drop off the top rope to defeat the champion in front of a sold-out Madison Square Garden crowd. Koloff was the only World Champion Albano managed.

Over the next three decades, the captain guided an unmatched sixteen tag teams to the coveted World Wrestling Federation World Tag Team Championship. Famous duos included the Executioners, the Valiant Brothers, the Yukon Lumberjacks, the Moondogs, Mr. Fuji & Mr. Saito, the Wild Samoans, the US Express, and the British Bulldogs. He also led Pat Patterson, the Magnificent Muraco, and Greg Valentine to the Intercontinental Championship, and managed Andre the Giant, Jimmy "Superfly" Snuka, George Steele, the Fabulous Moolah, Baron Mikel Scicluna, the Spoiler, Professor Toru Tanaka, Ken Patera, and Ray "Crippler" Stevens. Albano was also a three-time recipient of the *Pro Wrestling Illustrated* "Manager of the Year" Award in 1974, 1981, and 1986, as well as winning the Editor's Award in 1994.

Perhaps Albano's defining moment in professional wrestling was when he became a driving force behind the Rock-N-Wrestling Connection of the mid-1980s. Along with pop culture icon Cyndi Lauper, Albano was at the forefront of a war with onetime allies "Rowdy" Roddy Piper and Fabulous Moolah. This reached its boiling point at "The War to Settle the Score" and set the table for heated bouts at the historic first *WrestleMania.* Once *the* most controversial and despised manager in World Wrestling Federation history, Albano is now the most loved. This sinner-to-saint metamorphosis propelled his career into the mainstream. He was later seen in Lauper's famous video, "Girls Just Wanna Have Fun." Albano's love for music grew; for a brief time in 1986 he managed the acclaimed rock band NRBQ, and was celebrated in their song "Captain Lou" on the album *Lou and the Q.* Albano even stepped into the recording studio and performed vocals. As the 1980s came to an end, Albano entered semi-retirement. In 1987 he appeared on the hit show *Miami Vice,* and in 1989 he starred in the hit TV show *The Super Mario Bros. Super Show!* Albano also appeared in *Wise Guys* and an episode of the sitcom *227* during its first season.

In 1993 Albano returned to World Wrestling Federation and, alongside Wild Samoan Afa, co-managed his last championship tandem of Fatu & Samu, the Headshrinkers. This was Albano's final run with World Wrestling Federation. In 1996 his countless contributions to professional wrestling and his five-decade career were celebrated as the "Manager of Champions" took his rightful place in the WWE Hall of Fame.

"Classy" Freddie Blassie

FROM: **St. Louis, MO**

HEIGHT: **5'10"**

WEIGHT: **220 lbs.**

WHILE GROWING UP IN THE SOUTH SECTION OF ST. LOUIS, A YOUNG FRED BLASSIE WAS CAPTIVATED BY PRO WRESTLING. THE SEVENTEEN-YEAR-old, who supported himself as a butcher, made his in-ring debut in 1935. During World War II Blassie joined the U.S. Navy. While defending our country, he won the seventh Naval District Championship in boxing and wrestling. After being discharged in 1946, Blassie returned to wrestling and soon became one of the most hated wrestlers in the world, shocking fans when he sank his teeth into his opponents and spat out their blood for all to see. During his chilling interviews, Blassie filed his teeth as he described the demise of his opponents.

In 1962 he earned the name "Vampire" when he traveled to Japan and feuded with the father of Japanese *puroresu,* Rikidozan. Audiences on all continents loathed Fred Blassie, and he was often the target of attacks by fans who wanted him eliminated from wrestling. He survived twenty-one stabbings and being doused in acid, and received countless death threats over the course of his career. Blassie fed off fans' hatred, using it as motivation to bring his squared-circle slaughters to new heights. He traveled the world for four decades and battled the likes of Lou Thesz, the Sheik, Haystacks Calhoun, "Golden Greek" John Tolos, the Destroyer, Gorgeous George, Dick the Bruiser, Bruno Sammartino, Antonino Rocca, Bobo Brazil, Killer Kowalski, Pedro Morales, and "Nature Boy" Buddy Rogers. In the early 1960s Blassie became one of the first wrestlers to be featured on mainstream television, appearing on *The Dick Van Dyke Show.*

After headlining cards promoted by all three generations of McMahons—Jess, Vincent James, and Vincent Kennedy—Blassie retired from active competition in 1973. He then embarked on a managerial career that brought as much havoc around the ring as it did success for his stable members. Blassie taunted fans, calling them "pencil neck geeks," and interjected himself in any way so his man emerged victorious. One of his more popular tactics was to wallop unsuspecting opposing wrestlers with his cane. The list of men Blassie guided to stardom includes Ivan Koloff, Ray Stevens, Stan Hansen, Killer Khan, Adrian Adonis, Dick Murdoch, Baron Mikel Scicluna, Blackjack Mulligan, "High Chief" Peter Maivia, George Steele, Iron Sheik, Nikolai Volkoff, Jesse "The Body" Ventura, and Hulk Hogan. In 1976, Blassie's expertise was even sought after by Muhammad Ali as he prepared for his boxer-vs.-wrestler match against Japanese legend Antonio Inoki. In the 1980s Blassie's managerial highlights included escorting rule-breaker Hulk Hogan to the ring against Andre the Giant at the "Showdown at Shea" supercard. He guided the Iron Sheik to victory over World Wrestling Federation Champion Bob Backlund in 1984. The team of Iron Sheik & Nikolai Volkoff were led by Blassie to tag team gold as they defeated the US Express for World Wrestling Federation World Tag Team Championship at the inaugural *WrestleMania.* Blassie even had his own movie with comedian turned inter-gender World Champion Andy Kaufman, *Breakfast with Blassie.*

Throughout the 1990s, Blassie was often seen in video packages that aired on WWE programming and made select public appearances. In 1994, a fifty-year career was celebrated as Blassie took his rightful spot among wrestling's immortals in the WWE Hall of Fame. In 2002 Blassie appeared backstage, giving an inspirational speech to WWE Superstars as they prepared for an invasion by fallen promotions WCW and Extreme Championship Wrestling at the *Armageddon* Pay-Per-View.

On June 2, 2003, "Classy" Freddie Blassie passed away at the age of eighty-five. As a result of his countless contributions to professional wrestling, Blassie's legacy will live in the hearts and minds of fans and Superstars forever.

Miss Elizabeth

FROM: **Frankfort, KY**

HEIGHT: **5'4"**

WEIGHT: **115 lbs.**

THIS UNIVERSITY OF KENTUCKY GRADUATE WAS INTRODUCED TO PRO WRESTLING AS A CAMERA OPERATOR WORKING AT HER FATHER'S LOCAL Kentucky television station. Subsequently, she became the announcer and show host for the local ICW wrestling promotion.

When World Wrestling Federation newcomer Randy Savage debuted in 1985, he did the unexpected and selected the then unknown Miss Elizabeth as his manager over established names like Bobby Heenan, Mr. Fuji, Jimmy Hart, and Johnny Valiant. Miss Elizabeth led Savage to success when he defeated Tito Santana in the Boston Garden on February 6, 1986, for the World Wrestling Federation Intercontinental Championship. George Steele's infatuation with the lovely Elizabeth fueled the feud between himself and Savage. At *WrestleMania 2,* Savage's jealous nature surfaced along with his penchant for violence when he soundly defeated "The Animal." Elizabeth stood by her man through the peaks and valleys of his career. When he lost the Intercontinental Championship to Ricky Steamboat at *WrestleMania III,* she helped ensure the successful progression of Savage's career.

Elizabeth consistently displayed her loyalty to Savage, especially during his *Saturday Night's Main Event* match with newly crowned Intercontinental Champion the Honky Tonk Man. When Savage was blindsided by the Hart Foundation and beaten down by the unscrupulous trio, Elizabeth stepped in front of Savage to protect him from a guitar smashed over his head. When the cowardly Honky Tonk Man threw her down to the mat, Elizabeth got up and went to the locker room for help. When she returned with Hulk Hogan, fans cheered in unison as Hogan and the Macho Man cleared the ring. Not only did she save her man from imminent danger, but she was responsible for forming one of the greatest alliances in World Wrestling Federation history as Savage and Hogan became known as the Mega Powers.

At *WrestleMania IV,* Miss Elizabeth led Savage to the ring an impressive four times as the "Macho Man" defeated Butch Reed, Greg Valentine, One Man Gang, and Ted DiBiase en route to becoming the undisputed World Wrestling Federation World Heavyweight Champion. At the first *SummerSlam* in August 1988, Savage and Hogan battled Ted DiBiase and Andre the Giant in a match dubbed "The Mega Powers vs. The Mega Bucks." The Mega Powers' secret weapon, Elizabeth, stepped onto the ring apron and removed her dress to reveal a stunning, strapless ensemble that halted the four-man brawl and left the Madison Square Garden crowd screaming for more. She managed both Savage and Hogan's careers until an argument between the two caused them to explode in the main event at *WrestleMania V.* Though she remained neutral during the bout, she disassociated herself from Savage when it became clear he had returned to his villainous ways. Elizabeth managed Hogan for a brief period, then took a sabbatical, returning to *WrestleMania VI* in the corner of Dusty Rhodes and Sapphire for their mixed-gender match against Randy Savage and Queen Sherri.

Elizabeth showed her soft spot for the "Macho Man" at *WrestleMania VII.* After Savage lost the Retirement match to Ultimate Warrior, Sensational Sherri entered the ring and kicked Savage when he was down. Elizabeth emerged from the audience and gave chase to the Sensational One. Even in the face of a lethal king cobra courtesy of Jake Roberts at *SummerSlam '91,* Elizabeth knew no fear, facing each of Savage's adversaries right by his side. In 1992, when Ric Flair made slanderous remarks about his alleged prior relationship with the beautiful manager, Elizabeth enjoyed double revenge at *WrestleMania VIII.* The "Macho Man" defeated Flair for his second World Wrestling Federation Heavyweight Championship, and she slapped the taste out of Flair's mouth. Later that year, without any fanfare, Elizabeth abdicated her position at ringside, and Savage continued without her.

In 1995 Elizabeth returned to the ring, but this time in World Championship Wrestling, once again leading Savage and Hogan to the ring. Over the next five years she was also valet for Ric Flair and the Four Horsemen, both factions of the nWo, and Lex Luger. After her WCW departure in 2000, Elizabeth vanished from professional wrestling.

To the shock of the wrestling industry, Miss Elizabeth tragically passed away on May 1, 2003, in a Georgia hospital. She is universally recognized as "The First Lady of Wrestling."

"Big" John Studd

FROM: **Los Angeles, CA**

HEIGHT: **6'10"**

WEIGHT: **364 lbs.**

FINISHING MOVE: **Double-arm suplex**

TRAINED BY KILLER KOWALSKI, BIG JOHN STUDD IS MENTIONED IN THE SAME BREATH AS OTHER FAMOUS GIANTS SUCH AS HAYSTACKS CALHOUN, Gorilla Monsoon, "Big Cat" Ernie Ladd, and Andre the Giant. Alongside his mentor, Studd terrorized World Wrestling Federation tag teams during the mid-1970s as one-half of the masked Executioners. On May 11, 1976, they defeated eventual two-time champions Tony Parisi & Louis Cerdan for the World Wrestling Federation World Tag Team Championship. The Executioners were stripped of their titles seven months later when World Wrestling Federation officials discovered they were using a third member illegally during matches. This mysterious member turned out to be longtime rule-breaker Nikolai Volkoff. Once stripped of the championship, the Executioners disappeared from World Wrestling Federation, and their identities remained a mystery for years.

In 1977, Studd relocated to the NWA's Mid-Atlantic territory, where he wrestled under the names Chuck O'Connor, Captain USA, and Masked Superstar II. While there, Studd held the Mid-Atlantic Tag Team titles with Ken Patera and Ric Flair. Studd devastated every territory he competed in, and no champion's reign was safe. While in the AWA, he battled Verne Gagne in several high-profile contests and fought Canadian greats Dino Bravo and Maurice "Mad Dog" Vachon. In the early 1980s, Studd ravaged Florida, feuding with Dusty Rhodes, Barry Windham, and Ron Bass. Studd was so committed to inflicting pain on opponents that he came to the ring with a stretcher, promising that anyone who faced him would be carried away from the ring on it.

"Big" John Studd landed in World Wrestling Federation in 1983. Now on a national platform, he was more ferocious than ever and immediately challenged Bob Backlund for his World Wrestling Federation Heavyweight Championship. Studd quickly became the lynchpin in the ill-famed Heenan Family stable and was the prime threat to the reign of the newly crowned champion Hulk Hogan. Studd held weekly Body Slam Challenges on World Wrestling Federation programming, in which the winner received $15,000 if they could hoist him over their shoulders and slam him to the mat. Studd went to any lengths to back the claim that he was wrestling's only true giant. To the dismay of Studd, one week Andre the Giant was a last-minute replacement for Chief Jay Strongbow. Determined to reduce the Giant's chances, Heenan interfered by holding Studd's trunks when Andre tried to get him up in the air. When Andre realized this, he went after Heenan, and one of the greatest feuds in wrestling history was born. These two giants met in the $15,000 Bodyslam Challenge at *WrestleMania;* though Andre won the match, their bitter feud was far from over.

At *WrestleMania 2* Studd was a favorite to win the World Wrestling Federation/NFL battle royal. After he eliminated hometown hero William "The Refrigerator" Perry, the Fridge tricked Studd, pulling him over the top rope and onto the Rosemont Horizon floor after the two shook hands. Studd was irate, and both men were restrained from fighting and ordered back to the locker rooms. In 1986, Heenan brought his two leviathans together, and Studd partnered with King Kong Bundy. The team, still one of the physically largest in World Wrestling Federation history, competed against the British Bulldogs, the Killer Bees, and the Machines. In their ongoing feud with World Wrestling Federation's top heroes, Bundy & Studd battled variations of teams in an array of tag match stipulations that featured Hulk Hogan, Andre the Giant, Junkyard Dog, Tito Santana, Ricky Steamboat, and Hillbilly Jim. By the end of the year, "Big" John Studd left the company.

After a two-year absence, Studd returned to World Wrestling Federation in 1988 and rekindled his feud with Andre. The difference now was that Andre was a member of the Heenan Family, and Studd was a fan favorite. The highlight of Studd's return came when he won *Royal Rumble 1988,* eliminating Ted DiBiase in the event's first Pay-Per-View airing. At *WrestleMania V,* he was special guest referee in a match that pitted his archenemy Andre the Giant against Jake Roberts. That event marked the last major World Wrestling Federation appearance Studd made, as that summer he once again left.

The mid-1980s also marked Studd's acting debut. He appeared in film and television throughout the remainder of the decade and into the early 1990s. In 1984, he appeared in *Micki & Maude* alongside foes Andre the Giant and Chief Jay Strongbow. In

1985 he appeared in Jackie Chan's *The Protector as* well as in *The A-Team,* with Mr. T. Studd also had roles in the TV dramas *Hunter* and *Beauty and the Beast* and was in the 1989 cult sci-fi thriller *Hyper Space.* In 1991, he appeared in *Harley Davidson and the Marlboro Man,* starring Don Johnson and Mickey Rourke, in addition to *The Marrying Man,* starring Alec Baldwin and Kim Basinger. With his heart still in the squared circle, Studd made select appearances on the independent scene and opened a wrestling school. His career hit a roadblock in 1993 when he was diagnosed with Hodgkin's disease and had to put his career on hold to battle the illness.

Sadly, after a seventeen-month struggle, this WWE legend succumbed to liver cancer on March 20, 1995, at the age of forty-six. That day wrestling was robbed of one of its true greats. On March 13, 2004, "Big" John Studd's two-decade career was honored by his induction into the WWE Hall of Fame.

The Rockers (Shawn Michaels & Marty Jannetty)

FROM: **San Antonio, TX & Columbus, GA**

COMBINED WEIGHT: **451 lbs.**

FINISHING MOVE: **The Rocker Dropper**

SHAWN MICHAELS AND MARTY JANNETTY WERE AN EXCITING PAIR OF HIGH FLYERS WHO STARTED WRESTLING TOGETHER IN REGIONAL promotions as the Midnight Rockers. In April of 1986 they debuted in the American Wrestling Association and swiftly shot up the tag team ladder, beginning a bloody feud with then champions Buddy Rose & Doug Somers. After beating the two in nontitle matches, these young lions defeated the cagey veterans on January 27, 1987, for their first AWA World Tag Team Championship. During that summer they took a brief hiatus, but they would return to the AWA to capture their second World Tag Team title, defeating Paul E. Dangerously's version of the Midnight Express.

In 1988, the Rockers debuted on World Wrestling Federation television and quickly gained a reputation as tag team specialists. Michaels and Jannetty stunned audiences around the country with their acrobatic double-team moves, seamless continuity, and impressive resiliency. The Rockers had classic matches with the Hart Foundation, Demolition, the Rougeau Brothers, and the Brain Busters. In addition, they battled the Twin Towers, Nasty Boys, Orient Express, and Power and Glory. The pair also displayed their ring versatility at *Survivor Series* and *Royal Rumble.* At *Survivor Series 1991,* a rift between the two showed when Michaels walked out on Jannetty during their match, accusing his partner of trying to take control of the team. Just as it appeared that the two were ready to reconcile on *The Barber Shop,* Shawn Michaels did the unimaginable. After embracing Marty Jannetty, he ruthlessly threw his longtime partner and best friend through the *Barber Shop* window. Fans around the world gaped in horror, and Marty Jannetty would be out of action for several months with critical internal injuries.

Michaels then became the pompous "Heartbreak Kid," and during the October 1992 episode of *Saturday Night's Main Event* he captured the World Wrestling Federation Intercontinental Championship by defeating the British Bulldog. When Jannetty returned, he sought revenge. On May 17, 1993, he defeated his former partner for the Intercontinental title. Michaels, however, would get the last laugh, regaining the title three weeks later. The remainder of the 1990s saw Shawn Michaels become known as "The Showstopper," winning every World Wrestling Federation championship possible. Marty Jannetty would stay in World Wrestling Federation through 1996, displaying his expertise in tag team wrestling as he captured the World Wrestling Federation Tag Team Championship with the 1-2-3 Kid. After some time away from the ring, Jannetty briefly competed in WCW. In March 2005 the two reunited on *Raw* for a special one-night-only appearance, defeating the team of La Resistance. These two great performers showed they could still rock-n-roll and slam-n-jam. During a February 2006 episode of *Raw,* Jannetty came to the aid of his former partner when an outnumbered Michaels was being attacked by the Spirit Squad.

During their years in World Wrestling Federation as a team, the Rockers never won the prestigious World Tag Team Championship, but they'll always be revered as one of the greatest duos of all time, and visionaries within the ranks of tag team wrestling.

Hercules

FROM: **Tampa, FL**
HEIGHT: **6'1"**
WEIGHT: **270 lbs.**
FINISHING MOVE: **The Torture Rack**

STARTING IN THE FLORIDA AND MID-SOUTH TERRITORIES DURING THE EARLY 1980S, HERCULES HERNANDEZ SPENT MOST OF HIS TIME CONCEALING HIS identity under masks. He feuded with "Hacksaw" Jim Duggan under the name Mr. Wrestling III. When his mask was removed, Hercules left Mid-South and joined the ranks of World Class Championship Wrestling. Once again a masked man, he went by the name of the Assassin. In April 1984 he was unmasked during a match with Jimmy Valiant and soon left Texas.

In 1986 Hercules Hernandez made his World Wrestling Federation debut in Trojan warrior garb, coming to the ring with "Classy" Freddie Blassie. Hercules's offensive repertoire consisted of powerful moves that could end a match at any time. His running clotheslines nearly decapitated opponents and could pull down the pillars of Rome. Once his full nelson or Torture Rack were cinched in, they were virtually inescapable. One of the strongest men in all of World Wrestling Federation, Hercules forced all Superstars to take notice and feel his wrath. At *WrestleMania 2* he met Ricky Steamboat and displayed his ability to compete with the lighter, quicker high flyers.

Over the next year Hercules altered his appearance by cutting his hair and coming to the ring with a steel chain. He became a member of the Heenan Family and a serious threat to World Wrestling Federation Champions. The new look and manager brought him immediate success, and on the March 14 episode of *Saturday Night's Main Event,* he won a twenty-man battle royal and outlasted participants including Hulk Hogan, Andre the Giant, Demolition, Paul Orndorff, Honky Tonk Man, Hillbilly Jim, and Koko B. Ware.

During this time Hercules feuded with Billy Jack Haynes. The two fought at *WrestleMania III* in the Full Nelson Challenge: whoever slapped the full nelson onto his opponent won. Going toe-to-toe, they ended up on the Silverdome floor, resulting in a double countout. Hercules then hit Haynes with his chain and busted him open.

Hercules's next battle was with Ultimate Warrior in a feud that proved to be the definitive power struggle. During their bout at *WrestleMania IV,* both men refused to give any ground. After the contest the two began a tug of war for Hercules's chain that resulted in the steel manacle breaking in half. Hercules also battled Bam Bam Bigelow, Brutus Beefcake, Don Muraco, and Jake Roberts.

In late 1988, Bobby Heenan showed his true loathsome colors, trying to sell Hercules to Ted DiBiase as a slave. Hercules vehemently refused and set his sights on getting revenge. With a new attitude, Hercules became a fan favorite. The height of his newfound popularity came at *Survivor Series 1988,* when he was a member of the Mega Powers team along with co-captains Hulk Hogan, Randy "Macho Man" Savage, Koko B. Ware, and Hillbilly Jim. Hercules defeated King Haku in the opening match of *WrestleMania V.* Other opponents that year included Ted DiBiase, Virgil, Greg Valentine, Dino Bravo, Mr. Perfect, and Earthquake.

During the last half of 1990, the Mighty One returned to his rule-breaking ways and with Paul Roma formed the team Power and Glory. These veterans combined brute strength with speed and ring finesse. The final piece of the puzzle came in the form of their manager, "Doctor of Style" Slick. The duo started strong and defeated the Rockers at *SummerSlam '90.* Later that year they were on the winning team at *Survivor Series,* and with teammates Rick Martel and the Warlord defeated Jake Roberts, Jimmy Snuka, and the Rockers. After a disappointing *WrestleMania VII* defeat at the hands of World Wrestling Federation World Tag Team Champions the Legion of Doom, they lost a six-man tag match with partner the Warlord at *SummerSlam '91* to British Bulldog, Texas Tornado and the Dragon. After a second loss to the LOD, Power and Glory split.

In late 1991 Hercules left the company. He appeared in WCW in 1992 as the masked Super Invader, led to the ring by Harley Race. The peak of his WCW tenure came in September of that year at the *Clash of Champions,* teamed with Rick Rude, Jake Roberts, and Vader to battle Sting, Nikita Koloff, and the Steiner Brothers in an Elimination match. In 1993 he arrived in New Japan Pro Wrestling and formed a team with American Scott Norton, the Jurassic Powers. On August 5, they beat the Hellraisers—Road Warrior Hawk & Kesuke Sasaki—for the IWGP World Tag Team Championship. They held on to the titles until January 4, 1994, when the Hellraisers regained the titles. That summer the team parted, and Hercules returned to the States.

For the remainder of the 1990s he traveled the country's independent circuit, wielding his chain and breaking opponents with his versions of the full nelson and Human Torture Rack.

The wrestling world lost this apostle of power on March 6, 2004, when he suffered a heart attack at his home in Tampa. Hercules will be remembered as one of wrestling's strongest men, possessing incredible tenacity and fury in the squared circle. His intimidating aura and paralyzing submission holds set the standard.

Slick

FROM: **Fort Worth, TX**
HEIGHT: **6'4"**
WEIGHT: **180 lbs.**

BEFORE HE BECAME KNOWN AS "THE DOCTOR OF STYLE," THIS 1987 SLAMMY AWARD WINNER GOT HIS START MANAGING IN TEXAS ALL-STAR Wrestling and moved through the territories of the NWA. He made his World Wrestling Federation debut in 1986, purchasing 50 percent equity interest in "Classy" Freddie Blassie's stable of wrestlers. He began by managing former World Wrestling Federation World Tag Team Champions Nikolai Volkoff & the Iron Sheik, then unveiled a new Superstar, the bleached-blond "Natural" Butch Reed. Reed was a flamboyant, tough-as-nails competitor who, with the Doctor of Style behind him, was a perennial contender for the World Wrestling Federation Intercontinental and World Heavyweight Championships.

During a 1988 episode of *Superstars of Wrestling,* Slick transformed the feared One Man Gang into "African Dream" Akeem. Slick paired his new creation with former prison guard the Big Boss Man and formed the Twin Towers. As the 1990s began, he brought World Wrestling Federation Superstars Hercules and Paul Roma together, calling the team Power and Glory.

Always ensuring he had a full stable of Superstars, he also managed the careers of the Warlord and Rick Martel.

After a brief hiatus, Slick returned to World Wrestling Federation in 1992 as an ordained minister. He appeared on World Wrestling Federation programming pontificating to audiences about the importance of knowing thyself and accepting the Lord. He attempted to save Kamala from a beating from his trainer, Kim-Chee, and make the Ugandan Giant see that he was more than a monster, but a man who deserved to be treated with dignity and respect like any other human being. His attempts at conversion proved futile, as Kamala soon reverted to his beastly ways. Shortly after this, Reverend Slick and World Wrestling Entertainment parted.

Today the Doctor of Style runs a ministry in his hometown of Fort Worth and makes appearances at local wrestling shows and conventions.

"Million Dollar Man" Ted DiBiase

FROM: **Various**

HEIGHT: **6'3"**

WEIGHT: **260 lbs.**

FINISHING MOVE: **The Million Dollar Dream**

DIBIASE GREW UP IN THE WRESTLING BUSINESS. WHEN HIS STEPFATHER, "IRON" Mike DiBiase, died in the ring of a heart attack, a fifteen-year-old Ted moved to Arizona to live with his grandparents. He received a scholarship to West Texas State University, where he was trained by Dory Funk Jr. and made his pro debut in 1975. DiBiase competed in Oklahoma and had his first major matches with "Killer" Karl Kox, Dick Murdoch, and Greg Valentine. While in Japan, Ted fought *puroresu* greats Giant Baba and Jumbo Tsurata. In 1976, DiBiase moved to the Mid-South Wrestling territory. Over the next three years he had noted bouts with the Spoiler, Harley Race, and Fritz Von Erich over the North American Championship.

DiBiase's first introduction to World Wrestling Federation fans came in 1979 when he was billed as the North American Champion. He was defeated by Pat Patterson, and the title became the World Wrestling Federation Intercontinental Championship. While in World Wrestling Federation, DiBiase competed in tag matches with partners Andre the Giant and Tito Santana. He was Hulk Hogan's opponent in his first Madison Square Garden appearance. In 1980 DiBiase returned to the Mid-South territory. By October 1983 Ted had won a twelve-man tournament to become the NWA National Champion. During this time he formed one of the territory's greatest tag teams with "Dr. Death" Steve Williams, and the duo were two-time Mid-South Tag Team Champions. DiBiase shocked the region when he turned against longtime friend and partner Junkyard Dog, but managed to regain fan favorite status in 1985 before he left the region.

In 1987, "Million Dollar Man" Ted DiBiase made his World Wrestling Federation debut with his bodyguard Virgil at his side. The Million Dollar Man was out to prove his motto: "Everyone has a price." Vignettes aired on television programming that showed people being willingly humiliated and degraded for money. DiBiase called fans up, asking them to perform for cash. When a fan agreed to do ten push-ups, when he reached the ninth one, DiBiase would put his foot on the fan's back, insuring his failure. DiBiase pulled this trick on a boy in Battle Creek—Rob Van Dam. At the end of his matches, DiBiase stuffed $100 bills in the mouths of fallen opponents to publicly disgrace them.

DiBiase's other obsession was the World Wrestling Federation World Heavyweight Championship. Ted even offered then champion Hulk Hogan money in exchange for pro wrestling's crown jewel. When Hogan refused, DiBiase became incensed. The Million Dollar Man hired Andre the Giant to defeat Hogan, and hand the title over to him. This twisted dream became a reality in February 1988. During *The Main Event,* Hogan's four-year title reign came to a tragic end. After a suplex from the challenger, Andre covered Hogan. Although Hogan got his shoulder up, the referee continued the count. This was one of the most controversial matches in World Wrestling Federation history. When the bell rang, Andre was given the belt and turned it over to DiBiase. After a thorough investigation, it was discovered that DiBiase had paid for an official to have plastic surgery so he would resemble referee Dave Hebner. DiBiase was stripped of the title by then President Jack Tunney. For the first time in World Wrestling Federation's famed history, it did not have a World Heavyweight Champion.

A fourteen-man, single-elimination tournament was created for *WrestleMania IV.*

Though DiBiase made it to the finals, he lost to Randy Savage. This match led to one of the biggest main events in history as the Mega Powers squared off against the Mega Bucks at the first *SummerSlam* in August of 1988. The Million Dollar Man continued to exhaust all of his resources to acquire the World Wrestling Federation Heavyweight Championship, but his attempts were unsuccessful. DiBiase did what any other millionaire who desired something would do: he created his own championship.

In mid-1989 DiBiase unveiled "The Million Dollar Belt," beautifully handcrafted, with precious 24k gold and diamonds so bright they blinded the human eye. DiBiase's championship schemes got grander when World Wrestling Federation introduced the *Royal Rumble.* Each year DiBiase promised to draw a high number, or make someone an offer they couldn't refuse, but his shortcuts only got him so far. The rest of the late 1980s were spent in battles with Hulk Hogan, Dusty Rhodes, and Jake Roberts.

As the 1990s dawned, DiBiase's unquenchable thirst for money and the World Wrestling Federation Championship intensified. Staying true to his reputation, DiBiase shocked the wrestling world when he introduced Undertaker at *Survivor Series 1990.* In 1991, DiBiase and his bodyguard Virgil broke ties, and the two fought at *WrestleMania VII.* In early 1992, he formed a successful tag team with fellow money lover Irwin R. Schyster—I.R.S. Together they were known as Money Inc. The two Superstars were quite successful, capturing the World Wrestling Federation World Tag Team Championship on three separate occasions. The first championship reign began on February 7, 1992, when they defeated the Legion of Doom, and lasted just over five months. They reclaimed the titles on October 13, 1992, when they defeated the Natural Disasters. They soon split with manager Jimmy Hart and, at *WrestleMania IX,* faced off against the team of Hulk Hogan & Brutus Beefcake. They dropped the titles to the Steiner Brothers on June 14, 1993, and regained them two days later. Money Inc. lost the title for the final time on June 19.

By 1994, injuries forced this wrestling mogul to retire from active competition. DiBiase returned to World Wrestling Federation as a manager and built his Million Dollar Corporation. This group of rule-breakers consisted of I.R.S., Bam Bam Bigelow, and Nikolai Volkoff. Their main purpose was to eliminate figures like Undertaker and Lex Luger. As the Corporation's list of enemies grew, so did the number of members within the faction. As a manager, DiBiase's penchant for creating controversy grew. He orchestrated the Undertaker vs. Undertaker bout at *SummerSlam '94.* The main event of Bam Bam Bigelow vs. Lawrence Taylor at *WrestleMania XI* was under his management. DiBiase recruited Tatanka, Psycho Sid, and the 1-2-3 Kid. By early 1996 the Million Dollar Corporation had disbanded and DiBiase debuted his greatest protégé ever in

"The Ringmaster" Steve Austin. "The Million Dollar Man" gave Austin the Million Dollar Belt and permission to use the Million Dollar Dream. Austin feuded with Savio Vega, and the two Superstars exchanged victories until May of 1996, when Vega defeated Austin in a Caribbean Strap match. This loss forced the Million Dollar Man to leave the company.

In late 1996, DiBiase arrived in World Championship Wrestling as the manager of the New World Order. DiBiase had a change of heart and managed the Steiner Bros. to the WCW World Tag Team Championship. Within a year, DiBiase left the organization. Throughout the late 1990s DiBiase appeared on the independent scene around the country, and in 1997 he released his book. *Every Man Has His Price: The True Story of Wrestling's Million Dollar Man.* In 2004 DiBiase returned to World Wrestling Federation as a road agent working with the Superstars of today. He has appeared sporadically on television, proving to fans that his motto is still true.

"Million Dollar Man" Ted DiBiase will always be remembered as one of the most ruthless and cunning villains. Always looking to get ahead by any means necessary, DiBiase stopped at nothing to get what he wanted. He was also one of the few Superstars of his era whose larger-than-life persona was equal to his tremendous technical ability inside the squared circle. If you don't believe it, ask him yourself.

Sensational Sherri

FROM: **New Orleans, LA**

HEIGHT: **5'7"**

WEIGHT: **132 lbs.**

FINISHING MOVE: **Sleeper hold**

SENSATIONAL SHERRI HAD ONE OF THE MOST SUCCESSFUL TRANSITIONS FROM WRESTLER TO MANAGER EVER SEEN IN THE INDUSTRY. SHE BEGAN her career in the early 1980s, and on September 28, 1985, she defeated Candi Divine for the American Wrestling Association's Women's Championship. Over the next year, the two feuded, exchanging the title on three separate occasions. During this period she also perfected the art of managing and led the team of "Playboy" Buddy Rose & "Pretty Boy" Doug Somers to the AWA World Tag Team titles. Sherri defeated Candi for the title on June 28, 1986, for the final time. She vacated the title soon afterward.

On July 24, 1987, Sensational Sherri made her World Wrestling Federation debut, defeating her mentor the Fabulous Moolah to become World Wrestling Federation Women's Champion. Sherri developed the reputation for doing anything to win as she defended her title against Debbie Combs, Velvet McIntyre, and Desiree Peterson, among others. Her feud with Moolah continued, and they were opposing captains at the first *Survivor Series.* Sherri held the title for an impressive fifteen months before losing it to Rockin' Robin on October 7, 1988, in France. In the early 1990s World Wrestling Federation eliminated the Women's Division, and Sherri returned to managing.

Sherri raked eyes, ran her nails down opponents' backs, kicked them when they were down—anything to give her man the upper hand. Her first Superstar was Randy Savage during his reign as "The Macho King." Sherri became "Sensational Queen," and the two sparked chaos throughout the company. They even appeared on an episode of *Lifestyles of the Rich and Famous* with Robin Leach. The pair feuded with Hulk Hogan and Miss Elizabeth, and Dusty Rhodes and Sapphire. During Savage's feud with Ultimate Warrior, Sherri tried to seduce Warrior into granting Savage a World Wrestling Federation World Championship match. When Warrior denied her advances, Sherri was determined to make him pay. The "Queen" and "King" cost the Warrior the World Wrestling Federation Championship at *Royal Rumble 1991.* This set up the Savage vs. Warrior Retirement match at *WrestleMania VII.* After Savage lost the match, Sherri kicked him while he was down, but she was thrown from the ring by former Savage valet Miss Elizabeth, who surprised everyone by making the save. Later that evening Sherri ran to ringside and helped Ted DiBiase escape from Virgil and Roddy Piper. A grateful DiBiase enlisted her services on the spot, and she began escorting the Million Dollar Champion to the ring. After DiBiase and Sherri

split, she offered her services to rising star Shawn Michaels. It was Sherri's voice on the popular entrance theme "Sexy Boy" that set the tone for Michaels's early singles success. World Wrestling Federation's greatest stars had to watch their step whenever the Sensational One was at ringside.

After leaving World Wrestling Federation, Sherri briefly competed in Extreme Championship Wrestling before she moved to WCW in 1994. Here she was known as "Sensuous" Sherri and managed Ric Flair when he clashed with Sting and Hulk Hogan. Sherri and Flair parted ways, and she then guided Harlem Heat to an amazing seven WCW World Tag Team Championships, as "Sista Sherri." During this time Sherri also had a torrid love affair with Col. Robert Parker. After leaving WCW in 1997, Sherri spent the rest of the 1990s touring the U.S. independent circuit. Then, during the March 24, 2005, episode of *SmackDown!* Sherri made a surprise appearance, singing a version of the song "Sexy Kurt" with Kurt Angle. Sherri became emotional when viewing a video retrospective of HBK's career. An irate Angle then attacked Sherri and put her in the Angle Lock for showing sentiment toward his *WrestleMania* opponent.

On April 1, 2006, Sherri's twenty-five-year career reached its pinnacle when she was inducted into the WWE Hall of Fame. Sherri redefined the women's role in sports entertainment and paved the way for today's WWE Divas.

Rick Martel

FROM: **Quebec, Canada**
HEIGHT: **6'**
WEIGHT: **236 lbs.**
FINISHING MOVE: **The Boston Crab**

FROM ONE OF CANADA'S MOST FAMOUS WRESTLING FAMILIES, RICK MADE HIS PRO DEBUT AT SEVENTEEN IN 1972. EARLY ON, MARTEL WON championships in various parts of the world, including being one-half of the International Tag Team Champions in Stu Hart's Stampede Wrestling in 1974 and the British Empire/Commonwealth Championship in New Zealand in 1977. Rick first received significant attention in 1980 when he landed in the NWA's Pacific Northwest territory. Immediately, Martel became one of the promotion's top stars, excelling in both the singles and tag team ranks. He captured the Pacific Northwest Heavyweight Championship on March 22, 1980. A successful tag team was formed with Roddy Piper, and they took the Pacific Northwest Tag Team Championship on several occasions. That summer Martel left the National Wrestling Alliance.

In the fall Martel burst onto the World Wrestling Federation scene, forming a popular tag team with veteran Tony Garea. Combining sound technical mat wrestling with exciting high-flying maneuvers, on November 8, 1980, they defeated the Wild Samoans. After a four-month title reign, they dropped the titles to the Moondogs before regaining them four months later. The team's second title reign ended on July 21, 1980, at the hands of Mr. Fuji & Mr. Saito. Soon after the loss Garea and Martel went their separate ways. Garea continued to compete in World Wrestling Federation, and Martel returned to the Canadian wrestling scene. In 1984 Martel went to the American Wrestling Association, and in May he stunned the wrestling world when he defeated Japanese legend Jumbo Tsurata for the AWA World Heavyweight Championship. Martel defended the title for close to nineteen months before he dropped it to Stan Hansen.

In 1987, Martel returned to World Wrestling Federation as part of the popular yet short-lived duo the Can-Am Connection. Soon after their *WrestleMania III* victory over the Magnificent Muraco & "Cowboy" Bob Orton, Martel's partner vanished after a prematch attack from the Hart Foundation. Still hungry for success, Martel formed an exciting team with Tito Santana. These two thrilling Superstars together were known as Strike Force. Martel and Santana gelled seamlessly, and were immediate contenders in the ultra-competitive World Wrestling Federation Tag Team Championship landscape. On October 27, 1987, in Syracuse, New York, Strike Force defeated the Hart Foundation when Martel's Boston Crab forced Jim Neidhart to submit. This was Martel's third World Wrestling Federation Tag Team title and Santana's second, and Strike Force spent the next five months defending the title. Then at *WrestleMania IV* their title reign came to an end when the fan favorites crossed paths with Ax & Smash, the deadly Demolition.

As the 1980s were coming to an end, so did Martel's humble attitude. After some time away from World Wrestling Federation, Strike Force returned at *WrestleMania V* to take on supreme ring technicians Arn Anderson & Tully Blanchard, the Brain Busters. After Santana mistakenly hit Martel with his patented flying forearm, Martel refused to tag back into the match. He then abruptly left the ring, leaving Satana to fend for himself against Heenan's henchmen. The Brain Busters capitalized on this, planting Santana with a spike piledriver from the middle rope to win the match. When "Mean" Gene Okerlund confronted Martel after the match, all he said was that he was sick and tired of carrying Santana, and that Tito was riding his coattails. This resulted in a bitter near-year-long feud between the former partners. Martel took on a new persona. "The

Model" Rick Martel was a pompous, self-centered egomaniac from Cocoa Beach, Florida. The Model came to the ring with slicked-back hair, a tuxedo jacket and bow tie or a sweater, depending on the season, and a spray bottle of his own fragrance, aptly called Arrogance. Once his battle with Santana concluded, the Model faced Koko B. Ware, Tatanka, Shawn Michaels, Razor Ramon, and Lex Luger. His biggest battle came when he blinded Jake Roberts by spraying him in the face with Arrogance. This resulted in the two fighting at *WrestleMania VII* in a Blindfold match. Heading into the mid-1990s, the Model continued to be a contender for both World Wrestling Federation Intercontinental and Heavyweight Championships.

In 1995 Martel left the company. He remained active and competed in independent promotions all over the world. In 1997, he resurfaced in World Championship Wrestling and feuded with Booker T over the WCW Television Championship. On February 16, 1998, Martel captured the TV title but dropped it six days later at *SuperBrawl VIII*. Unfortunately for Martel, his comeback was cut short when injuries forced him to retire after an incredible twenty-six-year career. In 2003 he made a surprise appearance at a World Wrestling Federation show in his home country, Canada.

After a three-decade career, Rick Martel is one of the most respected and popular legends, and one of Canada's favorite sons. A world champion everywhere he competed, Martel gave everything he had once he stepped through the ropes to do battle.

Pedro Morales

FROM: **Culebra Island, Puerto Rico**

HEIGHT: **5'10"**

WEIGHT: **235 lbs.**

FINISHING MOVE: **Boston Crab**

PEDRO MORALES BEGAN WRESTLING IN 1959 AND QUICKLY BECAME ONE OF THE MOST POPULAR LATIN STARS TO EVER SET FOOT IN THE squared circle. Morales possessed a blue-collar work ethic, coupled with powerful southpaw punches and a fiery Latin temper. Pedro was also an incredible technical wrestler, utilizing the Boston Crab like no other. He soon proved he could defeat anyone at any time, regardless of their size. Morales feuded with Freddie Blassie, the Sheik, Pampero Firpo, Moondog Mayne, and "Killer" Karl Kox. While Morales saw success in both singles and tag team ranks in regional promotions like the NWA, WWA, and

WWC, he finally rose to national prominence on February 8, 1971, when he defeated Ivan Koloff for the World Wrestling Federation World Heavyweight Championship. This was a historic event, as Pedro became the first Puerto Rican Heavyweight Champion. Pedro enjoyed a near-three-year title reign, with many classic matches displaying his scientific mat skills, impressive strength, and unequaled stamina.

No match was as heralded during his reign as World Wrestling Federation Champion than his September 30, 1972, match with mentor and friend Bruno Sammartino. These two heroes battled to a 75-minute draw in front of 41,000 people at Shea Stadium. Unfortunately, Pedro's magical title reign came to an end on December 1, 1973, when he met the wild Stan "The Man" Stasiak. During the next few years Morales formed successful tag teams with Pat Patterson and Rocky Johnson and captured the NWA World Tag Team and Florida tag titles.

Morales briefly returned to World Wrestling Federation. On August 9, 1980, with partner World Wrestling Federation Champion Bob Backlund, he defeated the Wild Samoans to capture the World Wrestling Federation World Tag Team Championship. Unfortunately, due to the rules at the time, the fan favorites were forced to forfeit the titles. As 1980 came to a close, Morales feuded with Ken Patera over the World Wrestling Federation Intercontinental Championship. On December 8 he toppled the Olympian, becoming the first Superstar to win all three major World Wrestling Federation Championships. Pedro lost the title to Don Muraco on June 20, 1981, but regained it later that year from the Magnificent One on November 23. After enjoying a fourteen-month championship reign, Pedro was again defeated by Muraco on January 22, 1983. Morales retired from full-time action in 1985 but did not disappear from the ring completely.

In 1986, Pedro participated in the *WrestleMania 2* World Wrestling Federation/NFL battle royal and formed a team with Tito Santana. After hanging up his boots for good in the late 1980s, Morales began a career in the broadcast booth as World Wrestling Federation's lead Spanish announcer.

Pedro Morales is sometimes overlooked when wrestling's greatest champions are discussed. In 1995, however, Pedro's five decades of excellence was celebrated as he was inducted into the WWE Hall of Fame. To know Pedro Morales's greatness, all you need to do is watch one of his classic matches.

The Wild Samoans (Afa & Sika)

FROM: **Samoa**

COMBINED WEIGHT: **645 lbs.**

FINISHING MOVE: **The Samoan Drop / double headbutt**

AFA AND SIKA COME FROM A LARGE FAMILY OF WRESTLERS, INCLUDING HIGH CHIEF PETER MAIVIA, JIMMY SNUKA, ROCKY JOHNSON, YOKOZUNA, and The Rock. Trained by his uncle Peter Maivia and Rocky Johnson, Afa began his pro career in the early 1970s. He then trained his brother Sika, and the two became one of wrestling's first dominant tag teams, the Wild Samoans. The team traveled to Stu Hart's Stampede Wrestling and held the Stampede International Tag Team Championship on two separate occasions. For the rest of the 1970s they would rip opponents apart throughout the NWA territories, winning championships along the way.

This trail of terror continued, and in 1980 they moved on to World Wide Wrestling Federation. On January 21, Afa & Sika made their Madison Square Garden debut against Tag Team Champions Tito Santana & Ivan Putski. The title did not change hands, but the Wild Samoans made an impact. Both men, as individuals, became contenders for Bob Backlund's World Wrestling Federation Heavyweight crown, shredding anyone that stood in their way of obtaining the World Tag Team Championship. On April 12, 1980, in the Philadelphia Spectrum, the Samoans defeated Santana & Putski for their first taste of World Wrestling Federation tag team gold. Afa & Sika held the titles for five months until they met the super-team of Bob Backlund & Pedro Morales in a Best-Two-Out-of-Three Falls contest at *Showdown at Shea*. Unfortunately, the fan favorites had to forfeit the titles because Backlund was reigning World Wrestling Federation World Heavyweight Champion. Officials held a tournament, and on September 8, 1980, Afa & Sika defeated the team of Tony Garea & Rene Goulet for their second World Wrestling Federation tag title reign. One month later they would drop the championship to the team of Tony Garea & Rick Martel. Afa & Sika battled the new champions for the remainder of the year in attempts to regain the title but were unsuccessful.

In late 1981 they arrived in Mid-South Wrestling, using "Big Cat" Ernie Ladd as their financial adviser. After winning the Mid-South Tag Team titles, they entered into a violent feud with Junkyard Dog and Dick Murdoch. Shortly after, the Samoans attacked Ladd and spawned a feud with their former business associate. After trying to find the right partner, Ladd recruited "Iron" Mike Sharpe and drove Afa & Sika out of the territory. In August 1982 they briefly appeared in Mid-Atlantic Championship Wrestling and defeated the Fabulous Freebirds for the NWA National Tag Team titles. Afa & Sika soon vacated the title and returned home to World Wrestling Federation, reuniting with their manager, Capt. Lou Albano.

The Samoans were more savage than ever. During interviews Afa & Sika would grunt in primitive dialect only understandable to Albano. They displayed pure acts of savagery by tearing at giant chunks of raw fish and eating it. On March 19, 1983, they defeated the team of Chief Jay & Jules Strongbow. During this time they also introduced a third member to their team, Wild Samoan Samula, and feuded with former mentor Rocky Johnson as well as Jimmy Snuka and Andre the Giant. The Wild Samoans' third and final reign as World Wrestling Federation World Tag Team Champions came to an end on November 15, 1983, in Allentown, Pennsylvania, courtesy of Rocky Johnson & Tony Atlas. During the match, Capt. Lou tried to hit Johnson with a solid oak chair. Instead, Albano hit Sika, putting his head through the chair and splitting him open. Tony Atlas covered Sika for the win. In 1984 the team left World Wrestling Federation. Sika would return in 1986 as a singles competitor managed by the Wizard. He challenged Hulk Hogan for his Heavyweight title and occasionally tagged with the "Ugandan Giant," Kamala.

In 1992, Afa returned to World Wrestling Federation and managed family members the Headshrinkers. In 1994 he co-managed them to the World Wrestling Federation World Tag Team Championship with Capt. Lou Albano. After his team dropped the titles to Shawn Michaels & Diesel, Afa left WWE to open the Wild Samoan Training Center with his brother Sika. It has become one of the premier wrestling schools in the world, with distinguished alumni including Paul Orndorff, the Junkyard Dog, Sensational Sherri Martel, Michael P.S. Hayes, Yokozuna, Bam Bam Bigelow, and Batista. Afa and Sika also promote live wrestling shows bearing the WXW flag.

The Wild Samoans will be remembered not only for being the most bizarre and unpredictable tandem, but also for their countless contributions to professional wrestling helping form future stars.

SUPERCARD/PPV HISTORY

SHOWDOWN AT SHEA

LOCATION: **Shea Stadium, Flushing, NY**

DATE: **August 9, 1980**

Forty thousand fans packed Shea Stadium for another World Wrestling Federation supercard. Never shown on American television, the 1980 *Showdown* saw great names like Fabulous Moolah, Pat Patterson, and Chavo Guerrero. It also hosted the first bout between Andre the Giant and Hulk Hogan. Heroes Pedro Morales & Bob Backlund joined forces against the Wild Samoans, and Bruno Sammartino fought against student-turned-enemy Larry Zbyszko in a steel cage.

Beverly Slade & Fabulous Moolah vs. Kandi Malloy & Peggy Lee

Fabulous Moolah and her partner Beverly Slade took no prisoners. The two made easy work of Kandi Malloy & Peggy Lee.

Dominic DeNucci vs. Baron Mikel Scicluna

The popular Dominic DeNucci met Baron Mikel Scicluna. In the end, DeNucci's eternal fight brought him the victory over the man from the Isle of Malta.

Angel Marvilla vs. Jose Estrada

Two championship hopefuls collided: Angel Marvella defeated the Puerto Rican wrestling legend.

The Hangman vs. Rene Goulet

This match saw a clash of two Canadian-born grapplers. Escorted to the ring by "Classy" Freddie Blassie, the Hangman was looking for any opportunity to get Goulet in his bear hug. Goulet wanted nothing more than to lock the Hangman in his deadly scorpion claw hold. To the disappointment and surprise of those in attendance, Hangman covered Goulet for the win.

Greg Gagne vs. Rick McGraw

Famous high flyer Gagne had his hands full with the rugged "Quick Draw." The match went back and forth, but in the end, Gagne picked up the victory.

Pat Patterson vs. Tor Kamata

The devious Tor Kamata Pearl-Harbored Pat Patterson before the bell rang, and Patterson fought the early portion of the match with his ring jacket still on. The Japanese martial arts expert showed his agility, hitting Patterson with a dropkick. Kamata then missed a big splash attempt from the top rope. This gave Patterson a chance to land a kneedrop from the top rope and take control. While both Superstars were in the corner, Kamata attempted to throw salt in the eyes of his opponent. Patterson ducked, and the salt flew in the eyes of official Dick Grohl. Kamata was disqualified, and Patterson was the victor.

Tatsumi Fujinami vs. Chavo Guerrero

"The Dragon" Tatsumi Fujinami stood across the ring from Mexican challenger Chavo Guerrero. This was an exchange of holds, attacks, and reversals from the opening bell. Just beyond the ten-minute mark, Fujinami defeated Guerrero and left with his Junior Heavyweight Championship title belt secure around his waist.

Antonio Inoki vs. Larry Sharpe

On this night in Flushing, Queens, the Japanese great bested journeyman Larry Sharpe to retain his World Wrestling Federation Martial Arts Championship.

Ivan Putski vs. Johnny Rodz

"Polish Power" Ivan Putski locked up with veteran rule-breaker "Unpredictable" Johnny Rodz. Putski's strength was too much for Rodz, and he scored the pinfall for the victory.

Andre the Giant vs. Hulk Hogan

This was the first ever meeting between "The Eighth Wonder of the World" and Hulk Hogan. Hogan was greeted with a sea of boos from the Shea Stadium crowd.

The Giant established control from the opening bell as he tossed Hogan into the corner from the lockup position. Hogan showed his strength when he did not budge after two consecutive Andre shoulder blocks. Hogan's blows glanced off the Giant, who counted with roundhouse rights and headbutts. When the referee got knocked out, Hogan attacked Andre from behind. Just as Andre flattened Hogan with a splash, a replacement official ran into the ring and counted the one, two, three.

World Wrestling Federation Intercontinental Championship: Ken Patera (champion) vs. "Mr. USA" Tony Atlas

Mr. USA was off to a fast start and got the champion in a press slam, tossing him across the ring. Patera retaliated with a kneelift and a monster clothesline. Atlas staggered Patera with a half-dozen headbutts before he scored a near pinfall. The Olympic strongman displayed his power and got his opponent in a press slam. Mr. USA regrouped with a middle-rope headbutt and standing vertical suplex. The fight poured out of the ring as the two exchanged left-and-rights on the Shea Stadium infield. As the referee counted, they slugged it out on the apron, with Patera unintentionally knocking Atlas back into the ring before the count of ten. The champion lost by countout, but the title did not change hands.

Bob Backlund & Pedro Morales vs. the Wild Samoans (champions)

Two top heroes battled the barbaric Samoans in a Two-Out-of-Three Falls melee. Morales & Backlund defeated the Samoans, capturing the World Wrestling Federation World Tag Team Championship.

Steel Cage Match: Bruno Sammartino vs. Larry Zbyszko

As the cage door locked, Sammartino attacked his former student. He threw Zbyszko from one side of the cage to the other as the crowd erupted. After finishing the youngster off with kicks to the head, Bruno Sammartino walked through the cage door victorious.

WRESTLEMANIA

LOCATION: Madison Square Garden, New York, NY

DATE: March 31,1985

This groundbreaking spectacular was viewed by over 1 million fans around the world on closed circuit television. A capacity New York City crowd witnessed wrestling history.

Tito Santana vs. the Executioner

Tito Santana was determined to exit *WrestleMania* victorious. The mysterious Executioner guaranteed his victory. Santana started off with a flurry of offense, and the Executioner was in trouble. After a slam back into the ring from the apron, Tito knocked the Executioner out with his patented flying forearm. The Executioner submitted within seconds.

S. D. "Special Delivery" Jones vs. King Kong Bundy

King Kong Bundy was set to make an impact. After an Avalanche and a Big Splash, Bundy demolished S. D. in record time and scored a pinfall in just nine seconds, a record that still stands today.

Ricky Steamboat vs. Matt Borne

Ricky Steamboat was in peak physical condition. His opponent, Matt Borne, was a rugged second-generation wrestler. Steamboat opened the match and displayed his martial arts expertise. When Borne got Ricky in a belly-to-belly suplex, Steamboat retaliated with a series of reverse knife-edged chops and a belly-to-back suplex followed by a flying double chop off the ropes. Steamboat then climbed to the top turnbuckle and flew across the ring onto Borne with his high-flying cross-body for the three-count.

David Sammartino (w/Bruno Sammartino) vs. Brutus Beefcake (w/Luscious Johnny Valiant)

David Sammartino, the son of Bruno Sammartino, was ready to make his mark. Brutus Beefcake wanted a victory and was not concerned with how it was obtained. Sammartino and Beefcake locked horns in a seesaw battle. Beefcake used his power, throwing Sammartino into the corner from the classic collar-and-elbow tie-up. Sammartino sent Beefcake reeling with his methodical attack. On rubber legs, Beefcake threw Sammartino out of the ring. Johnny Valiant picked Sammartino up and slammed him on the Garden's cement floor. Bruno threw Valiant into the ring. All four men were brawling, and the Sammartinos cleaned house. The match was ruled a no contest.

Intercontinental Championship: Greg "The Hammer" Valentine (champion, w/"Mouth of the South" Jimmy Hart) vs. Junkyard Dog

The Junkyard Dog started off the match with fast and heavy-hitting offense. JYD tagged "The Hammer" with roundhouse right hands and headbutts. Valentine bounced back and started to work on the JYD's legs. The champion and challenger exchanged rights and lefts. When Jimmy Hart climbed on the ring apron, JYD grabbed him, and Valentine slugged his own manager. Valentine raked JYD's eyes and sent him to the mat. He got on top of the Dog and used his feet on the ropes for leverage for the pin. The bell rang, and Valentine left the ring. Tito Santana ran in and explained what had happened to official Dick Groll, who ordered the match to restart. When Valentine was out on the floor, the count began. The next bell sounded, the Hammer was counted out, and Junkyard Dog won the match.

World Wrestling Federation World Tag Team Championship: The US Express (champions, w/Capt. Lou Albano) vs. Nikolai Volkoff & Iron Sheik (w/"Classy" Freddie Blassie)

This match pitted the speed and agility of the US Express against the experience and power of the Sheik & Volkoff. The champions cut the ring in half early and made a series of quick tags until Volkoff threw a stunned Rotundo into the Sheik's notorious curled boot. After getting worked over by both opponents, Rotundo tagged a fresh Barry Windham, who unloaded on the big Russian and hit him with his Bulldog. The Sheik broke the pin, and when the referee's back was turned, he nailed Windham from behind with Blassie's cane. Volkoff made the pin, and new World Wrestling Federation World Tag Team Champions were crowned.

The $15,000 Body Slam Challenge: Andre the Giant vs. "Big" John Studd (w/Bobby "The Brain" Heenan)

The match stipulation was simple: If Andre the Giant slammed "Big" John Studd, he won the match, and $15,000. If he didn't, he had to retire.

"Big" John Studd attacked Andre early. Andre bounced back with chops and a headbutt. The Giant hit Studd with heavy shots as the Garden crowd chanted, "Slam, slam!" Andre wore Studd down with rights to the face and kicks to his knees. With Studd wobbling, the Giant scooped his adversary up over his shoulders and slammed Studd to the canvas. That match was over, and Andre took his winnings and started throwing it to the fans. Bobby Heenan ran into the ring, stole the bag of money, and fled the Garden. Andre's amazing undefeated streak remained intact.

World Wrestling Federation Women's Championship: Leilani Kai (w/Fabulous Moolah) vs. Wendi Richter (w/Cyndi Lauper)

Both women exchanged holds, and Kai worked on Richter's left arm. Richter retaliated with power moves when a melee ensued outside on the floor. Fabulous Moolah grabbed Richter, and Cyndi Lauper made the save. Leilani Kai climbed to the top rope and flew off with a flying cross-body. Richter allowed Kai's momentum to work against her, and she rolled through the move. With Kai's shoulders down on the mat, Wendi Richter was the Women's Champion.

Hulk Hogan & Mr. T (w/Jimmy "Superfly" Snuka) vs. "Rowdy" Roddy Piper & "Mr. Wonderful" Paul Orndorff (w/"Cowboy" Bob Orton)

Drum and bagpipes began to play, and the Garden was flooded with boos as the ill-famed trio of Roddy Piper, Paul Orndorff, and "Cowboy" Bob Orton made their way to the ring. Then the heroic triad of World Wrestling Federation World Champion Hulk Hogan, Mr. T, and Jimmy Snuka emerged. The match started with Piper and T nose-to-nose in the center of the ring. After the two traded slaps, Mr. T shocked Piper when he reversed two sit-outs. After a few tags it was clear that the duo of Hogan and T complemented one another. A near brawl erupted when all four men were in the ring and Muhammad Ali took a swing at Piper in an attempt to restore order. Control of the match shifted as Orndorff and Piper settled into their own groove. "Mr. Wonderful" had Hogan locked in a full nelson when Orton jumped from the top rope and mistakenly knocked Orndorff out. Hogan turned away from the attack and pinned Orndorff for the win. Piper laid out referee Pat Patterson and left the ring with his bodyguard.

THE WRESTLING CLASSIC

LOCATION: Rosemont Horizon, Rosemont, IL

DATE: November 7, 1985

The Superstars of World Wrestling Federation took part in the ultimate test of courage, physical endurance, and mental strength. The luck of the draw would play a part, creating interesting match-ups and surprise endings.

ROUND 1, ALL MATCHES 10-MINUTE TIME LIMIT

Match #1: Cpl. Kirschner vs. Adrian Adonis (w/Jimmy Hart)

The Corporal charged the ring, ready for the street fighting tactics of Adrian Adonis. Kirschner had Adonis reeling. After the Corporal rose to his feet from a sitting rear chin lock, he attempted a vertical suplex. Adonis then stepped over and planted Kirschner headfirst with a modified version of a DDT. Kirschner's youthful exuberance and inexperience cost him the match.

Match #2: Dynamite Kid vs. Nikolai Volkoff

As Nikolai Volkoff began to besmirch the crowd, the Russian walked into the Dynamite Kid's flying dropkick from the top rope. Volkoff was down for the count in a matter of seconds.

Match #3: Ivan Putski vs. Randy "Macho Man" Savage (w/Miss Elizabeth)

Savage was a favorite to win, given his special training sessions with Jesse "The Body" Ventura. The Macho Man spat on Putski before they locked up. When Ivan broke a full nelson, he returned the favor. Savage exchanged rights and lefts with Polish Power. When Putski unloaded on the Macho Man with kicks in the corner, Savage hooked Putski's legs and got him on his back. Savage then lay on Ivan, putting his feet on the ropes for leverage and the win.

Match #4: Davey Boy Smith vs. Ricky "The Dragon" Steamboat

Steamboat possessed an edge in the speed department, and Smith had a power advantage. Davey Boy wore Steamboat down with a front facelock and was in control until the Dragon reversed a standing vertical suplex. Smith rebounded and connected with two dropkicks that sent a dazed Steamboat into the ropes. When Davey Boy ran at Ricky for a third dropkick attempt, he moved out of the way, and Smith flew into the ropes, seriously injuring his groin. The referee called the match, awarding it to Steamboat.

Match #5: Iron Sheik vs. Junkyard Dog

The Sheik started the bout with a sneak attack on the Dog, choking him with his robe and turban. JYD retorted with a series of headbutts. The Sheik retaliated, locking the Dog in his Camel Clutch. The Dog did not submit; JYD nailed the Sheik with a headbutt and got the win.

Match #6: Terry Funk (w/Jimmy Hart) vs. Moondog Spot

Funk proposed that both men leave together and accept a draw. Once on the floor, Funk attacked the Moondog from behind and tried to get back into the ring before the ten-count. Spot pulled Funk back onto the floor. When Spot charged his attacker, Funk unintentionally threw him over his shoulder and back into the ring. Spot made it back into the ring before the ten-count, and won the match via countout.

Match # 7: The Magnificent Muraco (w/Mr. Fuji) vs. Tito Santana

Muraco hit Santana early with powerful rights. Tito retaliated, starting to work on the left arm of the Magnificent One. Muraco then focused on Santana's left leg, power-slammed Santana, and went for a pinfall. As the referee counted, Tito put his foot on the rope. Believing he had won the match, Muraco made a celebratory gesture to the crowd. As he turned around, Tito wrapped him up in a small package for the victory.

Match # 8: "Mr. Wonderful" Paul Orndorff vs. "Cowboy" Bob Orton

Orndorff focused his attack on the cast of Orton's allegedly injured left arm. When Orton missed a flying head scissors and hurled into the ropes, Mr. Wonderful capitalized. While on the apron, the Cowboy adjusted his cast and walloped Orndorff in the head right in front of the referee. When the Cowboy attempted a pin, the official signaled for the bell, and Orton was disqualified.

ROUND 2, ALL MATCHES 15-MINUTE TIME LIMIT

Match #1: Dynamite Kid vs. Adrian Adonis (w/Jimmy Hart)

Dynamite set things off with quick armdrags, sending his opponent out of the ring. Adonis regrouped on the floor, and began to work on Dynamite's left knee. Adrian then turned Dynamite over into a Texas cloverleaf, but broke the hold when Dynamite reached the ropes. When Hart jumped on the apron, a distracted Dynamite Kid got rolled up. The Kid kicked out, sending Adonis into Hart's megaphone. Dynamite scored the pinfall.

Match #2: Ricky "The Dragon" Steamboat vs. Randy "Macho Man" Savage (w/Miss Elizabeth)

When the bell rang, Savage placed Miss Elizabeth between himself and the Dragon. Steamboat returned to his corner, and Elizabeth took her post on the outside. The "Macho Man" then Pearl Harbored his opponent. Steamboat came back with reverse knife-edged chops that sent Savage reeling. The Macho Man took everything Steamboat threw at him. With his back turned, Savage took out a pair of brass knuckles from his trunks. When the Dragon hoisted him up for a back suplex, Savage knocked Steamboat out in midair and pinned Ricky for the win.

Match #3: Moondog Spot vs. Junkyard Dog

Moondog Spot did not wait for the bell to ring but jumped JYD. An over-anxious Spot missed a Big Splash from the middle rope. Without an official on hand, the Junkyard Dog delivered one of his signature headbutts. The Dog covered his opponent, as well as counting the pinfall himself.

Match #4: Tito Santana vs. "Mr. Wonderful" Paul Orndorff

These two opponents shook hands in an ultimate show of mutual respect and sportsmanship before they locked up and displayed their supreme technical ring abilities. Tito entered the match with his left leg taped, and after an atomic drop from Orndorff, he was reeling in pain. Mr. Wonderful continued to wear him down with a single-leg grapevine. Tempers flared, and both men fought toe-to-toe on the floor. Santana hurled Orndorff into the steel ring post as both men were counted out and eliminated from the tournament.

The outcome of this match translated into a bye for the Junkyard Dog. Now the JYD awaited his opponent in the tournament finals.

World Wrestling Federation World Heavyweight Championship: Hulk Hogan (champion) vs. "Rowdy" Roddy Piper

The Hot Rod came to the ring with his band of bagpipes, while Hogan stepped through the ropes with the eye of the tiger. Once the bell sounded, this match turned into a Chicago Street Fight, with both men beating one another on the outside floor. Piper regained control after a Hogan onslaught and locked the champion in a sleeper hold. When the referee raised Hogan's arm and it dropped for the second consecutive time, Piper thought wrestling's ultimate prize awaited him. Unfortunately, Hogan's arm did not drop a third time, and the champion came back to life. When the official got knocked out, Piper resorted to his usual tactics, clobbering Hogan with a steel chair. Hogan got to his feet, and both men fought for the chair. The champion put Piper in a sleeper hold. In mere seconds, Piper's bodyguard, "Cowboy" Bob Orton, jumped Hogan from behind. While the two beat down Hogan, Mr. Wonderful stormed the ring, sending Orton and Piper back to the locker room.

ROUND 3, 20-MINUTE TIME LIMIT

Dynamite Kid vs. Randy "Macho Man" Savage (w/Miss Elizabeth)

Both the Dynamite Kid and Randy Savage possessed exceptional technical abilities and lightning-fast speed. This contest saw the upper hand shift, with both men going hold-for-hold and move-for-move. With the "Macho Man" perched on the top rope, Dynamite Kid hit him with a flying dropkick, sending Savage down hard on the top turnbuckle. In an incredible display of physical strength and control, Dynamite Kid delivered a super-plex while both men stood on the top rope. The force off the mat was so great that Savage turned and hooked Dynamite's leg for the win, turning defeat into victory.

THE TOURNAMENT FINALS—NO TIME LIMIT

Randy "Macho Man" Savage (w/Miss Elizabeth) vs. Junkyard Dog

In a stalling tactic, the Macho Man circled the ring with a steel chair. Savage then threw the chair at the Junkyard Dog, who caught it and began to repeatedly hit himself in the head with it. He was ready for war. Savage continued his cat-and-mouse game until he lost a collar-and-elbow tie-up power struggle. The JYD took the upper hand, until Savage came back and nailed the Dog with his patented flying ax-handle from the top rope. The Dog absorbed incredible amounts of punishment. He caught Savage coming off the top rope with a shot to the solar plexus. The Macho Man charged the JYD and was back-dropped over the top rope and out of the ring. Unable to return, Savage was counted out, and the Junkyard Dog was the winner of the sixteen-man Wrestling Classic.

WRESTLEMANIA 2

LOCATION: **Nassau Coliseum, Uniondale, NY; Rosemont Horizon, Rosemont, IL; The Sports Arena, Los Angeles, CA**

DATE: **April 7, 1986**

Three cities—Los Angeles, Chicago, and Uniondale, New York—were needed to host *WrestleMania 2*. As in the first *WrestleMania,* a host of celebrities participated in the event: then Los Angeles Dodgers manager Tommy Lasorda, Joan Rivers, Ricky

Schroeder, Cathy Lee Crosby, Ozzy Osbourne, Mistress of the Dark Elvira, and Ray Charles, who sang a soul-stirring rendition of "America the Beautiful."

"Mr. Wonderful" Paul Orndorff vs. the Magnificent Muraco (w/Mr. Fuji)

This bout saw more action outside of the ring than inside, as Mr. Wonderful and the Magnificent One traded shots from the opening bell. The fight intensified when it moved outside the ring and onto the Nassau Coliseum floor. Both Superstars were counted out.

World Wrestling Federation Intercontinental Championship: Randy "Macho Man" Savage (champion, w/Miss Elizabeth) vs. George "The Animal" Steele

Steele's unorthodox style put the champion off his game when the Animal caught Savage and took a bite out of his right calf. Whenever Savage was down and in a compromised position, instead of staying on the champion, Steele made motions toward Miss Elizabeth. This gave the Macho Man time to recuperate and resulted in blindside attacks. Both men continued to brawl, and the Animal proceeded to beat the champion with a bouquet of flowers. Again distracted, Steele first bit the turnbuckle and then moved toward Miss Elizabeth, resulting in another attack from Savage. Savage hooked Steele's legs using the ropes for leverage to get the win and retain his World Wrestling Federation Intercontinental Championship.

Jake "The Snake" Roberts vs. George Wells

Jake Roberts entered the ring at the Nassau Coliseum willing to accept nothing less than victory. Wells hit the Snake with high-powered offense, including a flying head scissors, a flying shoulder tackle, and a scoop slam. Wells almost scored an upset when he got a near pinfall after a powerslam off the ropes. The match's direction changed after a thumb to the eye by Roberts. Jake then caught Wells with a fierce kneelift as he came back into the ring. The Snake, sensing victory, dropped Wells with the DDT for the victory. Roberts untied his bag and unleashed his pet snake, Damien, onto his fallen opponent.

Special Boxing Match: "Rowdy" Roddy Piper (w/"Cowboy" Bob Orton & Lou Duva) vs. Mr. T (w/Smokin' Joe Frazier & Haiti Kid)

Mr. T started out with a peek-a-boo style, and Piper went for an early knockout, throwing wild left and rights. The last thirty seconds of the first round resembled a brawl, and punches were thrown after the bell rang. In the second round Piper stayed on the offensive and knocked T down twice. The Rowdy One came out of his corner confident, but Mr. T knocked Piper down with a left. Roddy returned to his feet, but then T hit him out of the ring. Visibly frustrated, the Hot Rod hurled a stool at Mr. T and moments later shoved referee Jack Lotz to the canvas. Piper then bodyslammed Mr. T, and a melee ensued inside the ring. Mr. T won by disqualification.

World Wrestling Federation Women's Championship: Fabulous Moolah (champion) vs. Velvet McIntyre

Moolah blindsided her opponent with heavy shots. McIntyre missed a Big Splash. With the wind knocked out of her, Moolah covered the challenger and scored the pinfall.

Flag Match: Cpl. Kirschner vs. Nikolai Volkoff (w/Freddie Blassie)

The winner of this match would wave the flag of his home country in victory.

The Corporal made relatively quick work of the Russian, nailing Volkoff with Blassie's cane. Old Glory stood tall in the Rosemont Horizon, and the Russian and his manager got a taste of their own medicine.

World Wrestling Federation/NFL Over-the-Top-Rope Twenty-Man Battle Royal

This was another wrestling first. Superstars were put in the ring with some of the NFL's best. Participants included Andre the Giant, "Big" John Studd, Hillbilly Jim, Bruno Sammartino, Pedro Morales, the Hart Foundation, Iron Sheik & Nikolai Volkoff, and the Killer Bees. From the NFL were William "The Refrigerator" Perry, Russ Frances, Bill Fralic, and many more, along with guest judges Dick Butkus and Ed "Too Tall" Jones. The bell sounded, and it was pure bedlam. The first men eliminated were King Tonga and Jimbo Covert. Hometown favorite William "The Refrigerator" Perry did not hesitate and eliminated Tony Atlas before he locked horns with "Big" John Studd. Studd eliminated the Fridge, but Perry had the last laugh: while shaking Studd's hand, he pulled him out of the ring. The final four were Andre the Giant, Russ Francis, and the Hart Foundation. The Harts dumped Francis out of the ring with relative ease. As the crowd chanted "Andre, Andre," he knocked Jim Neidhart out of the ring with a big boot. Andre then caught Bret Hart on the top rope and dumped him onto his partner on the outside, for the win.

World Wrestling Federation World Tag Team Championship: The Dream Team (champions, w/"Luscious" Johnny Valiant) vs. the British Bulldogs (w/Capt. Lou Albano & Ozzy Osbourne)

The contest started with the Bulldogs taking their offense right to Greg Valentine. The Hammer went toe-to-toe with the Dynamite Kid. More quick tags on the part of the challengers resulted in a double shoulder block to the Hammer. As Capt. Lou and Ozzy looked on, the Dream Team had the upper hand, but Valentine refused to pin Davey

Boy Smith after a shoulder-breaker, and Davey Boy rammed Valentine into the cranium of his partner the Dynamite Kid. The Hammer was out. Smith went for the cover, and with Beefcake unable to get in the ring to break the pin, the British Bulldogs were the new World Wrestling Federation World Tag Team Champions.

Ricky "The Dragon" Steamboat vs. Hercules Hernandez

Hernandez charged Steamboat at the onset, but Ricky's quickness enabled him to control the match. The Dragon's offense continued until Hernandez caught him in a devastating slingshot. Hercules demonstrated his raw power, until he missed a Big Splash from the top rope. Steamboat climbed to the outside and hit Hercules with his trademark high-flying cross-body for his second straight *WrestleMania* victory.

Uncle Elmer vs. "Adorable" Adrian Adonis (w/"Mouth of the South" Jimmy Hart)

As Adrian Adonis and his manager entered the ring, they sprayed perfume in Elmer's direction. Elmer's heavy offense sent the Adorable One reeling. Elmer continued to use his weight to his advantage, but when he missed a legdrop, Adonis connected with a headbutt from the top rope and exited victorious.

Tito Santana & Junkyard Dog vs. Terry & Hoss Funk (w/"Mouth of the South" Jimmy Hart)

The Dog & Santana took the fight to the Funks. Utilizing their double-team tactics, the Funks wore down Santana & JYD. When the referee was distracted, Terry Funk whaled Junkyard Dog in the back of the head with Mouth of the South's megaphone. Funk covered JYD for the win.

World Wrestling Federation World Championship: Hulk Hogan (champion) vs. King Kong Bundy (w/Bobby "The Brain" Heenan)

As Hogan's "Real American" theme hit, the L. A. Sports Arena rose to its feet. Hogan scaled the cage and sat on top of it ripping his T-shirt, signifying that *Hulkamania* was running wild. As the cage door closed, the injured Hogan came out with a superpowerful offense. Bundy was in trouble. The Walking Condominium attacked Hogan's ribcage. Bundy called for the door, but Hogan denied him victory. Throughout the match both men used the cage as a weapon, and Bundy was bloodied and bashed. The champion finished Bundy off with his signature legdrop and then left the cage, retaining his title.

Hernandez takes control of the match, effortlessly tossing Billy Jack Haynes.

WRESTLEMANIA III

LOCATION: **Pontiac Silverdome, Pontiac, MI**
DATE: **March 29, 1987**

An indoor record-setting crowd of 93,173 packed the Pontiac Silverdome to witness the amazing card, headlined as arguably the greatest championship match in history as Hulk Hogan clashed with Andre the Giant. This *WrestleMania* had all the components needed to be a classic: outrageous stipulations, championship bouts, midgets, and celebrities.

Can-Am Connection vs. the Magnificent Muraco & "Cowboy" Bob Orton (w/Mr. Fuji)

Muraco's power moves were no match for the Can-Am's quick tags and double-team maneuvers. The fan favorites showed incredible continuity and were on a roll until Orton caught Zenk with a knee. The ring-savvy veterans wore their opponent down until Zenk tagged in a fresh Rick Martel. Suddenly, all four men were in the ring. A dropkick sent Orton out of the ring, and Martel pinned Muraco with a flying cross-body with a little help from his partner.

Billy Jack Haynes vs. Hercules Hernandez (w/Bobby "The Brain" Heenan)

Haynes neutralized Hernandez with reverse knife-edged chops and a barrage of lefts and rights. After a decapitating clothesline, Hercules took control. Billy Jack rebounded and slapped the full nelson on Hernandez. Hercules got to the ropes and used them for leverage, catapulting himself and his foe to the floor. The brawl continued outside, and both men were counted out. The match over, Hercules accosted Haynes with his chain and beat him to a bloody pulp.

Six-Man Tag match: Hillbilly Jim, Haiti Kid & Little Beaver vs. King Kong Bundy, Little Tokyo & Lord Littlebrook

Once the bell rang, the midgets mixed it up. Almost immediately Little Beaver performed hit-and-runs on the 440-pound King Kong Bundy. While Hillbilly and Bundy were exchanging shots, Little Beaver antagonized the monster for the last time. Bundy Avalanched Hillbilly and crushed him in the corner. Shockingly, Bundy then turned and picked up Little Beaver for a bodyslam. The behemoth then dropped an elbow, crushing the fan favorite. An unconscious Little Beaver had to be carried out by partner Hillbilly Jim.

Humiliation match: Junkyard Dog vs. "King" Harley Race (w/Bobby "The Brain" Heenan & Fabulous Moolah)

Escorted to the ring by his manager Bobby Heenan, "King" Harley Race also brought with him the queen of wrestling, the Fabulous Moolah. The Junkyard Dog entered the ring and started to clean house. Despite interference from the Brain, JYD had the upper hand and appeared poised to take Race's regal crown. The Dog was distracted by Heenan, however, and found himself on the receiving end of a belly-to-belly suplex. Race scored the pinfall, and JYD had to kneel before him in the center of the ring. The JYD gave a half-hearted bow and tagged Race with a thunderous chairshot. Race was knocked out, and the Dog left draped in the King's flowing majestic robe.

The Rougeau Brothers vs. the Dream Team (w/"Luscious" Johnny Valiant & Dino Bravo)

The Rougeaus were off to a great start until Raymond missed a flying cross-body out of the corner. Valentine & Beefcake cut the ring in half and calculated their attack. After a miscue from Brutus, the Rougeaus found themselves back in the match. Raymond hoisted the Hammer in an elevated bear hug, and Jacques landed on him in a Lou Thesz press. Raymond took Valentine's leg and flipped it into a pinfall position. With the official distracted, Dino Bravo landed a forearm smash from the middle rope onto Raymond. The Canadian Strongman then put Valentine on the laid-out Rougeau for the win.

Retirement match: "Rowdy" Roddy Piper vs. "Adorable" Adrian Adonis (w/"Mouth of the South" Jimmy Hart)

This match turned into a wild brawl, with both men exchanging whips from a leather belt. Piper threw Jimmy Hart into Adrian, sending both men out on the floor. Hart took a beating but came back to help Adonis. The Mouth hooked Piper's leg and then sprayed him in the face with Adonis's perfume. Piper got trapped in the Adorable One's Good Night Irene sleeper hold. Adonis broke the hold when he thought Piper's arm fell for the third time, and began his celebration. Then Brutus Beefcake came into the ring and brought the Hot Scot out of his daze. Adrian hit himself with his giant barber's shears, and Piper locked him in the sleeper hold. Adonis was out cold as the ninety-three-thousand-plus fans witnessed the birth of "The Barber." Piper helped Adrian regain consciousness, then showed him his new look. When Adonis got a glimpse of his reflection, he broke into a fit of rage and ran out.

British Bulldogs & Tito Santana (w/Matilda) vs. the Hart Foundation & Dangerous Danny Davis (w/"Mouth of the South" Jimmy Hart)

The Harts were on fire until Jim Neidhart broke a near pinfall and Bret Hart nailed Dynamite Kid with shots right between the eyes. The champions began their double-team tactics, and when Dynamite Kid was down on the mat, they tagged in Danny

Davis to take cheap shots on him. Strutting pompously in and out of the ring, Davis missed a slingshot splash. Dynamite tagged in the fiery Santana, and all six men were in the ring. When the referee wasn't looking, Davis cracked Davey Boy Smith with Jimmy Hart's megaphone and scored the pinfall for his team.

"The Natural" Butch Reed (w/Slick) vs. Koko B. Ware (w/Frankie)

Koko B. Ware got the crowd involved early and used his speed to counter the power of Reed, hitting him with lefts, rights, and a picture-perfect dropkick. Koko was on a roll, but he made a crucial error, putting his head down too soon for a backdrop. Reed took advantage and began to measure his opponent. When Koko bounced off the ropes with a flying cross-body, Reed rolled through the move and held the Birdman's tights for the win.

Slick attacked Koko with his cane after the bout. Tito Santana came in and ripped Slick's suit to shreds, then flew with Koko as they connected a double dropkick on the Natural.

World Wrestling Federation Intercontinental Championship: Randy "Macho Man" Savage (champion, w/Miss Elizabeth) vs. Ricky "The Dragon" Steamboat (w/George "The Animal" Steele)

The match started with Steamboat administering a series of deep armdrags. The Dragon started to work on the champion's left arm, and Savage fought back. Both wrestlers exchanged hold and near pinfall attempts, and the fight spilled out on the floor. Savage hit the Dragon with his double ax-handle from the top rope. Steamboat retaliated with a single hand-chop from the top turnbuckle. The Macho Man was in serious trouble, barely managing to kick out of several near falls. A reversed Irish whip sent Steamboat into referee Dave Hebner. Savage landed his flying elbow drop, but no count could be made. When the champion left and returned to the top rope with the timekeeper's bell, George "The Animal" Steele threw Savage down to the mat. The Macho Man went for a scoop slam; Steamboat reversed it into a small package in the center of the ring and became the new World Wrestling Federation Intercontinental Champion.

Jake "The Snake" Roberts (w/Alice Cooper) vs. Honky Tonk Man (w/"The Colonel" Jimmy Hart)

Jake pulled out all the stops and leveled Honky Tonk early with his patented short-arm clothesline. A well-schooled Honky Tonk Man got out of Jake's DDT. Honky started to soften Jake up for his Shake, Rattle & Roll neckbreaker. With the crowd chanting "DDT, DDT," Jake got his second wind and hit Honky Tonk with hard shots. The Snake went for a DDT attempt when Jimmy Hart hooked Roberts's leg. Honky Tonk came from behind and got Roberts in a roll-up. Using the top rope for leverage, Honky Tonk scored an upset victory over Roberts.

With his man gone, Jimmy Hart was left in the ring with Alice Cooper and Roberts. When the snake Damien was taken out, Alice Cooper brought him up close and personal to Hart, and the Colonel had an anxiety attack. Honky Tonk returned, and the two scurried out of the Silverdome.

The Killer Bees vs. Iron Sheik & Nikolai Volkoff

The bell rang, and all four men were in the ring. The Bees utilized quick tags and double-team moves against the Sheik, who fought back and went to work on Brunzell. While Sheik had Jumping' Jim cinched in the middle of the ring, "Hacksaw" Jim Duggan made his presence known, chasing Volkoff around the ring. Duggan turned and nailed Sheik with his two-by-four right in front of the official. This resulted in the Bees being disqualified.

World Wrestling Federation World Heavyweight Championship: Hulk Hogan (champion) vs. Andre the Giant (w/Bobby "The Brain" Heenan)

The two men met in the center of the ring for an epic stare-down. After Hogan hit Andre with roundhouse rights, the champion went for the big slam. Andre fell on top of Hogan and got a near three-count. Andre laid into Hogan, stepping on his back while his face was on the canvas. The giant's attack was devastating as he used his 500-plus pounds to crush Hogan in the corner while delivering a huge headbutt. Andre missed a second headbutt attempt but connected with his twenty-two-inch boot. Andre had Hogan squeezed in a bearhug in the center of the ring, and Hulk was in serious trouble. As referee Joey Marella raised Hogan's arm for the third time, he kept it raised and began to fight out of the move. With the crowd behind him, Hogan slugged Andre with shots to the head. Hogan was sent to the floor after a boot from the Giant. Battling on the floor, Hogan lifted the mats and attempting a piledriver on the concrete floor. Back in the ring, Hogan sidestepped another boot from Andre and knocked Andre off his feet with a clothesline. Feeling a power surge, Hogan did the unimaginable. He scooped the seven-foot-four Andre above his shoulders and slammed him on the mat. Seizing the moment, Hulk bounced off the ropes and landed his trademark legdrop for the win.

In that instant, Hulk Hogan ended Andre the Giant's fifteen-year undefeated streak and secured his place as one of the greatest wrestlers of all time. In front of almost one hundred thousand spectators, Hogan proved once and for all that *Hulkamania* was the most powerful force in the universe.

SURVIVOR SERIES

LOCATION: Richfield Coliseum, Richfield, OH

DATE: November 26, 1987

The original *Survivor Series* marked the first time a wrestling event revolved around team-based elimination matches. The combinations and possibilities were virtually endless as teams of five tried to survive. Wrestlers could be eliminated via pinfall, submission, count-out, disqualification, or—at the referee's discretion—in the event of an injury.

Randy "Macho Man" Savage (captain, w/Miss Elizabeth), Ricky "The Dragon" Steamboat, "Hacksaw" Jim Duggan, Jake "The Snake" Roberts & Brutus "The Barber" Beefcake vs. Honky Tonk Man (captain, w/"The Colonel" Jimmy Hart), Danny Davis, "King" Harley Race (w/Bobby "The Brain" Heenan), Hercules & "Outlaw" Ron Bass

As the match got under way, Beefcake kicked things off with Hercules. The Barber started off strong and handed out hiplocks to Hercules, Harley Race, and Danny Davis. Roberts, Savage, and Steamboat all made quick tags and got their licks in against Davis. The first elimination of the match came when "Hacksaw" Jim Duggan sent "King" Harley Race over the top rope, and both men brawled to a double countout.

"Outlaw" Ron Bass took the walk to the locker room after a Brutus Beefcake high knee. The Barber's night was soon over, when he walked into Honky Tonk's Shake, Rattle & Roll. Roberts quickly stepped in and traded shots with Honky Tonk. After landing in the wrong corner, Roberts connected with his vicious short-armed clothesline, planted Danny Davis with a DDT, and picked up the pinfall. After taking a beating from the Honky Tonk Man and Hercules, Jake turned the tide of the match and tagged in the Dragon. Steamboat laid into Hercules and set up the Mighty One for the Savage's trademark flying elbow drop. After the tag, Savage leaped from the top rope and crushed Hercules for the pin.

The match was now a one-on-three, and Honky Tonk was across the ring from Savage, Steamboat, and the lethal Jake "The Snake" Roberts. To the delight of the crowd, all three men got in on the Honky hit parade. After an atomic drop from the "Macho Man" sent him over the top rope, the Honky Tonk Man left the ring and was counted out.

SURVIVORS: Randy Savage, Ricky Steamboat, and Jake Roberts.

Fabulous Moolah (captain), Rockin' Robin, Velvet McIntyre & the Jumping Bomb Angels vs. Sensational Sherri (captain, Women's Champion), the Glamour Girls (Women's Tag Team Champions, w/"Mouth of the South" Jimmy Hart), Donna Christanello & Dawn Marie

The Women's Champion and the pride of Ireland, Velvet McIntyre locked up, and after a quick tag to Fabulous Moolah, she cleared the ring. McIntyre was soon back in the ring and eliminated Donna Christanello with a shoulder straddle into a forward roll. After a tag to Rockin' Robin, Sherri's team took the upper hand until Robin surprised Dawn Marie with a flying cross-body. It was now three to five in favor of Moolah's team. Japan's Jumping Bomb Angels—Noriyo Tateno & Itsuki Yamazaki—wowed the crowd with their speed and high-flying maneuvers. Rockin' Robin was eliminated by Sensational Sherri. Captain Fabulous Moolah was pinned after a Glamour Girls—Leilani Kai & Judy Martin—double clothesline. Velvet soon found herself on top of Sherri's shoulders. She used her flexibility to roll Sherri up for the pin. McIntyre was sent packing when Kai gave her a slingshot across the throat. Leilani was pinned, and Judy Martin was left to fight for herself. A dropkick sent Jimmy Hart flying off the ring apron; the Angels were too much, and Judy Martin was eliminated.

SURVIVORS: The Jumping Bomb Angels

Strike Force (captains), the Young Stallions, the Rougeau Brothers, the Killer Bees & the British Bulldogs vs. the Hart Foundation (captains), the Islanders (w/Bobby "The Brain" Heenan), Demolition, the Bolsheviks (w/Slick) & the New Dream Team (w/"Luscious" Johnny Valiant)

The added rule in this contest was that when one man was eliminated, his partner was also eliminated.

Nikolai Volkoff and Rick Martel started the match, tagging out to their partners. Tito hit Boris Zukhov with his flying forearm, and the Bolsheviks were history. Demolition came in and looked awesome. Jacques Rougeau telegraphed a flying cross-body, Ax covered, and the Rougeaus were eliminated. Smash was pummeling Dynamite Kid, and he elbowed the referee. Disqualification: Demolition was sent back to the locker room. As Tito battled Jim Neidhart, the Anvil scored a quick pin, eliminating the champions thanks to an elbow from the Hit Man.

The pace of the match quickened. The British Bulldogs were eliminated after Haku connected with a reverse thrust kick to the head of Dynamite Kid. Remaining: the Hart Foundation, the Islanders, the New Dream Team, the Killer Bees, and the Young Stallions. Jim Powers took a beating at the hands of Dino Bravo. The Hammer was tagged in and went for his figure-four leglock. Unbeknown to Valentine, Powers tagged his partner, Paul Roma. The Hammer leaned in to apply the figure four, and Roma pinned him with a sunset flip from the top rope. Two teams remained on each side. When Jim Brunzell scooped Bret Hart for a bodyslam, Islander Tama came in and dropkicked Hart onto the Killer Bee. Brunzell allowed the Hit Man's momentum to carry him through, so Hart was eliminated. The Bees and the Stallions now had a two-to-one advantage.

Heenan's Islanders controlled the pace of the match despite being outnumbered. Tama was fighting a sunset flip from Brunzell when a masked B. Brian Blair catapulted himself over the top rope and pinned the Samoan for the victory.

SURVIVORS: The Killer Bees and the Young Stallions

Hulk Hogan (captain), "Mr. Wonderful" Paul Orndorff, "The Rock" Don Muraco, Ken Patera & Bam Bam Bigelow (w/Sir Oliver Humperdink) vs. Andre the Giant (captain, w/Bobby "The Brain" Heenan), One Man Gang, King Kong Bundy, "The Natural" Butch Reed (w/Slick) & "Ravishing" Rick Rude

Hogan's team, a well-oiled machine, made frequent tags that threw the team of Andre the Giant off balance. After a double clothesline from "Mr. Wonderful" and Hogan, the captain landed his big legdrop on Reed. After Patera and the One Man Gang simultaneously knocked each other down with clotheslines, the Gang fell on Patera for the pin. Orndorff faced off against Rick Rude. When Orndorff gave the sign for the piledriver, King Kong Bundy clobbered him from behind. Rude used the opportunity to eliminate the Master of the Piledriver. After a powerslam from Don Muraco, Rude was gone, and it was now three versus three.

Hogan, Muraco, and Bigelow stood across from Andre, Bundy, and Gang. Muraco ran into a headbutt from Andre and was pinned by One Man Gang. Bam Bam Bigelow battled both the Gang and Andre, and when he tagged Hogan, the champion and his foe slugged it out. Bundy pulled Hogan out onto the floor. After he slammed Bundy and Gang, Hogan was counted out and told if he did not leave the ring area, the match would be awarded to Andre's team. When King Kong Bundy missed his Avalanche, Bigelow connected with his slingshot splash. Bam Bam continued to fight and miraculously covered the One Man Gang when the Gang missed a Big Splash from the top rope. It was now the Beast from the East against the Eighth Wonder of the World, but, Bam Bam's impressive heroics came to an end when Andre caught him in a double under-hook suplex for the victory.

SOLE SURVIVOR: Andre the Giant

ROYAL RUMBLE

LOCATION: Copps Coliseum, Hamilton, Ontario

DATE: January 24, 1988

The *Royal Rumble* aired live in January on the USA Network. The original *Rumble* featured twenty wrestlers. Two men started alone, and every two minutes another was added. A man is eliminated when he is thrown over the top rope and his feet touch the arena floor. The *Rumble* is one of the "classic five" Pay-Per-View events, along with *WrestleMania, Survivor Series, SummerSlam,* and *King of the Ring.*

Special weightlifting exhibition by Dino Bravo

Canadian strongman Dino Bravo broke the world bench press record, setting the new unofficial record at 715 pounds. The validity of this achievement is questionable, however, as Bravo's spot man was the ethically challenged Jesse Ventura.

Ricky "The Dragon" Steamboat vs. "Ravishing" Rick Rude (w/Bobby "The Brain" Heenan)

Steamboat faced Rude in a match that saw both men exchange holds and trade pinfalls. As Steamboat flew through the air, Rude threw the referee in front of him to bear the brunt of Steamboat's one-handed chop. Rude lifted Steamboat in a backbreaker, hoping to confuse the dazed referee and get the win, but was still disqualified.

World Wrestling Federation World Tag Team Championship, Two-Out-of-Three Falls: The Glamour Girls (champions, w/"Mouth of the South" Jimmy Hart) vs. the Jumping Bomb Angels

It appeared early on that the Glamour Girls—Leilani Kai & Judy Martin—were going to have an easy night. Kai scored the first pinfall on Itsuki with a modified bodyslam, but the Angels' continuity and speed were too much for the ground attack of the Glamour Girls. Itsuki got a sunset flip on Kai, and then the Angels hit Judy Martin with a double dropkick from the top rope.

Hulk Hogan–Andre the Giant contract signing

With President Jack Tunney on hand, Hogan and Andre signed a contract for a championship rematch, to be seen during a special episode of NBC's *Main Event*. Hogan arrived alone, but Andre's evil entourage of Bobby "The Brain" Heenan, "Million Dollar Man" Ted DiBiase, and Virgil were close behind.

"Hacksaw" Jim Duggan beats the odds and wins the *Rumble.*

Two-Out-Of-Three Falls Challenge. The Young Stallions vs. the Islanders (w/Bobby "The Brain" Heenan)

Unfortunately for the Stallions—Paul Roma & Jim Powers—Roma was seriously injured when Tama threw him over the top rope early in the first fall. Roma was counted out, and the first fall went to the Islanders—Haku and Tama. At the start of the second fall, the Islanders focused their attack on Roma's injured leg, and Haku cinched him into a half crab. The pain was too great, and Roma submitted. The Islanders left victors.

The *Royal Rumble*

"Hacksaw" Jim Duggan won the first Royal Rumble match when he eliminated the powerful One Man Gang. Before being eliminated, the Gang eliminated one-fourth of the competion.

PARTICIPANTS IN ORDER OF ENTRY	ORDER OF ELIMINATION
1. Bret Hart	1. Tito Santana, by Bret Hart and Jim Neidhart
2. Tito Santana	2. Boris Zukhov, by Jake Roberts
3. Butch Reed	3. Harley Race, by Don Muraco
4. Jim Neidhart	4. Jim Brunzell, by Nikolai Volkoff
5. Jake Roberts	5. Jim Neidhart, by Hillbilly Jim
6. Harley Race	6. Butch Reed, by Hillbilly Jim
7. Jim Brunzell	7. Sam Houston, by Ron Bass
8. Sam Houston	8. Bret Hart, by Jim Duggan
9. Danny Davis	9. B. Brian Blair, by One Man Gang
10. Boris Zukhov	10. Jake Roberts, by One Man Gang
11. Don Muraco	11. Nikolai Volkoff, by Jim Duggan
12. Nikolai Volkoff	12. Hillbilly Jim, by One Man Gang
13. "Hacksaw" Jim Duggan*	13. Danny Davis, by Jim Duggan
14. Ron Bass	14. Ultimate Warrior, by One Man Gang
15. B. Brian Blair	15. Junkyard Dog, by Dino Bravo
16. Hillbilly Jim	16. Ron Bass, by Don Muraco
17. Dino Bravo	17. Don Muraco, by Dino Bravo and One Man Gang
18. Ultimate Warrior	18. Dino Bravo, by Jim Duggan
19. One Man Gang	19. One Man Gang, by "Hacksaw" Jim Duggan
20. Junkyard Dog	

* Rumble winner

WRESTLEMANIA IV

LOCATION: **Trump Plaza, Atlantic City, NJ**

DATE: **March 27, 1988**

Over 19,000 packed Trump Plaza, while over 10 million people watched on Pay-Per-View. The World Wrestling Federation World Heavyweight Championship was vacant. The only way to crown a new champion was to hold a fourteen-man tournament of the world's top contenders.

TWENTY-MAN OVER-THE-TOP-ROPE BATTLE ROYAL

1. B. Brian Blair
2. Bad News Brown*
3. Boris Zukhov
4. Bret Hart
5. Danny Davis
6. George Steele**
7. Hillbilly Jim
8. Jacques Rougeau
9. Jim Neidhart
10. Jim Powers
11. Jim Brunzell
12. Junkyard Dog
13. Ken Patera
14. Harley Race
15. Nikolai Volkoff
16. Ron Bass
17. Paul Roma
18. Raymond Rougeau
19. Sam Houston
20. Sika

ORDER OF ELIMINATION

1. Sam Houston, by Danny Davis
2. Sika, by Junkyard Dog and Hillbilly Jim
3. Jim Neidhart, by George Steele
4. B. Brian Blair, by Bad News Brown and Jacques Rougeau
5. Raymond Rougeau, by Jim Brunzell
6. Jim Brunzell, by Jacques Rougeau
7. Ron Bass, by Junkyard Dog
8. Hillbilly Jim, by Boris Zukhov and Bad News Brown
9. Danny Davis, by Paul Roma
10. Jim Powers, by Bad News Brown
11. Nikolai Volkoff, by Ken Patera
12. Boris Zukhov, by Ken Patera
13. Ken Patera, by Bad News Brown
14. Jacques Rougeau, by Harley Race
15. Harley Race, by Junkyard Dog
16. Paul Roma, by Bad News Brown
17. Junkyard Dog, by Bad News Brown and Bret Hart
18. Bret Hart, by Bad News Brown

*Battle Royal winner.

**George Steele never officially entered the match.

Bobby Heenan was on the receiving end of Matilda's displeasure over the outcome of the match.

WORLD WRESTLING FEDERATION WORLD HEAVYWEIGHT CHAMPIONSHIP TOURNAMENT

FIRST ROUND

"Hacksaw" Jim Duggan vs. Ted DiBiase (w/Virgil, Andre the Giant)

Duggan opened with heavy rights that sent DiBiase out of the ring. Hacksaw charged into the corner and caught a Million Dollar boot to the face. Both men traded shots. When Duggan set for his three-point stance, his leg was hooked by Andre. Then Duggan caught a roundhouse right from Andre and a knee to the back by DiBiase. DiBiase pinned Hacksaw.

"The Rock" Don Muraco (w/ Superstar Billy Graham) vs. Dino Bravo (w/Frenchie Martin)

Muraco had the advantage until Bravo connected with big elbow drops. Back on his feet, Muraco began to work on Bravo's left leg, getting him in a step-over toe hold. The two powerhouses collided with a double clothesline. Muraco came off the ropes with a flying forearm. To avoid the impact, Bravo pulled the referee into the line of fire. With the referee knocked out, Bravo hooked Muraco in his side suplex. The referee came to and signaled for the bell, and Bravo was disqualified.

Ricky "The Dragon" Steamboat vs. Greg "The Hammer" Valentine (w/"Mouth of the South" Jimmy Hart)

The two men met in the traditional collar-and-elbow tie-up. Steamboat jumped ahead early and utilized his quickness with his signature deep armdrags. Valentine regrouped and began to wear down Steamboat. The Dragon returned with a martial arts attack. When Ricky hit Greg with his flying cross-body, the Hammer changed the momentum and pinned Steamboat.

Randy "Macho Man" Savage (w/Miss Elizabeth) vs. "Natural" Butch Reed

Reed opened up with power moves, keeping Savage grounded. Telegraphing a back-drop attempt, Reed allowed Savage to turn the tables. Going to the top rope, Reed wasted time boasting about his superior masculinity to Elizabeth. Savage caught the Natural on the top rope and threw him to the canvas. The Macho Man made a top trip to the outside and landed his signature flying elbow drop for the win.

Bam Bam Bigelow (w/Sir Oliver Humperdink) vs. One Man Gang (w/Slick)

The One Man Gang took an early advantage with heavy shots to Bigelow. Bam Bam dodged a running corner attack and hit the Gang with rights, lefts, and headbutts. Bam Bam went to bounce off the ropes, but Slick pulled the top rope down, and Bigelow fell out onto the arena floor. Bam Bam was counted out.

Jake "The Snake" Roberts vs. "Ravishing" Rick Rude (w/Bobby "The Brain" Heenan)

This was the last match of the tournament's first round. Roberts took control with a painful left wristlock. Rude turned things around, forcing Roberts into the corner. Jake worked on Rude's left arm and wrist, until both men were eliminated from the tournament. This resulted in a second-round bye for the One Man Gang.

Grudge Match: Ultimate Warrior vs. Hercules (w/Bobby "The Brain" Heenan)

Hercules dropped the Warrior after three consecutive clotheslines. The fight soon made its way onto the floor as they traded power shots, until Hercules performed a reverse atomic drop coming out of the corner. He attempted to lock the Warrior in his full nelson, but failed. Warrior pushed off the middle turnbuckle suddenly, and both men's shoulders were down. As the referee counted, Warrior raised his right shoulder to win the match.

SECOND ROUND

Hulk Hogan vs. Andre the Giant (w/"Million Dollar Man" Ted DiBiase, Virgil, and Bobby "The Brain" Heenan)

Andre attacked Hogan immediately. Hogan came back with hard shots, giving Andre and DiBiase a double noggin-knocker. Andre regained control, catching Hogan in a chokehold. Getting back to his feet, Hogan nailed Andre with a clothesline in the corner, then DiBiase hit Hogan with a chair. After both men used the chair, the referee issued a double disqualification. The winner of the Muraco/DiBiase match would receive a bye into the finals.

Don "The Rock" Muraco vs. "Million Dollar Man" Ted DiBiase

DiBiase attempted to employ stall tactics, but Muraco would have none of it. Bringing DiBiase into the ring the hard way, Muraco was all business. The tables soon turned when DiBiase reversed a slingshot attempt by Muraco, sending him into the steel ring post. Mentor Superstar Billy Graham yelled for Don to get up and fight. DiBiase scored a surprise pinfall when he clotheslined Muraco with the top rope.

Randy "Macho Man" Savage (w/Miss Elizabeth) vs. Greg "The Hammer" Valentine (w/"Mouth of the South" Jimmy Hart)

Valentine connected with hard forearm shots to Savage. He dropped his patented Hammer elbow across Savage's throat. With both men now on the floor, Valentine unloaded on Savage. Savage exploded with a quick offensive, and "The Hammer" went for his infamous figure-four leglock. "Macho Man" got a hold of Valentine and turned him into a small package for the win.

World Wrestling Federation Intercontinental Championship: Brutus "The Barber" Beefcake vs. Honky Tonk Man (champion, w/"The Colonel" Jimmy Hart and Peggy Sue)

After hitting Honky with some rights, Beefcake went for the psychological edge and messed up Honky's hair. The champion was in trouble. Beefcake missed an elbow, and

Honky Tonk beat his challenger. After a botched Shake, Rattle & Roll attempt, the Barber got Honky Tonk in the sleeper hold. The champion's title reign was in serious jeopardy. Jimmy Hart jumped on the ring apron and knocked the referee out with his megaphone. When the referee regained consciousness, he awarded the contest to Brutus via disqualification.

Special Six Man Tag Challenge: The British Bulldogs (w/Matilda) & Koko B. Ware (w/Frankie) vs. the Islanders & Bobby "The Brain" Heenan

The two power men of the respective teams, Davey Boy Smith and Haku, locked up, evenly matched. Koko B. Ware was tagged in and took care of the Islanders. Soon after, "The Brain" took the best of Koko, and the Islanders jumped him. With help from Haku and Tama, Heenan pinned the fallen Koko B. Ware for the victory.

TOURNAMENT SEMI-FINALS

Randy "Macho Man" Savage (w/Miss Elizabeth) v. One Man Gang (w/Slick)

One Man Gang caught Savage in the corner with roundhouse rights. Using his weight, Gang was in control. While the referee was preoccupied, One Man Gang tried to jab Savage with Slick's cane. The referee called for the bell, and One Man Gang was disqualified.

World Wrestling Federation World Tag Team Championship: Strike Force (champions) vs. Demolition (w/Mr. Fuji)

Demolition Smash started off like a jackhammer against Rick Martel. The champions used their speed and superior teamwork to counter Demolition's unrelenting attack. After a fierce clothesline from Ax on the apron, Demolition cut the ring in half. Out of nowhere, Tito hit Ax with his flying forearm, then tagged in Rick Martel. Going for the win, Martel got Smash in the Boston Crab. Ax cracked Martel in the back of the neck with Mr. Fuji's cane. Smash then covered a lifeless Martel for the Tag Team Championship.

World Wrestling Federation World Heavyweight Championship Finals: Randy "Macho Man" Savage (w/Miss Elizabeth) vs. "Million Dollar Man" Ted DiBiase (w/Virgil and Andre the Giant)

Savage and DiBiase exchanged holds and reversals. The Macho Man, realizing that Andre's interference would give his opponent the upper hand, consulted with Miss Elizabeth. She headed to the locker room, returning with Hulk Hogan. Savage was on the receiving end of a terrible beating, yet he displayed incredible resilience. He tried to end the match quickly with his flying elbow drop but missed. DiBiase got Savage in his Million Dollar Dream. As the referee's back was turned to deal with Andre, Hogan nailed DiBiase with a chair. With the Million Dollar Man laid out, Savage leapt from the top rope, landing his trademark flying elbow drop for the win.

SUMMERSLAM 1988

LOCATION: **Madison Square Garden, New York, NY**

DATE: **August 29, 1988**

With scores to settle after *WrestleMania,* the company created *SummerSlam.*

The British Bulldogs (w/Matilda) vs. the Fabulous Rougeau Brothers

The tension between these two teams was evident when Davey Boy Smith attacked Jacques at the bell. It seemed that Dynamite Kid and Davey Boy Smith were set to return to their winning ways. Both teams traded near pinfalls, and the Rougeaus landed a middle rope, belly-to-back-suplex to Dynamite Kid. The Kid eventually powered out of an abdominal stretch and tagged a fresh Davey Boy Smith. The Bulldogs hit Jacques with their signature maneuver. Unfortunately, the bell rang before the pinfall, and the two teams wrestled to a time-limit draw.

Ken Patera vs. Bad News Brown

Showing his ruthless methods in front of his hometown crowd, Bad News Brown Pearl Harbored Patera before the bell even rang. Patera charged out of the corner with a vicious clothesline. After a bear hug, Patera tried to pin Bad News. Failing, Ken attempted to get Brown in his full nelson, then missed a running charge. It was bad news for Patera when Brown connected with his ghetto blaster for the pinfall.

"Ravishing" Rick Rude vs. Junkyard Dog

Rude tried to attack JYD from behind, but the Dog was wise to Rude's tactics and connected with his signature headbutts. Rude rebounded—climbing to the top rope, he pulled his tights down, revealing another pair with the image of Cheryl Roberts on them. A furious Jake Roberts rushed the ring and attacked Rude, and the Junkyard Dog was disqualified.

Powers of Pain (w/the Baron) vs. the Bolsheviks (w/Slick)

The Powers of Pain ran to the ring, sending the Russians to higher ground. Warlord and Barbarian ruled the ring. However, Slick's shenanigans gave his men a temporary advantage. The Bolsheviks hit Warlord with all their weaponry, but they could not get

The Bolsheviks show they can also give pain to the Powers of Pain.

him off his feet. After a running powerslam from the Warlord and a flying top-rope headbutt by the Barbarian, Boris Zukhov was covered for the pinfall.

World Wrestling Federation Intercontinental Championship: Honky Tonk Man (champion, w/"Colonel" Jimmy Hart) vs. Ultimate Warrior

As his music hit, Ultimate Warrior hit the ring and unloaded on Honky Tonk Man. Still in his entrance gear, Honky Tonk was reeling. The Warrior Press Slam and Splash ended the longest Intercontinental Championship reign in record time.

"The Rock" Don Muraco vs. Dino Bravo (w/Frenchie Martin)

The bell rang, and both men hit one another with the same superloaded artillery they used during their first encounter five months prior. The Garden crowd behind him, Muraco was in control. When Frenchie Martin appeared on the apron, his strategy worked. With Muraco distracted, Bravo caught Muraco in his trademark side suplex for the win.

World Wrestling Federation World Tag Team Championship: Demolition (champions, w/Mr. Fuji and Jimmy Hart) vs. the Hart Foundation

Demolition came to the ring with Mr. Fuji and Jimmy Hart in hopes of throwing the Hart Foundation off their game. The bell sounded, and the Excellence of Execution convincingly handled both members of Demolition. Ax & Smash took control and handed Neidhart a beating. After Neidhart chased Jimmy Hart away from the ring, he returned to get the tag from a hurting Bret Hart. The Anvil was unstoppable, and after a powerslam got a near three-count on Smash. Now all four men were in the ring. Neidhart nailed Mr. Fuji off the apron, and Jimmy Hart returned to the ring area. As Bret tried to finish Smash off with a piledriver, Ax creamed Hart with the megaphone. Smash covered Hart for the win.

Koko B. Ware vs. Big Boss Man (w/Slick)

Thanks to Slick's help, the Boss Man jumped Koko and used his weight advantage. Boss Man crushed Koko with an avalanche but refused to pin him. After he missed a top rope splash and another avalanche, the Birdman retaliated with his own offense. Koko nailed the former corrections officer with a series of dropkicks. The Boss Man powered out of the pin attempt, regrouped, and caught Koko in his patented sideslam for the win.

Jake "The Snake" Roberts vs. Hercules

The power of Hercules was shown in the opening minutes of the match. When Jake attempted his DDT, Hercules was able to escape from it and wear Roberts down. As the match progressed, Roberts patiently waited. When Hercules attempted a scoop slam, Roberts slid out of the move and nailed Hercules with the DDT for the one-two-three.

Hulk Hogan & Randy "Macho Man" Savage (w/Miss Elizabeth) vs. Andre the Giant & "Million Dollar Man" Ted DiBiase (w/Virgil), Guest Referee Jesse Ventura.

The bell sounded, and the Mega Powers—Hogan & Savage—were off to a quick start, beating the Million Dollar Man from pillar to post. Hogan tagged in but his adrenaline got the best of him. He attacked Andre on the apron, and the Mega Bucks were able to capitalize. Tagged in, the Macho Man was a house of fire until he missed a charge in the corner. The tide turned once again. DiBiase missed his backward reverse elbow from the middle rope, Savage tagged Hogan in, and he took the fight to the Mega Bucks. All four men were now in the ring. Andre sent Savage and Hogan out on the arena floor. Elizabeth was arguing with the referee when she did the unimaginable and ripped her dress off. This gave her team just enough time to regroup. After Andre was sent to the floor, DiBiase got bodyslammed and hit with Savage's famous flying elbow drop. To ensure victory, Hogan immediately followed up with his legdrop. Hogan pinned DiBiase, and Jesse Ventura started a slow count, After two, Savage slammed Ventura's right arm down for three, and the win.

SURVIVOR SERIES 1988

LOCATION: Richfield Coliseum, Richfield, OH

DATE: November 24, 1988

The second *Survivor Series* amazingly had so many scores to settle, co-captains were added.

Ultimate Warrior (co-captain), Brutus "The Barber" Beefcake (co-captain), Sam Houston, the Blue Blazer & "Jumpin' " Jim Brunzell vs. Honky Tonk Man (co-captain, w/"The Colonel" Jimmy Hart), "Outlaw" Ron Bass (co-captain), Danny Davis, Greg "The Hammer" Valentine & Bad News Brown

The match started as Beefcake and Valentine slugged it out. Danny Davis, tagged in, gave Beefcake everything he'd got. Brutus reversed an Irish Whip, catching Davis. Valentine came back in and worked over Beefcake. The Barber then tagged the Blue Blazer, who worked a quick offense before he tagged another high flyer, Jumpin' Jim Brunzell. He hit Valentine with a dropkick, but the savvy veteran tagged out to Bad News Brown. Bad News beat the stuffing out of Brunzell, and when he attempted a comeback, News raked his eyes. Brown nailed Brunzell with the ghetto blaster and the pinfall. Brutus and Sam Houston worked on the arm of Bad News, but Houston got

DiBiase takes a savage hit from "The Macho Man."

caught in the attack. Valentine mistakenly hit News with a clothesline. Bad News Brown walked out on his team for the second time at *Survivor Series.*

The team led by Warrior and Beefcake were up four to three. After Sam Houston exchanged shots with Ron Bass, Houston, caught in a powerslam, was pinned. Warrior, making his first appearance in the match, cleaned house. After a tag to the Blue Blazer, the aerial attack resumed. The masked man took aim at Bass, Honky Tonk Man, and Valentine. Honky Tonk Man threw Blazer off the ropes, and he crashed down to the mat on his knees. Turning his shin guard around, Valentine locked the Blazer in his figure-four, and the masked acrobat submitted. The Barber, back in the ring, received a beating from the remaining three Superstars. Showing his toughness, Brutus escaped a Shake, Rattle & Roll, kicked out of a pin attempt by Bass, and spoiled Honky Tonk's attempt off the top rope with a fist to the midsection. Brutus got Honky in a sleeper hold. Both men ended up fighting on the floor and were counted out by the referee.

This left the Ultimate Warrior to battle Greg Valentine and Ron Bass. At first, Valentine and Bass were able to capitalize on the numbers advantage, until Warrior leveled both men with ax-handles to the face.

SOLE SURVIVOR: Ultimate Warrior

Powers of Pain, the Rockers, the British Bulldogs, the Hart Foundation & the Young Stallions vs. Demolition (Tag Team champions, w/Mr. Fuji), the Brain Busters (w/Bobby "The Brain" Heenan), the Bolsheviks, the Fabulous Rougeau Brothers (w/"Mouth of the South" Jimmy Hart) & Los Conquistadors.

Davey Boy Smith handled both Conquistador #1 and the Rougeaus. After a tag to Shawn Michaels, who also tagged in his partner Marty Jannetty, the Rockers got nailed by the Bolsheviks and Ax of Demolition. Arn Anderson entered; Jannetty rebounded with a dropkick and ended up trading blows with Tully Blanchard. When Jacques Rougeau missed a flying cross-body, Jannetty tagged Dynamite Kid. The match saw its first team eliminated when Bret Hart rolled Raymond Rougeau up in a small package. Hart now faced Nikolai Volkoff. After some tags on the Powers of Pain team, Hart was on the receiving end of a series of Demolition double ax-handles. The World Tag Team Champions were pulverizing their opponents, and became stronger as the match went on.

Jim Powers hit Boris Zukhov with a flying cross-body, but the Bolshevik surprised everyone when he rolled through the move and pinned the Young Stallion. Last year's survivors were now eliminated. Shawn Michaels returned and got a near pinfall on Zukhov after a middle-rope fist drop. The Barbarian and Ax exchanged blows, Michaels catching Volkoff with a shot to the abdomen. Then Marty Jannetty was tagged in and pinned Volkoff with a sunset flip. Smash quickly came in, and Jannetty was punished for his pinfall by one of the Conquistadors, Ax, and Arn Anderson. Jannetty tagged out to a fresh Davey Boy Smith. A cagey Tully Blanchard tagged in Ax. Demolition took it to Barbarian and traded tags with Los Conquistadors and the Brain Busters that prevented Barbarian from making a tag. The tables turned when Barbarian caught Anderson with a boot to the side of the head and tagged in Marty Jannetty. The Rockers and the Hart Foundation worked together against the Brain Busters. When Jannetty and Anderson brawled, their partners got involved. All four men were disqualified and fought all the way back to the locker room.

Dynamite Kid and Smash entered the ring. Barbarian, Warlord, and Davey Boy Smith scrapped with the Tag Team Champions. The Dynamite Kid was eliminated after a clothesline from Smash, and the Powers of Pain were left to battle Demolition and Los Conquistadors. After the Warlord missed a corner attack, Demolition pounded away on him. Mr. Fuji pulled down the top rope, and Smash was counted out. Ax and

Fuji argued, and Ax was hit with Fuji's cane. Ax slammed Fuji to the floor, and the Powers of Pain made the save. Fuji remained in their corner. Los Conquistadors were no match for the Powers of Pain, and after getting tripped up by Mr. Fuji, Barbarian came off the top with a headbutt for the win.

SURVIVORS: Powers of Pain

Jake "The Snake" Roberts, "Hacksaw" Jim Duggan, Scott Casey, Tito Santana & Ken Patera vs. Andre the Giant (w/Bobby "The Brain" Heenan), Dino Bravo (w/Frenchie Martin), "Ravishing" Rick Rude, Mr. Perfect & Harley Race

Ken Patera displayed his raw power against Rick Rude, Dino Bravo, and Mr. Perfect. When he tagged Jake Roberts, the crowd went wild. The Snake worked on the arm of Mr. Perfect before he brought in Tito Santana. Ken Patera was eliminated courtesy of a Rude Awakening. Rick, Andre, and Harley Race all worked over Scott Casey. Casey got caught in Bravo's signature sideslam, and the Roberts and Duggan team was at a three-to-five disadvantage.

Tito Santana unloaded on Dino, Bravo, and Mr. Perfect. The pace of the match changed when "Hacksaw" Jim Duggan got hit with a headbutt from Andre on the ring apron. Santana returned, Harley Race missed a clothesline, and Tito connected with his flying forearm for the pinfall. Andre made his first official entry into the match and chocked the life out of Santana. Acting on instinct, Tito got himself over Andre for a sunset flip. Andre flattened Santana for the pinfall.

Down two to four, the team of Roberts and Duggan needed to act fast. Hacksaw came in and sent Andre into the ropes with a powerful clothesline. Duggan and Roberts capitalized on the situation until Andre escaped and beat Jake. The remaining members of the opposition all laid into Roberts. Jake fought back, hitting Dino Bravo with a short-arm clothesline, but his DDT attempt was thwarted by Rick Rude. The Snake tagged Hacksaw in, who whaled at Bravo with roundhouse rights. When Frenchie Martin interfered, Duggan grabbed his trusty two-by-four, nailed Bravo with it, and was disqualified. Jake "The Snake" Roberts was alone, battling against four of World Wrestling Federation's most lethal Superstars.

As Roberts squared off with Mr. Perfect, Hennig, Rude, and Bravo dominated Roberts. Rick Rude forgot who he was in the ring with. "The Snake" pulled Rude's tights and planted him in the canvas with the DDT for the pinfall. A rested Andre came in and attacked Roberts from behind with a choke. After he disregarded the referee's warnings, refusing to break the chokehold, Andre was disqualified. Not wanting to make the mistakes of his teammates, Mr. Perfect came into the ring and pinned Roberts.

SURVIVORS: Mr. Perfect, Dino Bravo

Hulk Hogan, Randy "Macho Man" Savage, Hercules, Koko B. Ware & Hillbilly Jim vs. "Million Dollar Man" Ted DiBiase, Akeem, Big Boss Man, Haku & the Red Rooster

Savage locked up with his nemesis, the Million Dollar Man. They traded holds and blows until the Macho Man got the best of the exchange. The mighty Hercules entered the ring, and DiBiase tagged the Red Rooster. The Mega Powers showed great teamwork when Hogan and his protégé Hillbilly Jim hit Haku with a double boot to the face. Koko B. Ware nailed Red Rooster with a top-rope missile dropkick. Ware tagged in Hogan, who dropped Rooster with a boot, then set him up with a scoop slam. Perched on the top rope, the Macho Man landed his trademark flying elbow drop, and the Red Rooster was eliminated.

Savage beat on King Haku. Escaping from a Hercules standing side headlock, Haku tagged "The African Dream" Akeem. Hercules fought the monster off and tagged Hillbilly Jim. Akeem ended Hillbilly's night with a clothesline and Air Africa splash. After the Birdman flew from the top rope, he tagged in Hogan, and after quick strikes from Macho Man and Hercules, Koko was brought back in. The Big Boss Man caught Ware in his devastating sideslam for the one-two-three. The Savage and Hogan team now faced a three-to-four deficit.

Hogan endured a lengthy beating from the Boss Man, Haku, and DiBiase until he retaliated with roundhouse rights and an atomic drop. Hogan tagged Hercules, and he rocked DiBiase with a kneelift and a clothesline. Distracted by Virgil, Hercules got rolled up near the ropes by the Million Dollar Man and was eliminated. As DiBiase basked in his achievement, he was rolled up in turn and pinned by Savage. Haku entered the ring and attacked both Savage and Hogan, handing things over to the Big Boss Man. Though he looked to be in control, Haku did not attempt a pin after he sideslammed Hogan. From the top rope, Boss Man missed a Big Splash. This allowed Hogan to tag in a pumped-up "Macho Man." Due to interference from Slick, Savage's offensive campaign was cut short, and he was now caught in Big Boss Man's bear hug.

Outside the ring, Slick taunted Miss Elizabeth and forced Hulk Hogan to make the save. The Twin Towers ambushed Hogan and handcuffed him to the ropes. The Boss Man's merciless attack got him counted out by the referee. In a fit of rage, Boss Man beat Hogan with his nightstick. Then Boss Man entered the ring and attacked the Macho Man, who was handling both Akeem and Haku. The official disqualified Akeem, but not before he crushed Savage with the Air Africa splash. It was now down to two men, and Haku took full advantage of Savage's severely weakened state. As Haku pounded on the Macho Man, Slick and Heenan were forced to leave ringside.

During the commotion, Elizabeth was able to get the keys to the handcuffs back and free Hogan. When Haku connected with a reverse crescent kick, Savage was sent flying into the corner and unintentionally tagged Hogan. Hammering away on Haku, Hogan delivered a scoop slam, a big boot, and his trademark legdrop to pin Haku.

SURVIVORS: Hulk Hogan, Randy "Macho Man" Savage

ROYAL RUMBLE 1989

LOCATION: **The Summit, Houston, TX**

DATE: **January 15, 1989**

The second *Royal Rumble* was poised to eclipse all the stellar achievements of its predecessor. This year's event was the *Rumble's* Pay-Per-View debut. Every World Wrestling Federation Superstar wanted entry into what was now the most famous battle royal in wrestling.

Six Man Tag—Two-Out-of-Three Falls: The Hart Foundation & "Hacksaw" Jim Duggan vs. the Rougeau Brothers (w/"Mouth of the South" Jimmy Hart) & Dino Bravo (w/Frenchie Martin)

After a Dino Bravo side suplex, the Rougeaus connected with their Bombs Away and scored the first pinfall on Bret Hart. Dual slingshot splashes landed on Raymond from the Harts. Hacksaw dropped a big elbow and picked up the all-important second pinfall. A battle of Canadian pride ensued between Dino Bravo and Bret Hart. When Hacksaw leveled Bravo with his two-by-four, the Hit Man picked up the win.

Women's World Championship: Rockin' Robin (champion) vs. Judy Martin

From the opening bell it was the aerial moves of Robin against the mat skills of Martin. On the middle rope, Rockin' Robin leaped off and hit Martin with a flying cross-body to retain the title.

The Super Posedown: Ultimate Warrior vs. "Ravishing" Rick Rude (w/Bobby "The Brain" Heenan)

Striking poses to display his incredible physique, Rude became visibly perturbed by boos from the crowd. The response to Warrior became louder with each pose. Rude reached his boiling point and attacked Warrior from behind, knocking him cold. Rude taunted the fallen Intercontinental Champion. When the Warrior came to, he attacked everyone in the ring and charged to the locker room to search for Rude and his manager, Heenan.

A classic grudge match between Race and Haku.

Battle for the Crown: Haku (w/Bobby "The Brain" Heenan) vs. Harley Race

The technically sound and notoriously tough Harley Race threw everything he had at Haku. Haku retaliated with combination power and martial arts moves. Race climbed to the top rope for his signature diving headbutt but lost his gamble. After a sidekick to the head by Haku, he also lost the match.

The Royal Rumble

Now a thirty-man fight, this *Royal Rumble* was harder than the first to win.

ORDER OF ENTRY

1. Ax
2. Smash
3. Andre the Giant
4. Mr. Perfect
5. Ronnie Garvin
6. Greg Valentine
7. Jake Roberts
8. Ron Bass
9. Shawn Michaels
10. Bushwacker Butch
11. Honky Tonk Man
12. Tito Santana
13. Bad News Brown
14. Marty Jannetty
15. Randy Savage
16. Arn Anderson
17. Tully Blanchard
18. Hulk Hogan
19. Bushwacker Luke
20. Koko B. Ware
21. Warlord
22. Big Boss Man
23. Akeem
24. Brutus Beefcake
25. Red Rooster
26. Barbarian
27. "Big" John Studd*
28. Hercules
29. Rick Martel
30. Ted DiBiase

*Rumble winner

ORDER OF ELIMINATION

1. Smash, by Andre the Giant
2. Ronnie Garvin, by Andre the Giant
3. Jake Roberts, by Andre the Giant
4. Ax, by Mr. Perfect
5. Andre the Giant, by himself
6. Honky Tonk Man, by Tito Santana and Bushwacker Butch
7. Ron Bass, by Shawn Michaels and Marty Jannetty
8. Greg Valentine, by Randy Savage
9. Shawn Michaels, by Randy Savage and Arn Anderson
10. Marty Jannetty, by Arn Anderson and Tully Blanchard
11. Mr. Perfect, by Hulk Hogan
12. Tito Santana, by Arn Anderson
13. Bushwacker Butch, by Bad News Brown
14. Koko B. Ware, by Hulk Hogan
15. Bushwacker Luke, by Hulk Hogan
16. Arn Anderson, by Hulk Hogan
17. Tully Blanchard, by Hulk Hogan
18. Warlord, by Hulk Hogan
19. Bad News Brown, by Hulk Hogan
20. Randy Savage, by Hulk Hogan
21. Hulk Hogan, by Akeem and Big Boss Man
22. Big Boss Man, by Hulk Hogan
23. Red Rooster, by Ted DiBiase
24. Brutus Beefcake, by Ted DiBiase and Barbarian
25. Hercules, by Ted DiBiase and Barbarian
26. Barbarian, by Rick Martel
27. Rick Martel, by Akeem
28. Akeem, by "Big" John Studd
29. Ted DiBiase, by "Big" John Studd

WRESTLEMANIA V

LOCATION: Trump Plaza, Atlantic City, NJ

DATE: April 2, 1989

This was the second year wrestling's biggest event emanated from Trump Plaza.

Hercules vs. "King" Haku (w/Bobby "The Brain" Heenan)

Hercules entered and cleared the ring with his fifteen-foot steel chain. While he measured the King with elbow drops, Hercules was distracted by his former manager and clothesline to the floor. Herc hit Haku with a belly-to-back suplex. Using a bridge for the pin, Hercules got his shoulder up in time for the victory.

The Rockers vs. the Twin Towers (w/Slick)

The Rockers utilized their agility, continuity, and high-flying maneuvers against the mighty Twin Towers, Akeem and Big Boss Man. The Towers used their sizable weight advantages to ground the aerialists. A brief comeback by the Rockers saw them hit Akeem with a double shoulder tackle off the middle ropes. The Boss Man received a double dropkick. A Big Splash from "The African Dream" Akeem handed the Rockers a crushing loss.

Brutus "The Barber" Beefcake vs. "Million Dollar Man" Ted DiBiase (w/Virgil)

Beefcake was unstoppable, stunning the Million Dollar Man early. DiBiase took a breather when out on the floor. Eventually, DiBiase locked Beefcake in his Million Dollar Dream. After Brutus made it to the ropes, he cinched DiBiase in a sleeper. Virgil made his presence felt and allowed his man to regain the advantage. Eventually, both men fought on the arena floor to a double countout.

The Bushwackers vs. the Fabulous Rougeau Brothers (w/"Mouth of the South" Jimmy Hart)

Luke and Butch threw the Rougeaus off course with their unconventional wrestling methods. Jacques and Raymond used effective double-team maneuvers, but they took their eyes off their opponents. The Bushwackers hit Raymond with their signature battering ram. In a major upset, the Wackers used the double stomachbreaker for the win.

Blue Blazer vs. Mr. Perfect

The Blue Blazer took control from the onset, striking Mr. Perfect with a series of offensive moves that sent him reeling to the floor. Perfect's winning streak hung in the balance. The Blazer missed a Big Splash from the top rope. Mr. Perfect collected himself and scored the win with his Perfect Plex.

Determined to keep his title, the Warrior tries to crush Rude.

World Wrestling Federation World Tag Team Championship: Demolition (champions) vs. the Powers of Pain & Mr. Fuji

The champions—Ax & Smash—took the challengers off their feet with quick tags and crushing power moves. The Powers of Pain got back into the match when Ax went after Mr. Fuji. Warlord & Barbarian brought Fuji in only when a Demolition member was laid out on the canvas. Their strategy backfired when Fuji missed a Bonzai Drop from the top rope. Ax tagged an anxious Smash, who erupted with rights and lefts. Trying to throw his ceremonial salt in Smash's eyes, Fuji hit Warlord. Demolition then crashed down on Fuji to retain the titles.

"Rugged" Ronnie Garvin vs. Dino Bravo (w/Frenchie Martin)

Bravo clubbed Garvin from behind, using his power to neutralize his opponent. All of a sudden, Garvin exploded and had Bravo on his heels. Bravo came back to get Garvin in his finishing side suplex for the victory.

Strike Force vs. the Brain Busters (w/Bobby "The Brain" Heenan)

Strike Force—Tito Santana & Rick Martel—looked to bust the match open when they cleared the ring with double dropkicks. Martel went for an early submission with his Boston Crab on Arn Anderson, and Tito followed up with a figure-four on Tully Blanchard. After Anderson broke up consecutive pinfall attempts, Santana inadvertently caught Martel with his flying forearm. Victim to the double-team tactics of Anderson and Blanchard, Tito finally fought back. However, Martel refused to make the tag and left his longtime partner alone in the ring. The Busters planted Santana with a crippling spike piledriver for the win.

Jake "The Snake" Roberts vs. Andre the Giant (w/Bobby "The Brain" Heenan), with Special Guest Referee "Big" John Studd

Andre tore the cover off one of the turnbuckles in his corner and immediately threw Roberts headfirst into the steel. The Giant used his size, strength, and weight to abuse Roberts. Jake fought back, and Andre was tangled in the ropes. Thanks to his manager, Andre regained the upper hand and sent the Snake to the outside. Andre began to argue with John Studd. Ted DiBiase ran out from the back and tried to steal the snake Damien. Jake and Damien made the save and cleared the ring. The Snake was the victor via disqualification.

The Hart Foundation vs. the Honky Tonk Man & Greg "The Hammer" Valentine (w/"The Colonel" Jimmy Hart)

Bret Hart dominated and sent Honky Tonk and Valentine crashing to the mat. After a missed elbow, Honky Tonk and Valentine worked the Hit Man over until Hart tagged in his partner, Jim Neidhart. The Anvil handed out one beatdown after the other. Bret finally executed the Honky Tonk Man with a megaphone shot to the face.

World Wrestling Federation Intercontinental Championship: Ultimate Warrior (champion) vs. "Ravishing" Rick Rude (w/Bobby "The Brain" Heenan)

Ultimate Warrior rushed the ring and manhandled Rick Rude. The challenger was fading fast until the Warrior missed a splash. Rude executed a piledriver and chinbreaker, then landed a Russian Leg Sweep for a near pinfall. Warrior fought back, but thanks to quick thinking from Rude and help from Heenan, the new Intercontinental Champion was Rick Rude.

"Hacksaw" Jim Duggan vs. Bad News Brown

The match turned into an all-out street fight. When Bad News got control, the fight went out onto the floor. Hacksaw ducked an attempted ghetto blaster. Once Duggan connected with his three-point-stance clothesline, Brown brought a chair into the ring. Hacksaw introduced his two-by-four, and both men fought to a double disqualification.

Red Rooster vs. Bobby "The Brain" Heenan (w/Brooklyn Brawler)

Heenan came to the ring holding his ribs and was seconded by henchman-for-hire the Brooklyn Brawler. Rooster made quick work of his former mentor/manager. It was all over when Heenan missed a shoulder tackle and rammed right into the steel ring post.

World Wrestling Federation World Heavyweight Championship: Randy "Macho Man" Savage (champion) vs. Hulk Hogan

From the first collar-and-elbow tie-up, Hogan used his power to set the tone for the match. Savage resorted to less than admirable ring tactics, and Hogan was busted open. Savage jumped out of the ring, had choice words for Miss Elizabeth, and forced her to leave the ring area. Hogan sent Savage to the floor after an Irish Whip into the corner. The Macho Man rebounded and landed his double ax-handle across Hogan's throat as he was pressed against the steel barricade. Poised on the top rope, Savage dropped his famous flying elbow. It appeared *Hulkamania* was on its last legs. As the referee raised his hand to make the final three-count, Hogan launched Savage off him, now impervious to the Macho Man's shots. Hogan connected with his signature legdrop to become World Wrestling Federation World Heavyweight Champion for the second time.

SUMMERSLAM 1989

LOCATION: **The Meadowlands, East Rutherford, NJ**

DATE: **August 28, 1989**

The second *SummerSlam* saw a fantastic lineup of grudge matches and evenly matched contests.

The Hart Foundation vs. the Brain Busters (w/Bobby "The Brain" Heenan)

Bret Hart worked Tully Blanchard's arm in a series of textbook armdrags. Arn Anderson tried to interfere. Hit Man tagged in Jim Neidhart, who also went to work on Arn's arm. After getting double-teamed in the corner, Anderson tagged Blanchard. After a brief Brain Busters double-team, the Hit Man tossed both Blanchard and Anderson from the ring. Bret whipped Jim into the corner, but Arn moved his partner out of the way. Neidhart crashed into the corner, and Anderson stomped the life out of him. When Arn came off the ropes, Bret kneed the Enforcer in the back. Neidhart tagged Bret, and the Hit Man destroyed both men. After Anderson was caught trying to interfere, all four men brawled in the ring. Hart slingshot Neidhart into Blanchard, then Neidhart powerslammed the Hit Man onto Tully Blanchard. With the referee out of position—thanks to Bobby Heenan—Neidhart went after the Weasel. Anderson dropped a double ax-handle from the middle rope to the back of Hart's neck. Anderson pinned Hart and covered his head so the referee didn't know he was not the legal man. A win for Brain Busters.

"The American Dream" Dusty Rhodes vs. Honky Tonk Man (w/"The Colonel" Jimmy Hart

Honky Tonk tried to attack Rhodes. To get under Honky's skin, Dusty messed up his hair. "The American Dream" had total control until "The Colonel" distracted Dusty. This allowed Honky Tonk time to regroup and nail Rhodes in the midsection with a megaphone. Slowing the pace of the match down, Honky Tonk wore down Dusty with a rear chinlock. Finally on his feet, Dusty missed a corner attack and Honky threw him into the referee. With the official knocked out, Honky tied Dusty up and called for his guitar. Their plan backfired when Dusty moved out of the way and Hart smashed the guitar over Honky Tonk's head. Rhodes dropped his famous big elbow and got the win.

The Red Rooster vs. Mr. Perfect

Both men met in the center of the ring, and a shoving match ensued. Perfect took control with an armdrag, hip toss, and fireman's carry. The Rooster collapsed when he tried

Honky Tonk Man knows he has to get a quick win or the wily Rhodes will beat him.

to reverse a slam attempt. Perfect connected with a standing dropkick and locked the Rooster in the Perfect Plex for the win.

The Rockers & Tito Santana vs. the Fabulous Rougeaus (w/"Mouth of the South" Jimmy Hart) & Rick Martel (w/Slick)

The Rockers and Santana cleaned house. When the villains regrouped, each of them tangled with Marty Jannetty. The Rougeaus focused on Santana's back. Martel entered and stomped on his former partner. The three Canadians kept Tito in their corner and worked on his back with illegal double-team moves. After Santana surprised Raymond with a sunset flip, Rougeau returned with a sleeper hold. Attempting another double-team move, Jacques accidentally nailed Raymond with a high knee. Finally, Santana tagged in Shawn Michaels, who unloaded on the Rougeaus. Santana hit Martel with his flying forearm. After Marty Jannetty chased Jimmy Hart, Jacques clubbed Marty from behind. Martel nailed Jannetty and illegally pinned him for the win.

World Wrestling Federation Intercontinental Championship: "Ravishing" Rick Rude (champion, w/Bobby "The Brain" Heenan) vs. Ultimate Warrior

The Warrior raced to the ring and dominated with his intensity. The Warrior press-slammed Rude out of the ring and onto the arena floor. Warrior's dominance continued until Rude caught him on the top rope and sent him crashing onto the turnbuckle. Rude attacked the Warrior's back with forearm smashes and a standing vertical suplex, but the Warrior broke the Rude Awakening. When Rude resorted to a sleeper hold, the Warrior countered with a jawbreaker. Both wrestlers were out. Warrior returned with several clotheslines that almost decapitated the champion. Warrior hit Rude with a piledriver and a powerslam, but he could not pin him. Rude got his knees up during the Warrior's splash and followed up with a fist drop from the top rope. "Rowdy" Roddy Piper appeared at ringside and entered a war of words with the champion. With Rude's attention on Piper, Warrior regrouped, and German-suplexed Rude from the middle turnbuckle. Connecting with a flying shoulder tackle, a gorilla press slam, and finally a Warrior Splash. Ultimate Warrior was the new Intercontinental Champion.

Demolition & "Hacksaw" Jim Duggan vs. the Twin Towers (w/Slick) & Andre the Giant (w/Bobby "The Brain" Heenan)

Duggan wasted no time getting the upper hand for his team. As he tagged out, Demolition worked on Akeem's arm. After a rake to the eyes of Ax, Akeem tagged in the Big Boss Man, who brawled with both Ax and Smash. All three members beat on Ax. Akeem missed a charge in the corner, and Ax tagged in Smash. Displaying his raw power, Smash slammed the Twin Towers one after the other. Then Andre the Giant took all the air out of the Demolition member, and a six-man scramble ensued. With the referee turned away, Duggan walloped Akeem with his two-by-four. Smash covered Akeem for the win.

Hercules vs. Greg "The Hammer" Valentine

Special ring announcer Ronnie Garvin insulted Valentine, and Hercules blindsided the distracted Hammer with furious fists and a scoop slam. Valentine went to the outside, then he and Garvin stared one another down. Hercules rolled up Valentine and almost pinned him, then nearly caught him in a double ax-handle off the top rope. The resourceful Valentine lured Hercules into the corner, pinning him with his foot on the ropes for the win.

Jimmy "Superfly" Snuka vs. "Million Dollar Man" Ted DiBiase (w/Virgil)

In typical "Million Dollar Man" fashion, DiBiase attempted to jump Snuka from behind. Snuka sent wrestling's tycoon over the top rope with an atomic drop. The resourceful DiBiase caught Snuka in a clothesline across the top rope, followed by a vertical suplex. "Superfly" retaliated with chops and a diving headbutt off the top rope. Making another climb to the outside, Snuka was distracted by Virgil. An attack from the Million Dollar Man resulted in Superfly getting counted out. A fired-up Snuka cleared the ring and landed his Superfly Splash on Virgil.

Hulk Hogan & Brutus "The Barber" Beefcake (w/Miss Elizabeth) vs. Randy "Macho Man" Savage (w/Sensational Sherri) & Zeus

When both teams entered the ring, a brawl erupted and Beefcake sent Savage out. Hogan hit Zeus with everything he had, but he didn't budge. Zeus got Hogan in a choke, and when Beefcake tried to break the hold, he ended up in a bear hug. Both Savage and Zeus assaulted Hogan and kept him in their corner. The fate of the Hogan Beefcake duo looked bleak until the Macho Man missed a splash off the rope. Hogan tagged in a fresh Beefcake. The Barber unloaded on Savage and got him in the sleeper hold. Macho Man broke the hold and tagged in Zeus, but Beefcake got him in a sleeper too. When the referee was distracted, Savage nailed Beefcake with Sherri's loaded purse. The Barber was down, Savage went after Elizabeth, and Zeus choked the life out of Beefcake. Beefcake regrouped and tagged Hogan, who pounded away at his former partner until Zeus attacked. Savage then climbed to the top rope and dropped his flying elbow. Unstoppable, Hogan blasted Zeus with Sherri's purse. He followed up with a bodyslam and his patented legdrop for the win.

SURVIVOR SERIES 1989

LOCATION: **The Rosemont Horizon, Chicago, IL**

DATE: **November 23, 1989**

The third *Survivor Series* saw the final chapter in the Hulk Hogan-Zeus saga.

The Dream Team: "The American Dream" Dusty Rhodes, Red Rooster, Brutus "The Barber" Beefcake & Tito Santana vs. the Enforcers: Big Boss Man, Bad News Brown, "The Model" Rick Martel & Honky Tonk Man

Santana and Martel locked up, then it was Rhodes and Big Boss Man. "The Dream" tagged in Beefcake, Boss Man tagged in Honky Tonk. Honky worked on Brutus's leg. The first man eliminated was Santana, pinned by Martel. Dusty Rhodes came in and took it to "The Model," connecting with a dropkick and following up with an elbow. The Red Rooster landed in a Boss Man bear hug. Rooster bit the Boss Man to escape. After Rooster brought Bad News Brown in the hard way, News retaliated and set up a double-team. Accidentally hit in the face by Boss Man, Bad News left for the second consecutive year. "The Barber" now was battling the Boss Man. After a tag to the Honky Tonk Man, Beefcake caught him with a high knee and eliminated him. Beefcake fought out of a rear chin lock from Martel, pinning him with a variation on a sunset flip. The Dream Team now held a three-to-one advantage. After a tag from the Barber, Red Rooster mounted an offense against Boss Man, who caught him in a sideslam. Rhodes and Beefcake tagged in, keeping a fresh man in the ring. Rhodes hammered away at Boss Man. Ducking a clothesline, Rhodes came at the former prison guard with a flying cross-body. With the referee's three-count, it was victory for the Dream Team.

SURVIVORS: Dusty Rhodes & Brutus "The Barber" Beefcake

The 4x4s: "Hacksaw" Jim Duggan, "Rugged" Ronnie Garvin, Hercules & Bret "Hit Man" Hart vs. the King's Court: "Macho King" Randy Savage, Dino Bravo, Earthquake & Greg "The Hammer" Valentine

When Savage saw Ronnie Garvin was his opponent, he tagged in Hacksaw Duggan. Hercules came in and soon tagged in Bret Hart. Bret worked on Valentine's arm and brought Hacksaw back. Garvin came in with chops and a sleeper hold. Valentine made it back to his corner and tagged in Dino Bravo. Unloading on Garvin, Bravo missed an elbow, allowing Ronnie to tag Hercules. When Bravo reversed an Irish Whip, he sent Hercules into the corner. Bravo tagged Earthquake, who crushed Hercules for the pin.

Duggan came in and tried to get Quake down, Hart got on all fours, and Earthquake fell over him and onto the mat. Garvin entered the match, hitting Earthquake with everything he had. Quake tagged in Dino Bravo, who worked Garvin over. The Hammer was tagged in. Garvin tagged Duggan, who leveled the Hammer, eliminating him. Dino Bravo jumped in, hitting Duggan from behind. Hacksaw tagged Garvin, who delivered his Garvin Stomp. He then tagged in the Hit Man, who convincingly handled both the Macho King and Bravo. Garvin's Irish Whip was reversed, and he was caught in Bravo's side suplex for the three-count.

The 4x4s were down to two members. Hart ended up in a Bravo bear hug. Then Bret was triple-teamed in the King's Court corner. Bravo tagged Savage, who landed the flying elbow drop for the pin. Duggan took the fight to the three villains and threw Savage and Bravo into Earthquake. Duggan tried to fight back, but went over the ropes after Queen Sherri pulled them down. Hacksaw was eliminated.

SURVIVORS: "Macho King" Randy Savage, Dino Bravo & Earthquake

Roddy's Rowdies: "Rowdy" Roddy Piper, Jimmy "Superfly" Snuka & The Bushwackers vs. the Rude Brood: "Ravishing" Rick Rude, Mr. Perfect & the Rougeau Brothers

Mr. Perfect Pearl Harbored Cousin Luke. He missed a knee drop, and all the Rowdies bit him. It was Jacques Rougeau against Jimmy Snuka. Superfly introduced Jacques to a flying headbutt and then the Superfly Splash for the pinfall. Rick Rude jumped Snuka and tagged Mr. Perfect. Piper atomic-dropped Perfect and tagged Raymond Rougeau. When Rougeau telegraphed a back-drop attempt, Piper connected with a piledriver and eliminated him.

Mr. Perfect and "Ravishing" Rick were left to beat the odds against the Roddy Rowdies. Perfect got beaten by Piper and the Bushwackers. Cousin Butch paused to greet the crowd, and Mr. Perfect rolled him up for the pin. Perfect tagged in Rude, who got hit by Butch off the top rope. Cousin Luke was planted on the canvas with a Rude Awakening for the one-two-three. It was Perfect and Rude versus Piper and Snuka. Piper took it to both Perfect and Rude, but when he speared Rude out of the ring, Piper and he were counted out. Snuka got caught in the Perfect Plex and was eliminated.

SOLE SURVIVOR: Mr. Perfect

The Ultimate Warriors: Ultimate Warrior, Jim "The Anvil" Neidhart & the Rockers vs. the Heenan Family: Andre the Giant, Bobby "The Brain" Heenan, Haku & Arn Anderson

The Rockers jumped Arn Anderson and Haku. Andre smashed Michaels and Jannetty's heads together and choked Jim Neidhart. The Warrior blitzed the ring, clotheslined Andre from behind, sent him over the top rope, and the Giant was counted out. Warrior soon tagged in the Anvil, who traded shots with Haku. Arn Anderson was brought in, and when the Anvil went after him, Jim was hit with a Haku thrust kick and eliminated. The Rockers double-teamed Haku until they gave him and Double A superkicks. Haku caught Marty Jannetty with a martial arts kick. The Brain tagged in and stomped on the Rocker for the pin.

Now it was Arn Anderson in with the Warrior, who tagged in Shawn Michaels and threw him on top of Arn for a near pinfall. Arn tagged in Haku. Shawn Michaels hit Haku with a flying cross-body and eliminated him. It was Ultimate Warrior and Shawn Michaels versus Arn Anderson and Bobby Heenan. Arn traded rights and lefts with Michaels. Shawn Michaels was caught with a spinebuster and eliminated. Ultimate Warrior fought Arn Anderson, hoisting him up in the gorilla press slam and pinning him. The Warrior threw Heenan into the corner. Heenan tried to walk out, but Warrior dragged him back and leveled him with a flying shoulder block and a splash for the win.

SOLE SURVIVOR: Ultimate Warrior

The *Hulkamaniacs*: Hulk Hogan, Demolition & Jake Roberts (w/Damien) vs. the Million Dollar Team: "Million Dollar Man" Ted DiBiase, Zeus & Powers of Pain

Jake "The Snake" Roberts took Damien, his snake, and slid him into the ring. Zeus yelled for Hogan to face him. Tagged in by Roberts, Hogan met Zeus for a stare-down. After an eye-rake and a bodyslam, Zeus popped up. Choking Hogan, Zeus refused to break the hold, and the referee disqualified him. DiBiase entered the match and hammered away at Hogan, who caught DiBiase with a boot and tagged the Snake. DiBiase got hammered by Demolition and Hogan at the same time. As Ax battled both Warlord and Barbarian, he was tripped by former manager Mr. Fuji. The Warlord then dropped an elbow for the pin. Both teams were even at three.

Smash came in and fought until he got a thumb to the eye and a Barbarian boot to the face. After a blind tag from DiBiase, Barbarian nailed Smash with a top-rope clothesline. The Million Dollar Team regained control of the match. A Hogan slam on Barbarian was stopped by the Warlord. The Powers of Pain then double-teamed Hogan, trying to render him immobile with a spike piledriver. Since they did not adhere to the referee's count, both men were disqualified. Hogan was slapped into DiBiase's Million Dollar Dream. As Hogan's arm was about to drop for the third time, Roberts broke the hold. A tenacious DiBiase put Hogan back in the hold, but he broke it by ramming his opponent into the corner. Roberts was tagged in and delivered his wicked short-arm clothesline to DiBiase. Roberts dragged Virgil into the ring and gave him the DDT. DiBiase landed a Million Dollar Fist Drop on Jake, and the Snake was eliminated.

The Million Dollar Man then hit the motionless Hogan with elbows. Hogan rose from a reverse chin lock, and the two clotheslined one another as they came off the ropes. DiBiase blocked an atomic drop attempt and got Hogan into a belly-to-back suplex. Hogan nailed the Million Dollar Man with a boot to the face and his signature legdrop for the win.

SOLE SURVIVOR: Hulk Hogan

Andre turns his title
over to DiBiase in front
of a stunned crowd.

TITLE HISTORY

The World Wrestling Federation Heavyweight Championship

"Holiday Jeers"

December 26, 1983—the Iron Sheik defeats Bob Backlund

The Sheik attacked Backlund's weak back. Locked in the dreaded camel clutch, Backlund was trapped. The champion's manager, Arnold Skaaland, threw in the towel, ending the match, though Backlund didn't give up, nor was he pinned.

"A Cultural Movement Conceived"

January 23, 1984—Hulk Hogan defeats the Iron Sheik

Showing his superhuman strength, Hogan rose from the mat during the Sheik's Camel Clutch and ran backward into the turnbuckle, crushing the Sheik. Hogan then hit his legdrop. Hogan's historic title reign would last over four years.

"A Sinister Plot"

February 5, 1988—Andre the Giant defeats Hulk Hogan

This was a power struggle from the opening bell. After a suplex, Andre went for a cover, and although Hogan got his shoulder up, the referee counted three and awarded the match to Andre, who handed the championship over to "Million Dollar Man" Ted DiBiase. According to President Jack Tunney, when Andre handed the belt over to DiBiase, he vacated the title.

"Beating the Odds"

March 27, 1988—Randy "Macho Man" Savage defeats "Million Dollar Man" Ted DiBiase

With ally Hulk Hogan at ringside, Savage was on the road to destiny. Savage hit his signature flying elbow drop and covered DiBiase for the pin, becoming the undisputed World Wrestling Federation World Heavyweight Champion.

"The Mega Powers Explode"

April 2, 1989—Champion Hulk Hogan defeats Randy "Macho Man" Savage

Savage looked to have things well in hand, hitting a bleeding Hogan with his patented flying elbow drop. In typical Hogan fashion, he pressed Savage off him in a powerhouse kickout that almost sent the Macho Man out of the ring. Impermeable to pain, Hogan rallied to level Savage with his big boot and legdrop for his second championship.

World Wrestling Federation Intercontinental Heavyweight Championship

"A New Champion"

April 21, 1980—Ken Patera defeats Pat Patterson

Patera connected with a kneedrop from the middle turnbuckle to Patterson's back and went for the cover. The referee, who was recovering from an earlier collision with the champion, counted to three. Sadly for Patterson, the official failed to notice his foot was under the rope.

"The Triple Crown"

December 8, 1980—Pedro Morales defeats Ken Patera

On this night at Madison Square Garden, Pedro Morales defeated Olympic strongman Ken Patera. Morales became the first to hold World Wrestling Federation World, Tag Team, and Intercontinental Championships, a feat known today as the Triple Crown.

"A Shocker in Philly"

June 20, 1981—Don Muraco defeats Pedro Morales

"The Magnificent" Don Muraco stunned fans all over the world when he defeated Pedro Morales. Morales's title reign came to an end after Muraco hit him with a foreign object unseen by the referee, since he was knocked out.

"The First Two-Time Champion"

November 23, 1981—Pedro Morales defeats Don Muraco

During a Texas Death match, Pedro Morales hit Muraco with his own foreign object for the three-count. Morales became the first two-time World Wrestling Federation Intercontinental Champion.

"Muraco's Revenge"

January 22, 1983—Don Muraco defeats Pedro Morales

Muraco's weight advantage became the deciding factor when Morales attempted a scoop slam and his injured knee buckled on him. Landing on Pedro, Don Muraco won his second Intercontinental Championship.

"Arriba Santana"

February 11, 1984—Tito Santana defeats Don Muraco

During a back-and-forth contest, Tito Santana made the most of his opportunity to win the Intercontinental title. Tito caught Muraco in a sunset flip for the win and his first World Wrestling Federation singles championship.

"Dropping the Hammer"

September 24, 1984—Greg "The Hammer" Valentine defeats Tito Santana

At one point, Tito Santana thought he had pinned Valentine after a flying forearm, but Valentine's leg was outside the ring. After Valentine smashed Santana in the back with a knee, he hooked Tito's leg for the pinfall and Intercontinental title.

"Tito's Return"

July 6, 1985—Tito Santana defeats Greg "The Hammer" Valentine

Tito Santana was the challenger for Greg "The Hammer" Valentine's Intercontinental Championship—inside a fifteen-foot-high steel cage. When Santana scaled the cage and kicked the door in the Hammer's face, he had his second World Wrestling Federation Intercontinental Championship.

"Macho Madness"

February 8, 1986—Randy "Macho Man" Savage defeats Tito Santana

In this Boston Garden rematch, Savage defeated Santana after he knocked him unconscious with a foreign object while in a belly-to-back suplex.

"A Triumphant Comeback"

March 29, 1987—Ricky "The Dragon" Steamboat defeats Randy "Macho Man" Savage

During an Intercontinental title defense, Savage took the timekeeper's bell, jumped from the top rope, and crashed down on Steamboat's throat, crushing his larynx. This time when the "Macho Man" grabbed the timekeeper's bell and went to the top rope, George Steele threw Savage off. Steamboat rolled Savage up in a small package and won.

"Cool, Cocky & Bad"

June 2, 1987—Honky Tonk Man defeats Ricky "The Dragon" Steamboat

Ricky Steamboat crossed paths with the Honky Tonk Man. A shocked crowd watched Honky Tonk reverse an inside cradle, holding the ropes for leverage, on his way to victory.

"The Ultimate Destiny"

August 28, 1988—Ultimate Warrior defeats the Honky Tonk Man

The Honky Tonk Man issued an open challenge to the locker rooms, and the Ultimate Warrior answered. After a guerilla press slam and a splash, one of the longest title reigns ended in a record time of ten seconds.

"Simply Ravishing"

April 2, 1989—"Ravishing" Rick Rude defeats Ultimate Warrior

The two were set to meet at *WrestleMania V.* With a little help from his manager Bobby "The Brain" Heenan, "Ravishing" Rick Rude won the match.

"A True Warrior"

August 28, 1989—Ultimate Warrior defeats "Ravishing" Rick Rude

The Ultimate Warrior wanted to avenge his loss. When Roddy Piper made his way to ringside, Rude was diverted, and Warrior leveled him with a flying shoulder block. The Ultimate One then hit his guerilla press slam and splash to defeat Rude, becoming one of the few to hold the Intercontinental title on two separate occasions.

World Wrestling Federation World Tag Team Championship

"A New Era"

April 12, 1980—The Wild Samoans defeat Ivan Putski & Tito Santana

The Wild Samoans—Afa & Sika—with their unorthodox wrestling style and bizarre behavior, were an almost unbeatable team. In Philadelphia's Spectrum, they defeated "Polish Power" Ivan Putski & Tito Santana, after Santana missed a flying cross-body and was flattened with a Samoan Drop.

"A Fans' Dream Team"

August 8, 1980—Bob Backlund & Pedro Morales defeat the Wild Samoans

Bob Backlund & Pedro Morales defeated the Wild Samoans—Afa & Sika—in a Two-Out-Of-Three Falls contest, but were forced to forfeit the titles due to rules disallowing a champion—Backlund—to hold two different titles.

"A Wild Return"

September 9, 1980—the Wild Samoans defeat Tony Garea & Rene Goulet

The Wild Samoans—Afa & Sika—were hungry to regain the title. After a double body-slam on Goulet, the Samoans captured their second Tag Team Championship.

"Mat Wrestling Prevails"

November 8, 1980—Tony Garea & Rick Martel defeat the Wild Samoans

The Samoans' second title reign was short-lived. Garea & Martel captured the tag title after a Martel sunset flip.

"The Day of the Dogs"

March 17, 1981—The Moondogs defeat Tony Garea & Rick Martel

The Moondogs—King & Rex—were a barbaric tandem managed by Capt. Lou Albano. When Moondog King nailed Garea in the head with his bone, Rex covered him for the one-two-three in a controversial win.

"A Dog's Old Tricks"

July 21, 1981—Tony Garea & Rick Martel defeat the Moondogs

Garea & Martel recaptured the gold when Martel pinned Moondog Spot with a sunset flip as Spot attempted to choke out Tony Garea with his bone.

"Japanese Reign"

October 13, 1981—Mr. Fuji & Mr. Saito defeat Tony Garea & Rick Martel

With Capt. Lou Albano in their corner, Mr. Fuji & Mr. Saito were two of the most dangerous men in the world. Fuji threw salt in Rick Martel's eyes as he flew off the top rope with a flying cross-body. This enabled Saito to roll through the move and pin the blinded and stunned Martel for the win.

"Native American Heroes"

June 28, 1982—Chief Jay & Jules Strongbow defeat Mr. Fuji & Mr. Saito

With special guest referee Ivan Putski, the Strongbows knew they would receive a fair shot at the tag titles. The match saw the tide change many times, but in the end Jules pinned Mr. Fuji after he missed a dive attempt.

"Double Trouble"

July 13, 1982—Mr. Fuji & Mr. Saito defeat Chief Jay & Jules Strongbow

In a Two-Out-of-Three Falls, Fuji & Saito bested the Strongbows to become champions. This was Fuji's fifth time as a co-holder of World Wrestling Federation Tag titles.

"The Chiefs Triumph"

October 26, 1982—Chief Jay & Jules Strongbow defeat Mr. Fuji & Mr. Saito

The Strongbows were all too familiar with the antics of Fuji & Saito and their manager Capt. Lou Albano. Just over the three-minute mark, Chief Jay pinned Mr. Saito with the Lou Thesz press for the title.

"A Third Reign of Terror"

March 8, 1983—The Wild Samoans defeat Chief Jay & Jules Strongbow

Chief Jay was pinned after a brutal double clothesline and Samoan Drop. This win put the Wild Samoans in an elite category, holders of the Tag Championship on three separate occasions.

"Mr. USA & the Soulman"

November 15, 1983—"Mr. USA" Tony Atlas & Rocky Johnson defeat the Wild Samoans

Rocky Johnson & Tony Atlas could no longer be ignored. In a no-disqualification bout, Capt. Lou Albano accidentally broke a chair over Afa's head. This knocked out the Samoan, and Atlas scored the pinfall victory.

"Roughhousing Rules"

April 17, 1984—Adrian Adonis & Dick Murdoch defeat "Mr. USA" Tony Atlas & Rocky Johnson

Adrian Adonis & Dick Murdoch joined forces to become one of the toughest tandems. Adonis & Murdoch ended the five-month reign of Atlas & Johnson when Adonis rolled up Johnson from behind for the pin.

"USA, USA!"

January 21, 1985—The US Express defeat Adrian Adonis & Dick Murdoch

Barry Windham & Mike Rotundo—the US Express—had their first taste of tag team gold thanks to a sunset flip by Barry Windham on fellow Texan Dick Murdoch.

"The Cold War Is Waged"

March 31, 1985—Iron Sheik & Nikolai Volkoff defeat the US Express

The US Express—Barry Windham & Mike Rotundo—used their speed and agility to outmaneuver Sheik & Volkoff for much of the contest. The experience of the Iron Sheik showed when he knocked Windham out with "Classy" Freddie Blassie's cane. Nikolai Volkoff made the cover for the win.

"A Wild One"

June 17, 1985—The US Express defeat Iron Sheik & Nikolai Volkoff

When Mike Rotundo or the Sheik had the other in a pinning predicament, their partners reversed the pin when the referee was not looking. Fortunately for the Express, the last pin position to be reversed was seen by the referee, who counted one-two-three.

"Tough & Tougher"

August 25, 1985—The Dream Team defeat the US Express

Barry Windham & Mike Rotundo faced a new duo managed by "Luscious" Johnny Valiant. Things got out of control when Greg Valentine pinned Barry Windham after Beefcake stuck Valiant's lit cigarette in Windham's eye.

"The Bite of the Bulldogs"

April 7, 1986—The British Bulldogs defeat the Dream Team

The Dream Team—Greg Valentine & Brutus Beefcake—held the titles for nearly seven months. The Bulldogs—Davey Boy Smith & Dynamite Kid—were a top team. After Valentine was rammed into Dynamite's head, Smith covered the Hammer for the win.

"A Numbers Game"

January 26, 1987—The Hart Foundation defeat the British Bulldogs

The Dynamite Kid was knocked out with Jimmy Hart's megaphone before the match officially started. Referee Danny Davis permitted questionable double-team tactics on Davey Boy Smith, and after a double DDT and the Hart Attack the Hart Foundation's ten-month championship reign began.

"When Lightning Strikes"

October 27, 1987—Strike Force defeat the Hart Foundation

Tito Santana & Rick Martel—Strike Force—came out of nowhere. Each man knew what it took to be a successful tag team. Their five-month championship reign began when Martel got the Anvil to submit while locked in his Boston Crab.

"Walking Disasters"

March 27, 1988—Demolition defeat Strike Force

Demolition—Ax & Smash—got their shot at Strike Force. It looked like Martel & Santana would retain the championship. Then Ax cracked Martel's head with Mr. Fuji's cane when the referee was not looking. Smash covered the lifeless Martel for the victory.

"A Two-Out-of-Three Falls Classic"

July 18, 1989—The Brain Busters defeat Demolition

The Brain Busters—Arn Anderson & Tully Blanchard—were threats to Demolition's championship reign. In the third and decisive fall, Arn Anderson pinned Smash after Blanchard tattooed him with a chair that was thrown into the ring by Andre the Giant.

"The Demos Will Get Ya"

October 2, 1989—Demolition defeat the Brain Busters

Demolition—Ax & Smash—were granted a championship rematch. Demolition came back bigger and badder than ever. They secured their second stint as champions after they hit Tully Blanchard with the Decapitation Elbow.

"A Colossal Defeat"

December 13, 1989—The Colossal Connection defeat Demolition

Demolition was never outsized nor outpowered. When they clashed with the Colossal Connection—Andre the Giant & Haku—they were. Ax and Smash were manhandled, and Andre landed on Ax with a massive elbow drop and covered him for Andre's first World Wrestling Federation World Tag Team Championship.

World Wrestling Federation Women's Championship

"The End of an Era"

July 23, 1984—Wendi Richter defeats Fabulous Moolah

Wendi Richter did what many considered the impossible—ended the three-decade title reign of Fabulous Moolah. Richter lifted her shoulder on a bridged roll-up.

"Moolah's Purse"

February 18, 1985—Leilani Kai defeats Wendi Richter

Wendi Richter's opponent was the ruthless Leilani Kai. The champion had the energy of the eighties pop star—Cyndi Lauper—in her corner, but Kai brought the championship experience of the Fabulous Moolah. When Lauper fell under attack by Moolah, Richter tried to help and got tagged with Moolah's purse. This made the champion susceptible to a roll-up and a pinfall by Kai.

"Richter's Retribution"

March 31, 1985—Wendi Richter defeats Leilani Kai

Leilani Kai would not be able to retain her title despite Fabulous Moolah's presence at ringside. Leilani hit Richter with a flying cross-body, but Wendi rolled through for the pinfall.

"The Return of Moolah"

November 25, 1985—Fabulous Moolah defeats Wendi Richter

The Masked Spider Lady shocked the wrestling world when she pinned Wendi Richter. The only thing more shocking than Richter's loss was when the masked wrestler's identity was revealed: Fabulous Moolah.

"An Upset Down Under"

July 3, 1986—Velvet McIntyre defeats Fabulous Moolah

Velvet McIntyre caught the Fabulous Moolah off guard at an event in Australia and defeated her. Unfortunately for McIntyre, her stunning upset victory did not translate into a lengthy title reign.

"Moolah's Hat Trick"

July 9, 1986—Fabulous Moolah defeats Velvet McIntyre

Determined to prove that Velvet McIntyre's victory was beginner's luck, Moolah beat McIntyre just six days later.

"Master vs. Apprentice"

July 27, 1987—Sensational Sherri defeats Fabulous Moolah

Fabulous Moolah enjoyed a year-long reign as champion before she stood opposite her student Sensational Sherri. Blocking a bodyslam attempt into the ring, Sherri reversed it into a cradle for the pinfall and her first championship.

"She Rocks in the Tree Tops"

October 7, 1988—Rockin' Robin defeats Sensational Sherri

Rockin' Robin came to the ring with her sights set on the richest prize in women's wrestling. After she planted Sherri with a bulldog, her dream came true.

In 1990, the Women's title was deemed inactive and did not return to World Wrestling Entertainment until 1993.